HARVEST
OF
THE PALM

Overleaf: An elder of the
Rotinese state of Termanu.

HARVEST

OF THE PALM

Ecological Change
in Eastern Indonesia

James J. Fox

HARVARD UNIVERSITY PRESS
Cambridge, Massachusetts
and London, England   1977

Publication of this book has been aided by a grant
   from the Andrew W. Mellon Foundation

Library of Congress Cataloging in Publication Data

Fox, James J   1940-
   Harvest of the palm.

      Bibliography: p.
      Includes index.
      1. Economics, Primitive—Indonesia—Sunda Islands,
Lesser.   2. Ethnology—Indonesia—Sunda Islands, Lesser.
3. Borassus.   4. Palms—Indonesia—Sunda Islands, Lesser.
I. Title.
GN635.I65F68   301.5'1'095986   76-52996
ISBN 0-674-38111-4

For Irmgard

Preface

SINCE I HAVE come to this study indirectly and have drawn upon different aspects of my research to produce this book, I feel that it is essential to provide some personal background to it. Any anthropologist who has put in a long period of fieldwork inevitably faces the task of relating, in an intelligible fashion, the bewildering array of interrelated factors that combine to create a particular culture. The question is always one of where to begin and how to proceed. The problem is by no means an easy one to solve, for it is impossible to proceed in all directions and at all levels simultaneously. This book is my choice of a starting point. It is intended as the first volume of several that will describe in full my researches on the Indonesian island of Roti: it provides a general setting for subsequent volumes. The fact that relatively little is known of the history and ethnography of the peoples of the outer arc of the Lesser Sunda Islands has prompted me to write this broadly based study first, rather than a more specific monograph. I am acutely aware, however, of what I have not included, and I can only hope that future volumes will expand upon and clarify what I have chosen to concentrate on in this study.

Another reason for providing personal background is to emphasize a theoretical point. From the outset, I want to make clear that this is not a study that I conceived in the field. It has grown slowly over a course of years that has included two periods of fieldwork. Only gradually, through a great deal of historical research, have my perspectives changed and my focus widened from a few villages on Roti, to the island as a whole, to the arc of islands of which Roti is a part. One of the arguments I advance in this book concerns

developments that have been occurring on separate islands over a long period. I doubt whether any individual on these islands could be fully aware of
the complex processes in which he is involved as a participant. The view of
an individual, no less than that of the anthropologist in the field, is limited
to his locality and to the traditions of his group. The implicit contention
throughout much of this book is that a historical dimension enables the
anthropologist to overcome some of the limitations imposed by intensive
fieldwork in a few localities. It offers both a counter to ethnographic narrow-
ness and a corrective to oversimplified generalizations. At the same time, the
anthropologist has a certain vantage point, for often historical records cannot
be understood without the intimate knowledge of the ethnographic situation that the anthropologist gains through his fieldwork.

A final, but no less important, reason for this personal preface is to represent anthropological analysis as a continuing process. The late Sir E. E.
Evans-Pritchard, Professor of Social Anthropology at Oxford University,
used to assure his students that it normally takes a full ten years to prepare
an intensive study of a single society. Although there is certainly no hard-
and-fast rule on the subject, it seems appropriate to portray the process of
analysis that goes into a monograph as dependent on far more than a few
forays into the field. A corollary of this, it seems, ought to be the ready acknowledgment by anthropologists that further analysis should continue even
after the publication of a particular book. Ethnographers should be among
the first to engage in the development and rethinking of their own published materials. For this reason alone, I feel compelled to indicate the stage
in the process of my thinking that this book occupies, and from which future
volumes, I would hope, may take their lead.

This research had its beginning at Oxford in 1962. I was directed initially
toward eastern Indonesia by my tutor and supervisor, Rodney Needham,
who had done field research on the island of Sumba. Clark Cunningham,
now at the University of Illinois, was then completing his doctoral dissertation on the Atoni peoples of Timor and he too urged me to do fieldwork in
the area. Fascinated but undecided, I went to Holland for language training.
In addition to Indonesian, I began to study the Kamberaas dialect of Sumbanese under Professor L. Onvlee of the Free University of Amsterdam and
contemplated research on some region of Sumba. Like its larger neighbor
Timor, Sumba seemed a fairly well-studied island compared to the two small
islands of Savu and Roti that lay between Timor and Sumba. A few short
published and unpublished reports on these two islands existed, plus some
excellent linguistic material and a general impression—based on this frag-

mentary knowledge—that on Savu and Roti could be found social systems of great comparative and theoretical importance. I resolved to study one of the islands, but could not decide on which of the two I preferred to concentrate. In the end, I avoided the dilemma by writing a dissertation based on all available sources for both islands. Armed with a copy of this thesis, my wife and I set out for Indonesia.

Within days of our arrival there in January 1965, we met both Rotinese and Savunese, who together assisted us in getting from Jakarta to Kupang on Timor. To both peoples I explained my resolution to do research on their islands. In actuality, most of my first fieldwork was done on the island of Roti. But whenever I encountered Savunese, particularly in the district capital (where there were not a few who expressed amazement that anyone would waste time on Roti before going to Savu), I continued my haphazard study of Savunese and always promised that eventually I would get on with that important part of my project. My situation was further complicated by the realization that there were peoples other than Rotinese and Savunese on the islands between Sumba and Timor. This was certainly indicated in the Dutch records, but my discovery of both the Ndaonese and Helong peoples seemed at the time to be of some importance, and I attempted to gather what information I could on these minority populations.

On Roti, I put in my first and longest period of research in the state of Termanu. The Lord of Termanu, E. J. Amalo, who was also the *camat* or district officer for central Roti, was altogether indifferent to what anthropologists do. He expected me to be historian to his realm and his court. In a society conspicuously conscious of class, rank, and status, this gave me a definite position. I was usually known as *mesen*, the Rotinese word for "schoolmaster," or *tou lasik*, "old man"—not because of my age, but because my interests were supposed to be in ancestral matters and my associates were to be the elders of the state. I gathered genealogies, recorded historical tales, and began an apprenticeship in Rotinese ritual language. National political events during 1965 and 1966 prevented mobility and fortunately (it seems now) diverted me from some of my attempts at direct inquiry. Effectively and not always gently, the Rotinese themselves forced me to abandon some of my preconceived research plans and steered me to what they considered important and what they wished me to record—little of which had anything to do with matters relating to their economy.

Some of the reasons for these attitudes are not difficult to imagine. Elders and many of the higher nobles are not actively involved in economic production; their interests lie elsewhere. Young men, many middle-aged men, and women of all ages labor; but the work they perform, the techniques they use, the strategies they employ, are not viewed as significant. They are commonplace and taken for granted. Ownership of property, on the other hand, is of great interest. Although an enormous amount of time is spent, especially by elders, in conducting or hearing litigation, Rotinese judge that information about property is not a subject for open inquiry. No Rotinese will willingly reveal his property holdings. Avoiding inquiries about property is not a skill unique to the Rotinese, but it is certainly one that these people have been masterful in developing. Nor is it a skill that Rotinese have developed only to avoid probing or meddling from the outside; it is something fundamental to their notions of contestation.

Of all the peoples of eastern Indonesia, the Rotinese have gained the reputation of being the most able at evading outside interference. F. J. Ormeling, former Director of the Geographical Institute of Jakarta, who carried out survey research on Timor in the early 1950's, accurately reports on this Rotinese trait (1956:225):

> [The] Rotinese community's reluctance to resign itself to official instructions is especially noticeable during the annual tax assessment. Many Rotinese cannot be found when, in the dry season, the tax commission travels around estimating the harvest to ascertain the population's annual income. On tax registers the name of Rotinese *kampung* (village) residents is often followed by the official remark *lari* (bolted). The Rotinese who are found and questioned usually pass themselves off in an extremely talented way as being needy and penniless.

I should point out that the Savunese, the other main group studied here, have been no less successful, but a great deal less obvious, in their evasion of tax registers and property enumeration. In 1954-1955 a Savunese, M. C. Radja Haba, was assigned to report on the conditions of animal husbandry on his native island. At just this time, in September 1955, an epidemic ocurred among the water buffalo and pig populations, and a team of veterinarians was rushed to the island to inoculate the animals. On page 1 of his undated report Radja Haba notes without surprise that on the basis of this inoculation campaign, the number of buffalo and pigs on Savu "appears to be more than eleven times the total registered" in the official records. As a Savunese, he properly concludes that "no exact information could be obtained as to how the animal wealth is distributed among the people."

Even though I had been assigned a role in the society, I was received as an outsider. The first time I asked about the ownership of certain property, I was told flatly that such questions were "police questions." I was not expected to act as a policeman. Eventually, and only gradually, I ceased to be a rank outsider. Precisely when this change occurred and was recognized by those with whom I was living, I cannot say: that a point was reached was confirmed by one particular event. Two government officials, themselves Rotinese but from a distant state, arrived in the village area where my wife and I had settled. They requested horses for official use, to ride to an eastern state. On that day, in the courtyard of one of the houses, I sat for hours with a group of local residents listening to a long, woeful recitation of the disasters of an epidemic that had struck this area, leaving hardly a horse from any of the herds. In the end, one old nag was found and the two officials left, one riding, one walking. I had played the game; for, only a week before, I had witnessed a roundup of 47 horses in that same courtyard.

In more than a year's residence in one small area, it is impossible not to learn something about who owns what. Still, there is a considerable difference between this casual accumulation of information and the systematic collection of data. One eventually gains some scattered knowledge through what a few acquaintances happen to reveal, but has little notion of how this relates to a large population. In systematic surveys under these conditions, one can only expect to arrive at an imprecise view; but presumably this view is representatively distorted for the entire sample. My analysis here is a compromise between the two methods. I use only "official" figures, all of which are available data. But I interpret these, in several instances, in the light of my own field information. This neither compromises individuals nor betrays the trust of my Rotinese friends.

When finally I left the island of Roti, I was saddled with a project that I had not originally expected to undertake. I had promised to write a history of the state of Termanu, using the voluminous political narratives and genealogies that had been thrust upon me. To judge from other anthropologists' experience, some change in research as a result of fieldwork is not unusual, and this project could at least be fitted to my intended study of the social organization of that state. As I conceived it—and still do partly conceive it—I needed to examine the narratives as political charters used in the ordering of social groups. My assumption was that these orally transmitted genealogies and tales were easily altered and therefore could hardly be reliable as historical information. In drafting a historical introduction to my doctoral dissertation, however, I discovered largely by accident that the name of one of the individuals, Fola Sinlae, in the dynastic genealogy of the Lord of Termanu occurred as signatory to a Dutch East India Company contract in 1756. This disturbing discovery again altered my research. If one name could be identified, it seemed likely that others could as well. I felt that I had to scour the archives. As it turned out, not just one, but *every* one—in proper succession—of the Lords of Termanu from 1662 to 1966 could be identified and dated in the archival records. In many cases, the narratives I had gathered reflected events recounted in the Dutch sources as well.

Dating the Lords of Termanu took four years of intermittent investigation. During one period of this research in the Netherlands, I discovered what were for me new sources of archival information. The most important of these were the *Timor Books* of the Dutch East India Company—the heavy, leather-bound, handwritten annual records that cover the years of the Company's post at Kupang from 1647 to 1798. In addition, I was able to locate in various archives numerous official colonial depositions, commission reports, personal manuscripts, and dozens of government "mail reports."

The Company records, government documents for the period to 1849, and a variety of other personal manuscript collections are to be found today in the General Government Archives (*Algemeen Rijksarchief*) in the Hague; similar documents for the period 1850 to 1899 are stacked to the ceiling in level after level of a massive, abandoned German bunker in Schaarsbergen that has been converted into an archive depot; while all mail reports for the twentieth century are kept in an archive collection of the Ministry of Internal Affairs in the Hague, following the dissolution of the Ministry of Colonies. Additional manuscript material can be found in the archives of the Royal Institute for Linguistics, Geography, and Anthropology in Leiden; in the Museum for the Tropics in Amsterdam; and in the mission house of the Dutch Reformed Church in Oegstgeest. Generally reckoned in meters of shelf space and calculated to run to kilometers, these archives form a vast accumulation of unpublished information on Indonesia.

In searching for a few names, I uncovered for Roti and Savu—two of Indonesia's least important islands—a formidable collection of historical materials. From so vast an accumulation of records, it would be imprudent of me to assume that I have found all that relates to these islands; yet the documents I managed to assemble cover, in some detail, three hundred years of these islands' history.

At just the time I was finishing these archival searches, I was awarded a year's fellowship at the Center for Advanced Study in the Behavioral Sciences in Stanford, California. I resolved that, having marshaled all the materials, I would write parallel histories of the state of Termanu—as told by Rotinese in their oral tradition and as evidenced by Dutch documents for much of this same period. A considerable portion of the manuscript of Termanu's history took shape at the Center and slowly is nearing completion, but it quickly became apparent to me that such a history would be almost unintelligible without a wider context. Studies of the islands in the outer arc of the Lesser Sundas are fragmentary, each confined to an island or a portion of an island and to a limited period. Still, the collected historical documents reveal that certain of the processes which I had momentarily glimpsed in 1965-1966, and which other commentators had occasionally noted, were not recent phenomena but had a long, recognizable history.

The present study is thus another diversion from my planned ethnography of Roti; it is an attempt to supply a context for this eventual ethnography. Dealing with those factors common to the area of which Roti is a part, it covers an appreciable period. In preparing this broader history, I have adopted a perspective that is, in a sense, external to the orientation of the individual participants in the various social systems I discuss. These individuals are involved in a complex of ecological and economic relations of which they are only partially aware. What is occurring is beyond the full comprehension of the participants, and present events are confined within certain limits as a result of past events. With a groundwork understanding of this situation, a further ethnography can make legitimate use of the anthropological device known as the "ethnographic present" and give a fuller account of the motivations of that segment of Roti's population with which I am best acquainted.

In August 1972 I submitted a draft manuscript of this book for publication and left California to do another year's fieldwork in eastern Indonesia. I spent the entire year continuing research on the islands of Roti, Savu, Ndao, and Timor. I was able to visit all these islands and gather new information. I was also appointed visiting lecturer in the history faculty at the recently founded University of Nusa Cendana in Kupang, and during my periodic stays in Kupang I was able to give a series of lectures, in Indonesian, based on my manuscript. I circulated copies of the manuscript among Savunese, Rotinese, and Timorese who could read it and give me detailed comments. The information I was uncovering in further fieldwork, the enthusiasm that attended my lectures, the discussions that followed them, and the careful readings given my manuscript confirmed for me that my arguments were not misdirected. I was supplied with so much additional evidence that I felt that I had no choice but to revise, expand, and update the earlier manuscript. I therefore wrote from Kupang and asked that the manuscript be withdrawn until I had an opportunity to rework it.

It has taken over two years since returning from Indonesia to find the time to make all my intended revisions. While these changes have not substantially altered the structure of the original study, the manuscript has grown considerably and minor amplifications seem to have crept in on virtually every page. Thus the present book has been a long time in preparation. As Evans-Pritchard predicted, it has taken approximately ten years since my first fieldwork to complete this initial study.

ACKNOWLEDGMENTS

In future publications I hope to be able to name a large number of the Rotinese and Savunese who have helped me over the years. Here I wish to thank those who were most directly responsible for assisting me in this study: Ernst Amalo and all the Amalo and Biredoko families of Fola-Teik in Masa-Huk, who supported me during my time in Termanu; Jeremias Kiuk and all the Kiuk families of Ingu-Beuk, whose juice I drank most often and whose tapping and cooking procedures I had the chance to observe at close hand; S. Adulanu, N. D. Pah, J. Pello, and L. P. Foeh for their patient instruction and assistance; and D. D. Bireludji, G. R. Manu, and Pa Nalle for their invaluable help to me on Savu. For directing me in my search for materials in the Dutch archives, I am grateful to F. G. P. Jaquet, and for assistance in my struggles to decipher seventeenth- and eighteenth-century documents, to Miriam van den Berg of the Algemeen Rijksarchief. I appreciate also P. E. de Josselin de Jong's unfailing aid to my research in the Netherlands, and that of J. Noorduyn who on behalf of the *Koninklijk Instituut voor Taal-, Land- en Volkenkunde* provided innumerable facilities for this project. Above all, I thank my tutor and supervisor at Oxford, Rodney Needham, who directed me to eastern Indonesia and supervised my research on Roti.

The research on which this study is based was originally supported by a U. S. Public Health Service fellowship (MH-23, 148) and a grant (MH-10, 161) from the National Institute of Mental Health; it was conducted in 1965-1966 in Indonesia under the auspices of the Lembaga Ilmu Pengetahuan Indonesia (LIPI). The continuation of the research was again supported by a NIMH grant (MH-20, 659) and carried out in 1972-1973 under the joint sponsorship of the LIPI and the University of Nusa Cendana in Kupang. Grants from the Clarke and Teschemacher funds of Harvard University aided in the preparation of maps and diagrams. The first draft of this book was written during the tenure of my fellowship at the Center for Advanced Study in the Behavioral Sciences at Stanford. To this institution and its staff, I express my heartfelt thanks. In the development of the statistical analyses used in this study, I have relied heavily on the assistance of Perry Gluckman and on the suggestions and comments of my colleague for the year, David Wiley.

I should also like to express my appreciation to all of those who commented on some portion of the manuscript: Erich Breunig, Frank Cooley, Clark Cunningham, William Davenport, I. H. Doko, E. K. Fisk, Shepard Forman, Charles Frake, Derek Freeman, David Maybury-Lewis, Joachim Metzner, Rodney Needham, F. J. Ormeling, Robert Pringle, Renato and Michelle Rosaldo, David Schneider, O. H. K. Spate, A. J. Toelle, Elizabeth Traube, Evon Z. Vogt, and Monica Wilson. Thanks are due Harold E. Moore, Jr., of the Bailey Hortorium of Cornell University for his identification of botanical specimens and his highly useful comments on my draft description of the lontar palm. I am grateful to all those who have kindly given permission to reproduce material for incorporation in this book: the Algemeen Rijksarchief, the Universiy of California Press, Martinus Nijhoff, the British Library Board, and the Mitchell Library, Library Council of New South Wales. I also wish to thank the government officials of Nusa Tenggara Timor, especially Governor El. Tari, K. Amalo, D. C. Saudale, and H. Ataupah. Finally I express my thanks to Professor Dr. Koentjaraningrat of the University of Indonesia, to Mohammed Sjah, Rector of the University of Nusa Cendana, and to the members of the history faculty and the Badan Lingkungan Peminat Sejarah Nusa Tenggara Timur: C. D. Bissilisin, J. Detaq, A. Nisnoni, M. A. Noach, A. Soh, and I. Toto.

Contents

TABLES

FIGURES

MAPS

ILLUSTRATIONS

HARVEST
OF
THE PALM

Introduction

IN *MAX HAVELAAR,* Multatuli's influential nineteenth-century novel on the Netherlands East Indies, a curious passage occurs. The eminently practical, hopelessly unimaginative coffee broker from Amsterdam, Batavus Drystubble, is given an odd collection of manuscripts. The bundle comes from a man named Scarfman, who describes himself as a poet and writer who has thought, worked, and witnessed much. Drystubble's interests are in business and the coffee trade; yet despite his disapproval of Scarfman, he agrees to leaf through his papers. Like the dissertations at a modern university, there are essays on all topics: On the origin of the aristocracy . . . On Russian statecraft . . . On Icelandic mythology . . . On the unnaturalness of schools . . . On the invention of chastity . . . On Moorish architecture . . . On Chinese shadow plays . . . On Malthus' theories of population in relation to subsistence . . . Among this assortment there is one title that impresses Drystubble: On the noneating people of the island of Roti, near Timor. To someone with a knowledge of Indonesia, the title refers to the fact that the people of Roti drink most of their meals instead of eating them. Drystubble, however, chooses to interpret it differently. Here, he feels, is a people who have managed to avoid the expensive, troublesome problems of eating. With mocking approval, he pencils in the annotation: "Living must be cheap there."

THE NONEATING PEOPLE OF ROTI

This book could be considered something of a substitute for Scarfman's imaginary manuscript. It deals with the topic that attracted Drystubble's

1

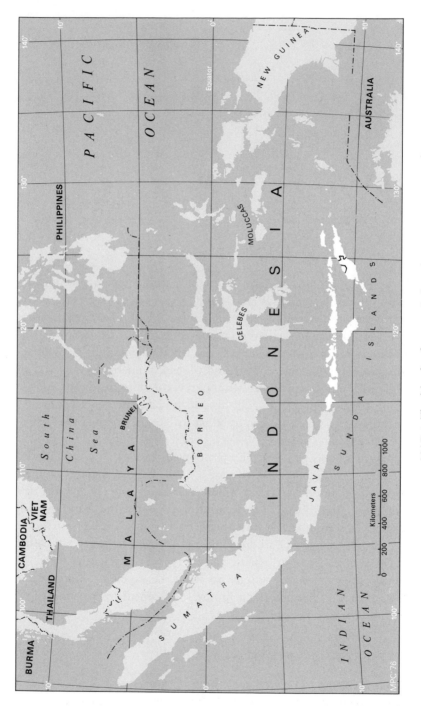

MAP 1 The islands of eastern Indonesia.

attention. That a people in the southern corner of eastern Indonesia should drink more meals than they eat is an unusual and interesting social fact. But that these people, the Rotinese—and their near neighbors, the Savunese—should derive, as Drystubble recognized, a distinct economic advantage from their unusual subsistence is of even greater interest.

This study involves more, however, than the description of a peculiar mode of food production limited by specific conditions. I intend to consider a continuing process of ecological deterioration, caused in part by a long history of human habitation and agricultural exploitation under adverse conditions. The focus is not a single island, but a chain of islands—the outer arc of the Lesser Sundas in eastern Indonesia, whose varying ecologies and specific histories provide the context for a comparison of several socially and linguistically distinct peoples. Map 1 shows these islands in their Indonesian setting. What has occurred on two of these islands—to state the situation in its most simplified form—is a partial reversion from agriculture to gathering with the seemingly curious consequence that present-day gatherers have a major advantage over the agriculturalists with whom they are now in competition.

Nothing in the social sciences, however, is simple. An inestimable factor of extreme importance to these islands has been a colonial presence, first of the Portuguese and then of the Dutch, from approximately the 1560's to the 1950's. Viewed to the present, this is a period of almost four hundred years during which the islands were affected by European influence. Despite this influence, the islands remained in the backwaters of European colonialism. They have had few products worth exploiting and consequently they have never experienced the massive intervention that characterized other areas of Indonesia. For the Dutch East India Company, the Timor area afforded small profit. After the demise of the Company and with the gradual decline in Timor's sandalwood trade, this area was administered at an economic loss by the Dutch colonial government.

Each of the island societies in this study responded differently, and at different times, to European presence in the area. Initially, the major issue was with whom to ally: with the Portuguese, who arrived first in the area and whose adherents, the Topasses or "Black Portuguese," formed their own renegade state and managed, with enormous bravado, to maintain enclaves on the islands; or with the Dutch, who arrived later and began methodically to assert their influence without ever ousting their trading rivals.

Although Christian influences reached these islands in the sixteenth century, the spread of Christianity in a coherent pattern began later, in the eighteenth century.[1] The local response was as varied as it was to political alliance. Both among these societies and within them, the range was from a headlong rush to conversion to a steady unyielding resistance. Both attitudes —and not one more than the other—affected the internal structure of each society. This was a two-way process. Native attitudes and various adaptive modes of livelihood created for the Dutch a number of stereotypes of the "traditional" nature of these societies. This stereotyping was by no means entirely erroneous; occasionally it was remarkably incisive, but it was always partial, presumptive, and, more importantly, a glimpse of societies already affected (directly or indirectly) by previous European involvement. At times, therefore, Dutch policy ran counter to the effects of previous policy. This study considers the complicated interaction of these influences in native life as an important factor along with more easily specified ecological, economic, and demographic variables. Dutch records on this area of Indonesia, although not as extensive or as accurate as those for other areas, offer a means of discerning these influences.

Rather than maintain a single methodological perspective—ecological, economic, or historical—I have attempted to fuse these several views. Like the field of social anthropology itself, committed as it is to cultural comparison without a strictly defined limitation on its point of view, this study covers a set of complexly interrelated topics. The thrust of my main argument is, however, concerned with the economic and social adaptations of various related groups in a specific ecological and cultural setting. As this study proceeds, the field of comparison is extended. My first concern is with a few small islands, then with these islands in a chain of islands, and finally with these same islands as representatives of a system of economic production that extends beyond the circumscribed area of eastern Indonesia.

THE OUTER ARC OF THE LESSER SUNDAS

The chain of islands that extends in a line eastward from Java is known as the Lesser Sunda Islands. Below this line is an outer arc of islands that stretches almost 1,000 kilometers (see Map 2). In climate the islands of this arc are affected by their proximity to Australia; characteristic features are a long dry season, low rainfall, and consequent semiarid conditions when compared with the more tropical areas of Indonesia. From east to west, the outer arc comprises seven habitable islands: Sumba, Savu which together with Raijua makes up the "Savu group," Ndao, Roti, Semau, and Timor. Within this range of islands is a gradation. The eastern and western ends of the arc swing upward to the north; thus west Sumba and east Timor are less dry than areas in the southern circumference of the arc. Timor is the largest island in the

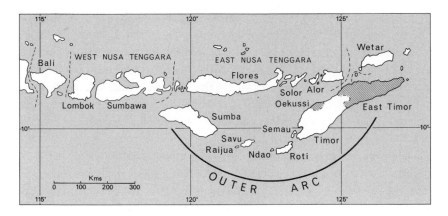

MAP 2 The outer arc of the Lesser Sunda Islands.

group. It has an area of over 30,000 square kilometers, and its situation is more varied. The rugged mountains that divide it create two sharply contrasting coastal plains: the northern coast is an area of low rainfall; the southern coast, especially its eastern extension, is an area of relatively higher rainfall. The focus of this study is on the drier regions of this outer arc.

The seven islands are inhabited by a diversity of peoples, among whom one significant difference is language. Linguistically, there is a dividing line that bisects the arc. The peoples of Sumba, Raijua, Savu, and Ndao speak separate but related languages that belong to the Sumba-Bima grouping of eastern Indonesian languages; the peoples of Roti, Semau, and most of Timor speak languages that belong to the class of assorted languages referred to as the Timor-Ambon group.

Timor and Sumba, the two large islands of the outer arc, are markedly different. Sumba has none of the broken mountainous terrain of Timor. Linguistically, Sumba is usually described as having a single language divided into dialects, although by the criterion of mutual intelligibility it might be more reasonable to conceive of these dialects, particularly those in west Sumba, as separate languages. On Sumba, in other words, it is possible to distinguish local languages or dialects; it is impossible to draw unequivocal lines to separate them. Sumba is characterized by continuous linguistic variation from east to west. Timor, on the other hand, has many languages and the discontinuities among them are marked. Furthermore, Timor is politically divided. East Timor and the enclave of Oekussi on the northern coast of west Timor were Portuguese territories, whose future noncolonial political status must now be decided. The peoples of east Timor are more complexly divided than those of west Timor. Where west Timor has three or four native languages, east Timor has at least a dozen. Several local populations, including an important group known as the Bunaq,[2] who straddle the border areas of central Timor, speak Papuan rather than Austronesian languages. Language thus reflects, to some extent, the history of this area as an avenue for different streams of migration—and recent movements continue to complicate the language situation.

The seven islands have over a million and a half inhabitants. In terms of Indonesia's estimated 130 million people, this figure seems insignificant. In terms of the size and limited area of these few islands, the population appears more considerable. No recent census reports for the Indonesian parts of the outer arc identify populations according to linguistic or ethnic group. In published accounts, the populations of the small islands—Raijua, Savu, Ndao, and Roti—are included with those of Timor. The following figures give an approximation of the island populations as of 1970-1971:[3]

Sumba	291,000
Raijua and Savu	51,000
Ndao	2,000
Roti	74,000
Semau	5,500
West Timor	694,000
Oekussi and east Timor	610,500
Total outer arc	1,728,000

There are indications that some of the arguments in this analysis may be applicable to the northern coastal regions of Oekussi and east Timor. Substantiating information, however, is scant and therefore cannot be brought within the scope of this study.[4] The analysis is less applicable also to the heavier rainfall areas of the south coast of west Timor—in general, the area of the Belu peoples. (Comparisons with this region are confined to the notes.) Similarly, the analysis applies less to the greener regions of west Sumba, although no attempt is made to delimit the borders of "west" Sumba. Since the present study is specifically of adaptations to semiarid ecologies, exclusion of these other regions defines a more precise focus. The following figures give an estimation of the population of the reduced study area:

East Sumba	104,000
Raijua and Savu	51,000
Ndao	2,000
Roti	74,000
Semau	5,500
West Timor	540,500 (without Belu)
	————
Total study area	777,000

This area includes six distinct native peoples: the Sumbanese, Savunese, Ndaonese, Rotinese, Helong (in some earlier literature, referred to as Kupangese), and Timorese (referred to in the anthropological literature as either Dawan or Atoni).[5] A fact of importance about this area is that it was a region, as was most of eastern Indonesia, of indirect Dutch rule. Prior to the arrival of either the Portuguese or the Dutch, there were petty kingdoms on Timor whose rulers controlled the cutting of sandalwood for trade with China. It is probable that at this time loosely defined states existed on other nearby islands, although none of them had sandalwood to trade. When the Portuguese and Dutch intervened, they recognized and legitimized their trading partners as the rulers of their respective states. Thus the Sumbanese, Savunese, Rotinese, and Timorese were divided among a differing number of rival rulers, while the Ndaonese and Helong were each accorded separate rulers.

The Portuguese arrived on independent trading vessels. The Dutch, however, came as officers and representatives of a single tightly organized trading company. This organization, the *Vereenigde Oostindische Compagnie,* or *V.O.C.,* had such an initial impact throughout the islands that most members of the small states recognized by the Dutch continued to refer to all subsequent forms of Dutch rule as "Company" (*Kompani*) or, in more elevated, personal terms, as "Mother-Father Company" (*Ina-Ama Kompani*). Under Company contracts, the rulers of these states were basically obliged (*a*) to make gifts of tribute, which in effect constituted a special form of elite trade, (*b*) to supply a levy of armed men in case of need, (*c*) to refuse trade with other powers, which usually meant the Portuguese but which included all unauthorized traders, either Chinese or Indonesians from other islands, and (*d*) to settle disputes among their states by Company-designated arbitration. Most matters of internal rule were left to individual rulers to be dealt with in terms of *adat* or native law.

This situation did not change much when the Netherlands government assumed the debts of the bankrupt Dutch East India Company and, after the disasters of the Napoleonic wars in Europe, formally in 1815 resumed control of Indonesia from the British. It was not until 1898 that native rulers of the Timor area renegotiated their previous Company contracts; not until 1901 that they signed a declaration recognizing the right of the Netherlands Indies government to tax their population; and not until 1907, under a policy of "intensification of rule," that the Dutch government attempted to "rationalize" the organizational structure of rule that until then they had sanctioned. This reorganization consisted chiefly in the coalescence of smaller states into larger administrative units. Titles and offices were changed, but informally the prior structure of rule was retained, or at least not radically altered. A number of schemes were tried, but all of these were ended by the Japanese occupation and were further modified after Indonesian independence was declared. To 1966, administrative units, roughly corresponding to the previous states and under local native authorities, were recognized as part of the bureaucratic structure of this province of the Republic of Indonesia.

Since 1966, there has been further administrative reorganization and a rearrangement of the old native states in new district (*kecamatan*) groupings. What is impressive, however, is the continuity and relative stability of the native states and, in particular, the local consciousness of each state's tradition. Since these states remain the basic units in each new bureaucratic scheme, administrative reshuffling seems only to emphasize their permanency at the expense of more inclusive divisions. Throughout the Timor area, dress and dialect reflect an individual's local identity. For most of the area, an estimated 90 percent or more of all marriages are contracted between members of the same state. And while it is common to find individuals who have ventured beyond their island or visited the provincial capital, it is rare—except in the case of the Ndaonese[6]—to encounter an individual who has spent a night or two in a state at any distance from his own. Details of these various states therefore figure prominently in any discussion of the area.

Included in the study area—and of importance to it—is the town of Kupang. Originally, Kupang was the site of a minor Portuguese fortification; this was abandoned, but in 1653 was garrisoned and enlarged by the Dutch. This Fort Concordia formed the nucleus of the Company's trading post and, like trading centers in other parts of the world, attracted a diverse population. By the earliest treaty with a Timorese native ruler, dating from the appearance of the Dutch at Kupang in 1613 rather than from their occupation of its fort, the Dutch were ceded a narrow coastal strip around the Bay of Kupang. This area too attracted "foreign" settlers. During the colonial period, Kupang became the administrative capital for the *Residentie van Timor en Onderhoorigheden;* after independence, Kupang became the capital of the Province of Nusa Tenggara Timur. In each administration Kupang grew further. Successive enumerations of the population of "Kupang" refer confusingly to the town and its environs, to various surrounding small states (Semau, Funai, Lesser Sonba'i, Amabi, Oefeto, Taebenu, Babau) that eventually were formed into the single "princedom" (*vorstendom*) of Kupang, or to the major "regency" (*kabupaten*) of Kupang which now includes the islands of Savu, Ndao, Roti, Semau, and the four large states of western Timor: Kupang, Amarasi, Fatule'u, and Amfoan. Today Kupang continues to act as a magnet; the regency of which it is the center is the fastest growing regency in eastern Indonesia. In one portion of this study, I shall consider Kupang's bureaucracy as a specialized niche in the general ecology of the area. The analogy, it is hoped, will not seem overstrained.

FORMAT OF THE BOOK

This study is divided into three unequal and dissimilar parts. The first of these is an attempt to examine the essential features of a somewhat unusual economic system that has developed on the small islands of the outer arc (Roti, Savu, and Ndao) and to contrast this system with those found on the large islands of the arc (Timor and Sumba). From the outset, my viewpoint should be apparent. The economies of both Timor and Sumba are of a "type"—slash-and-burn, or swidden, agriculture—about which there exists a considerable body of literature. Both Timor and Sumba have been the subject of a variety of researches, and their basic bibliographies comprise hundreds of titles. Roti, Savu, and Ndao, on the other hand, were infrequently visited and have been relatively overlooked. The existence of a distinctive population on Ndao can, for example, only be discovered by combing the literature, and those sentences containing accurate information on the island would hardly number one hundred.

My object has been to portray the orientation of the small islands in relation to their larger neighbors, to describe their economies in detail, and to demonstrate that these economies are better adapted to present ecological conditions and have the capacity to support far higher population densities than can the traditional economies of either of the large islands. In attempting to demonstrate this, I have had to focus on the varying emphases of the local economies within the minor regions of the small island of Roti. Much of this may at first seem like the unnecessarily dull litany of peculiar place names. Nonetheless, an examination of these microvariations is essential to the argument. To appreciate this will require more than the usual lingering glance at the maps in this book. Within the entire outer arc, my focus is on the driest regions; within these dry regions, my primary focus is on the smaller islands; and within these islands, my concern is with the states that constitute microsystems of the whole.

Part One is thus mainly concerned with outlining an economic model of two subsistence systems. As it happens, the economies of the small islands have now become established on the larger islands and can be shown to be advancing as the swidden systems contract. The focus of Part Two is to show how this has come about. What I have attempted to do is interweave a chronicle of events on four or five islands over a period of three hundred years, wherever possible allowing the participants to speak for themselves. Here again, my own viewpoint is obvious. I make no attempt to hide my special regard for the Rotinese and Savunese peoples, many of whom I know well, whose separate cultures and styles of life I can at times comprehend and appreciate, and whose actions seem to me understandable. At the present time, I have no comparable understanding of either the Timorese or the Sumbanese and would not claim that I can personally comprehend their way of life. I am thus no less biased than some of the Dutch officers whose one-sided views helped create the situation that now exists in the outer arc. Perhaps this is why their decisions, many of which I would indict, seem so eminently intelligible. Despite my obvious concern for the peoples involved, I hope I can convey with some detachment the course and consequences of the events that have occurred. In any case, Part Two provides historical documentation on the advancement of the Rotinese and Savunese, with their special economies, in the outer arc of the Lesser Sundas.

Part Three is a venture for which I claim no particular success. In it I reverse certain of my assertions about the unusual nature of the Rotinese and Savunese economy by indicating the extent to which similar economies occur in Asia, particularly in south India, Ceylon, mainland southeast Asia, and Indonesia. Instead of supporting a hundred thousand or so persons, economies of this type support millions. I had hoped, in describing three widely separate instances of this one type of economy, that I might be able to delimit its most essential features and arrive at some estimate of its capacity and limitations. Unfortunately, the comparative botany for this kind of study has not yet been worked out. Minimally reliable quantitative data are also not available and one might wait indefinitely for the material necessary to an ideal study. Part Three, therefore, is a comparative venture, based on presently available data, that may at best chart certain directions for the future study of this type of economy. Overall, I follow a general progression from the detailed examination of the smallest islands of the outer arc and their microdivisions, to the larger islands affected by their smaller neighbors, then from these islands to areas of comparative relevance in south and southeast Asia.

A NOTE ON NAMES

Proper names present a special problem in this study not simply because present usage is so variable, but because this is a historical study and both personal names and local place names have varied even more in the past than they do at present. One may take as an example the name for the island I refer to as Roti. Sixteenth- and seventeenth-century Portuguese documents begin with a profusion of names. The island was known as "Rotes," as "Enda" ("Eda" is, to this day, the Savunese designation for the island), and as "Savo" (*Sabo*) or "Savo Pequeno," which was supposedly intended to distinguish the island from what is actually the smaller island now known as Savu but then known as "Savo Grande." Early Dutch maps give the name as "Rotthe," which was miscopied by a later generation of cartographers as "Rotto." One early seventeenth-century map, however, labels the island by a native name. "Noessa Dahena" (*Nusa Dahena*) derives from an eastern dialect of Rotinese and can be translated literally as the "Island of Man." Apart from this one map label, the name never occurs again. By the mid-seventeenth century, Dutch East India Company documents introduced the name "Rotti," using three variant spellings: "Rotti," "Rotty," and "Rottij." This official designation continued into the twentieth century in modified form as "Roti."

In their folk traditions the Rotinese insist (justifiably, it would seem) that the name for their island is a Portuguese imposition. Furthermore, the name "Roti" is a Malay corruption of "Rote"—a corruption that engendered the pointless and now quite stale pun on the word "roti," which happens to mean "bread" in Indonesian. Local usage now favors "Rote," but this too is problematical, since \r\ and \l\ are used interchangeably among the island's nine dialects and a considerable portion of the population therefore refers to the island as "Lote." In the ritual language of the Termanu dialect, the full name is "Lote do Kale." In present-day Indonesia, most official documents originating from the island or the district capital use "Rote," while most documents issued by the central government give the name as "Roti." It is this name for the island, now fixed in most world atlases, that seems to be most widely accepted, and it is this name that I have adopted in this and other publications.

Savu's name has perhaps fared better than that of Roti. The Portuguese first designated the island as "Savo," and the Dutch altered it only slightly to "Savu." This has become the most generally accepted name for the island, although local Indonesian usage still varies between "Sabu" and "Sawu." As it happens, the Savunese language utilizes neither \s \nor\ v\, and the Savunese themselves refer to their island as "Rai Hawu," the "Island of Hawu." This is not a foreign designation, but a reference to an early founding ancestor. Since in this case both local and international usages vary and none is a correct rendering of the native name, I have chosen to adopt the older convention and continue to refer to the island as Savu.

In the case of other place names, worse problems arise. Throughout much of the Timor area, there are ritual language place names, ordinary language names for the same place, Malay and sometimes Dutch corruptions of these names, and possibly one or more ways of spelling the various corruptions. The name "Thie" might better be spelled "Ti," "Delha" as "Dela," "Mesara" as "Mehara," or "Timu" as "Dimu," but for the fact that a long tradition has established these slightly peculiar spellings. The recent adoption of "New Spelling" by the Indonesian government and its application to local names has further complicated the problem.

There are additional problems that go beyond simple spelling. For example, "Termanu" is the outsiders' name for Pada, a small but important state on Roti; Pada's ritual name, among others, is "Koli do Buna." To make matters worse, as part of a recent administrative reorganization of districts on Roti, most village areas have taken on new names for the official records. At one fell swoop, all the village names of Termanu were officially changed. Now even to begin to decipher recent records for comparison with past ones requires some knowledge of Rotinese ritual language, on which these name changes were based. To the local population, little has actually been altered; a certain deference has been paid to ancient tradition by the use of ritual names. To the outsider, this baffling change of names under the aegis of the Indonesian government's "New Effort" (*Gaya Baru*) campaign seems only to disguise the local situation.

There is no simple way out of this confusion of multiple names and spellings. Rather than attempt to keep up with all the shifts that have occurred recently and that are likely to continue, I have endeavored in this study to use the most widely recognized, historically established place names. (For other native terms in different languages, I use as close a phonemic rendering as is possible based on present studies of these languages.) I have also tried to be consistent. In quoting directly from historical sources, however, I have retained the spellings of the period and merely inserted in brackets, where necessary, the spelling adopted in this study. With the aid of maps, the places and areas to which I refer should be clearly recognizable.

A NOTE ON NUMBERS

In studies of this kind, analyses of quantitative data are indispensable. Among other things, social anthropology should be concerned with the formulation of theoretical and, where possible, formal models for the analysis of social systems. But in tentatively advancing these models, the anthropologist should have an equal concern for assessing their appropriateness to particular situations. Examining the history of a specific area offers the attractive possibility of judging a model in terms of a sequence of developments. Dutch records, although neither as extensive nor as accurate as those for other regions more important than the outer arc, provide some means to this end. The Dutch East India Company and the later colonial administration both were meticulous keepers of records. (One has only to see the sheer accumulation of records that do exist to appreciate the frequent criticisms made of this endless paperwork in the colonies.)

The problem for this kind of study is rather different. There are, of course, and will always remain major inadequacies in the data but more often the data that are available—many of them in unpublished form—are tantalizingly mismatched to the question one wishes to ask. The problem, then, is how to proceed: how to restructure or reinterpret the available information to bring it to bear, in some fashion, on the question at hand. The procedure offers no direct access, but instead a series of byways whose steps must be clearly marked. To give an example: for Roti, there exist population figures taken at intervals from 1831 to the present. This is information that many anthropologists would be delighted to have. Quite apart from the questionable accuracy of these figures (there being no information on precisely how they were obtained), there is the problem that each set was gathered independently for different reasons—by commission officers, missionaries, district officers, then later by Dutch and Indonesian census officials. In the breakdown of these figures, populations are sometimes identified in terms of clans, or states whose borders fluctuated, or religion, or ethnic group. Throughout this period, migration to other islands was an important factor. Nevertheless, in various instances no discrimination is made in the differing populations of an island; more disturbingly, the populations of several small islands may be lumped together without further analysis. For the demographer these numbers are not easily interpretable without an age pyramid or a means of estimating the birth rate of any one group or local area. The data are enough to be indicative, but insufficient to be conclusive.

A draft of this book was completed before I had the results of the various computer analyses now included. That these analyses considerably bolster my argument merits their inclusion. (To facilitate presentation, I confine to notes and appendixes discussion of the methods by which they were derived.) Presentation consists in a series of approximations based on separate lines of inquiry that are intended to advance the general argument.

PART ONE

The Ecology and Economies of the Outer Arc

CHAPTER ONE

The Contrast
of Economies

IN THE TYPOLOGY of Indonesian ecological systems de-
scribed in *Agricultural Involution,* Clifford Geertz has drawn a vivid contrast
between the intensive wet-rice cultivation of the densely populated inner islands of Indonesia and the diverse, multicrop, dry-field cultivation of the
less populated outer islands.[1] This typology admits a variety of possible com-
posites based on the two systems and, more importantly, the adaptation of
either to the cultivation of cash crops for a market economy. What this typology neglects is a third, as yet minor but increasingly important, ecological
system in the outer islands of Indonesia. This is not another form of agriculture, but a highly specialized form of gathering: the intensive utilization of
certain productive species of palm. The object of the present study is to examine specific forms of palm utilization and to consider their social implication in current developments in the outer arc of the Lesser Sundas of eastern
Indonesia.

Researchers in southeast Asia have made varying estimates of the carrying
capacity of swidden systems under specific conditions. Freeman sets a maximum density of 20 to 25 persons per square kilometer for the Iban of Sara-
wak; Conklin, a figure of 48 per square kilometer for the Hanunoo in the
Philippines; Van Beukering has estimated 50 per square kilometer as an absolute ceiling on the density of swidden populations in Indonesia.[2] What is
expected to occur when these limits are reached or exceeded is a progressive
deterioration of the entire system—a shortening of the fallow cycle and a
succession to grassland climax. As is well recognized, there are definable limits to swidden agriculture.

Most of Timor and, in general, the outer arc of the Lesser Sundas, evidence the extreme conditions that lead to swidden deterioration: (*a*) a short, irregular, wet monsoon season with low overall rainfall; (*b*) a prolonged dry season, often initiated by tropical cyclones and dominated by a dry westerly wind; and (*c*) impermeable, erosion-prone, margalitic soils that suffer extreme desiccation during the long dry season. In a classic study, Ormeling has documented the results of swidden cultivation under these conditions.[3] Timor, for most of the year, is a parched, arid island. The average annual precipitation for the whole of Indonesian Timor is below 1,500 mm, making it one of the driest islands in Indonesia.[4] The distribution of this rain is variable. Higher elevations receive a heavier rainfall than most coastal areas, and the south coast more rain than the north coast, which has a calculated average annual precipitation of less than 775 mm. Critical factors in this situation are uncertainties over the onset of the rains, which may begin any time between November and January, and the enormous fluctuation in rainfall from season to season. In some years the rains may fail to arrive, and a ''wet season'' will bring little or no rain. And when the rains do arrive, they cannot immediately penetrate the soil; instead, they rush off in deep gutted rivers to the sea. The island is highly eroded and retains only traces of primary forest and larger patches of secondary forest. It is given over to various kinds of rugged savannah of palm, eucalyptus, acacia, and cemara.

In this environment the Atoni, the major population of west Timor, remain primarily swidden agriculturalists.[5] They depend for their subsistence on the cultivation of dry rice, maize, and some millet. The 1930 census figures for the Atoni indicate a range of population density from north to south Timor of 19.5 to 26.5 persons per square kilometer.[6] Already in 1930 certain limits had seemingly been reached; the history of the Atoni since that time has been one of continued population increase and recurrent, ever more severe, periods of famine.

The major complicating factor in this simple equation was the near-simultaneous colonial introduction, after 1910, of Bali cattle and a quick-growing, shrub-size weed, *Lantana camara* L. Ironically, there is some indication that lantana seeds and Bali cattle may have come on the same ships from Java. The effects were incalculable. Cattle, originally distributed as part of colonial policy to the local rulers and headmen of Timor, have increased spectacularly since the thirties. To this day, the large herds on the island are controlled by descendants of the earlier rulers. Raised for the export market, these cattle do not contribute appreciably to the diet of the local swidden agriculturalists. Studies have shown that cattle-grazing in association with swidden farming can, in fact, impede savannah climax and allow a more rapid return of secondary forestation to field clearings.[7] In the case of Timor, the rapid spread of cattle has led to indiscriminate grazing and, in large areas, to undeniable overgrazing during the dry season that in turn only furthers erosion when the rains suddenly arrive. Cattle have also led to a conspicuous decline in water buffalo, the older indigenous animal, and have forced an inordinate increase in the labor that must be expended to construct strong fencing. Estimates of this time-consuming labor for the Atoni vary from a quarter to a third of total work output in the initial preparation of a swidden field.[8]

What has most effectively checked the spread of cattle, however, is lantana, the once seemingly harmless ornamental hedge shrub. Estimates are that from 25 to 50 percent of Timor is now covered by this fire-resistant weed. Where dense lantana grows, few other plants thrive. As it spreads, it smothers grasslands and prevents cattle-grazing. Despite the fact that it resists burning and increases requirements for field-clearing labor, the Atoni agricultural population favors the lantana. It is an excellent, rapid field restorative. In one area of Timor on which studies have been made, the unimpeded spread of lantana led to both a decline in water buffalo and the virtual elimination of cattle export, but at the same time it reduced the fallow period for swidden fields from fifteen to five years. On Timor, cattle and lantana vie as the chief factors affecting the development of swidden agriculture.

To combat the spread of lantana, the Dutch, in the 1930's, began the experimental planting of a drought-resistant, leguminous shrub, *Leucaena glauca* Benth, colloquially known as *lamtoro*. The first planting of lamtoro on abandoned dry fields was in Amarasi, a former state that now forms the southern portion of the regency of Kupang. Lamtoro spread to neighboring areas and was introduced in the Belu region; local government efforts continue to promote the planting of this shrub. Lamtoro's deep root system makes it even more difficult to clear than lantana and, although it has little attraction for the agriculturalist, its leaves and husks are an excellent source of rich green fodder for livestock. An accommodation over lamtoro has developed into what is officially known as the *paron* system. Under this system cattle still graze freely throughout much of the interior of Timor, but many head are now rounded up at an earlier age than previously and sold to the local inhabitants in Amarasi and other areas of the regency of Kupang. These cattle are kept tied and fattened on lamtoro before they are eventually sold for export or for slaughter in Kupang. The success of the paron system on Timor is still uncertain. The immediate gains have gone to middlemen who trade the cattle, and to those populations that have access to established lamtoro fields.

Since 1930 the island of Timor has seen dramatic changes. With the coming of independence after 1945, Kupang, as a provincial capital, experienced a boom and now has some buildings several stories tall. The government bureaucracy expanded enormously, and with it the population of Kupang. The string of towns connected with Kupang via the trunk road that winds its way into the interior expanded proportionally and even attracted people from other islands. Soe, Kefamnanu, and Atambua became important towns on the road, which opened the interior to truck transportation. The relatively rich areas of Belu, somewhat cut off from Kupang but supplied from the port of Atapupu, have received generous infusions of mission aid.

Ormeling estimated a 1952 overall population density for west Timor of 32 persons per square kilometer.[9] By 1961, based on official figures, Timor's population had grown to 40 persons per square kilometer and by 1971 the island had a density of 49 persons per square kilometer. But these figures are inflated by various factors that have little to do with the Atoni population, who depend upon swidden agriculture. They include a considerable number of civil servants and their dependents, who live in towns and are supported by government subsidy; a large influx of peoples from other islands; and the dense Belu population of the southern coast of Timor, where rainfall and soil conditions permit wet-rice agriculture and gardening. By excluding these factors, it is possible to gain a better estimate of the population density of the Atoni cultivators. Figures for the regency of north central Timor, an area of particular relevance in this study, show a population of about 34 persons per square kilometer for 1961 and, depending on differing areal calculations for the regency,[10] this population rose to between 38 and 44 persons per square kilometer by 1971. Although these figures include the inhabitants of the town of Kefamnanu and a good number of immigrants, they provide a more accurate estimate of the present density for swidden agriculturalists.

More than any other island in the province, Timor has been affected by the spread of a cash economy. Still, it is questionable whether this has yet had a profound effect on the subsistence patterns of the majority of the indigenous population. Those Atoni who have no close relative in the civil service, who have no stake in the herds of cattle that graze in their territory, and who are unfamiliar with the subtleties of trade must subsist by cultivating their dry fields under conditions of ecological deterioration, irregular rainfall, and decreasing yields. In official documents Timor is often referred to as a *daerah minus,* a "deprived area." The situation has become so much a fact of life on Timor that town dwellers have a common expression for what happens each year in the interior. The period (often lasting two to three months) when food supplies have begun to run out for the Atoni and their new harvest is not yet gathered, is described, in Indonesian, as *lapar biasa,* the "ordinary hunger period." Nineteenth- and early twentieth-century reports make no mention of an annual lapar biasa period but all too frequently in recent decades, especially in dry years, this lapar biasa has turned into a *lapar luar biasa,* an "extraordinary hunger period," or simply *lapar betul,* "true famine." The evidence indicates that a variety of factors combined to impinge upon the purely swidden economy of the Atoni as early as 1930. Under these circumstances, as the population began to approach and then surpass an approximate limit of 30 persons per square kilometer, serious deterioration set in and has progressively produced the present situation.

At the western end of the outer arc of the Lesser Sundas is the island of Sumba. Much of central Sumba is a grassy upland with patches of forest; the southern coast has a more broken, irregular mountainous terrain, while the northern coast forms a dry lowland. Compared to some of the lush tropical islands of Indonesia, this island is starkly dry. Its western side is less subject to the drying winds from Australia, more liable to receive rain during the west monsoon, and better suited for irrigated wet-rice agriculture. To the east the island becomes progressively drier. Meteorological data to substantiate these differences between east and west Sumba are limited and not entirely reliable. Recent government figures for 1966 and 1969 indicate, however, that east Sumba had an average of 884 mm of rain distributed over 70 days, whereas west Sumba received 1,826 mm of rain over 90 days.[11] West Sumba's rainfall would appear to be at least double that of east Sumba and better distributed over the growing season.

Most Sumbanese, and nearly all east Sumbanese, are swidden agriculturalists.[12] Rice, maize, or sometimes millet are planted in dry fields in varying proportions depending on the quality of the soil and the possibilities of rain.[13] Wet rice is grown extensively in west Sumba, and only in poor, dry areas of the island is sorghum planted. The factor that most affected this traditional economy was the development of a booming horse trade in the nineteenth century. Horses raised in the central highlands were traded via the eastern lowlands to Arab merchants on the coast. This trade developed prior to Dutch administrative control of the island; but once established, the Dutch fostered the trade and improved the breeding stock. Herds, as on Timor, are a preserve of local rulers, and increased wealth has not had a direct effect on subsistence patterns. Census figures for Sumba in 1930 show a population density of 31.4 per square kilometer in the agriculturally rich areas of west Sumba, with a population of only 9.6 per square kilometer for the dry regions of east Sumba.

Since 1930 Sumba has experienced few of the dramatic changes that have occurred on Timor. No towns the size of Kupang can be found on the island, and its isolation in relation to Timor has at times appeared to have increased. While cattle have replaced horses as a source of outside revenue, the lack of interisland transportation has tended to hinder export. By 1971 west Sumba's population had grown to roughly 45 persons per square kilometer; east Sumba's population, including immigrants to its coastal regions, had increased to only 14 persons per square kilometer. Although the east Sumbanese face the recurrent hardships of swidden cultivators in a dry, deforested land, they do not suffer, to the same extent, the "ordinary hunger period" of the Timorese.

Between Sumba and Timor lie the islands of Roti and Ndao, and the island group of Savu. All the climatic factors that affect Timor and the eastern half of Sumba are intensified on these islands. Both are bare and eroded and rifted by rough hills of limestone and clay. Based on Dutch figures gathered in the early part of this century,[14] Roti is reported to have an average annual precipitation of less than 1,165 mm, as compared to Timor's 1,500 mm. More revealing is that whereas the island has an average of 62 days of rain in the year, only 12 days of them occur during the eight months from April to November. A British hydrologist, M. Wainwright, who surveyed water resources on Roti, Savu, and Timor in 1972 concluded that Roti received even less rainfall than is indicated by the earlier Dutch reports. Rainfall data were available only from Baä, the small town that serves as the government and trading center for the island. He reports that "the average for Baä over the last 15 years is 960 mm but this includes amounts of 422 mm and 490 mm respectively for the years 1966 and 1970. The length of the dry season indicates that Baä is more arid than almost all parts of Timor, and it is probable that some parts of Roti are considerably drier than Baä.[15]

Conditions on Savu are even more extreme. As one nineteenth-century commentator exaggeratedly described his first impression of the island: "No greenery, no plants, no trees. Savu is like a lump of stone set in the middle of an immense sea."[16] Based on some scant figures for the island, Savu, for example, had only 491 mm of rain during 29 days in 1953, 601 mm of rain during 41 days in 1954, and then in the following year received 991 mm of rain during 47 days.[17] More recent figures reveal the extremes to which Savu is subject. In 1970, only 379 mm of rain fell during 14 days, all concentrated between the middle of January and the end of February; the next year, 1,724 mm of rain fell in 69 days.[18] Although 1,724 mm is not an unusually high rainfall even by Timor standards, sudden heavy rainfall (over 400 mm fell in January 1971) coming after ten months of parching heat can produce havoc by its dangerous rapid runoff. Wainwright, in his survey on Savu, concludes that while the northern and eastern parts of the island have a probable average range between 700 and 1,000 mm of rain, the southwestern parts of the island receive much less and have a possible range between 500 and 800 mm.[19] There can be little doubt, as far as rainfall is concerned, that conditions on Roti and Savu are far worse than on Timor; these conditions resemble those of east Sumba, which has a population density of a mere 14 persons per square kilometer.

Yet the population figures for these islands portray a different picture. In 1930, Roti had an average population of 49 persons per square kilometer; figures for 1971 give the island an average density of 61 per square kilometer and, if these figures are analyzed in terms of the individual small states that make up the island, certain states have population densities of up to 130 per square kilometer. Savu is even more densely populated. In 1930, the Savu group already had a population of almost 71 per square kilometer. The tiny off-shore island of Raijua, by itself, had about 114 per square kilometer. Savu's population by 1961 had risen to 90 per square kilometer and in 1971 had reached 102. Ndao, the little island off Roti's northwestern coast, surpasses both Roti and the Savu group in density of population. In 1971, by official records, this tiny island had a population density of 232 per square kilometer.

All of these densities outstrip those of Timor and Sumba: all of them exceed Van Beukering's population ceiling for swidden agriculture; and in their upper range they are comparable to the population densities in areas of wet-rice cultivation outside of Java and Bali. The typology of Indonesian ecological systems cannot account for them. It is necessary, therefore, to examine the economic base that supports these high population densities.

THE PALM ECONOMIES OF ROTI AND SAVU

The populations of Roti and Savu depend for their survival on utilization of the lontar palm, a distinct species of *Borassus* (*Borassus sundaicus* Beccari).[20] A second major fan-leaf palm, the gewang (*Corypha elata* Roxb.), grows extensively on Roti but not on Savu. Rotinese are able to make use of the gewang for various products that supplement those of the lontar, whereas the Savunese are oriented more exclusively to the lontar. The utilization of the lontar approaches near-total exploitation.[21] Both populations literally harvest palms for their daily needs. And they have created around them, with palms as the pivot, a complex diverse economy. In general, the palms are neither planted nor tended in their early growth, but they thrive in such superabundance on these islands that their number has not yet been fully exploited. The precise carrying capacity of this economic adaptation to palm utilization remains unknown.

The lontar is a solitary-stemmed, dioecious or separately sexed, fan-leaf palm that may attain a height of 90 to 100 feet and a diameter of 2 to 3 feet. The gewang resembles the lontar but slightly exceeds it in height and diameter: it is hermaphroditic and although it is also a fan palm, the blades of its leaves radiate, as they extend outward, in spear-shaped lengths. At the crown of the lontar grow large inflorescences. In the male lontar, these inflorescences sprout what are technically termed rachillae, separately paired spike-like branches, each of which droops from the crown like some long, slender phallus. The inflorescences of the female lontar develop large clusters of heavy fruit. In the lontar, these inflorescences begin to appear early in the life of the palm. In this respect, the gewang is remarkably different. It grows for over a hundred years before it suddenly develops a single enormous terminal inflorescence like an ornate tower, flowers in unison with other gewang scattered over a wide area, and dies.

By breeching the inflorescences of either of these palms, it is possible to extract a sweet juice. Although the Rotinese are always ready to seize the rare opportunity to tap gewang, they and the Savunese depend for their livelihood upon the annual yield of the lontar. The lontar blossoms twice a year, and both male and female provide large quantities of juice. To tap the male, the long, drooping rachillae are slivered at their tips after budding and their fibrous structure is crushed to initiate the flow of juice. For the female, these inflorescences must be forcefully pressed and cut at their ends before they have begun to fruit.

The juice of the lontar is gathered in leaf-buckets twice daily by climbers who must cut a further thin slice from the end of the inflorescences to continue the flow. Fresh from the tree, this juice may be drunk as it is. During the months of the tapping season, Rotinese and Savunese live largely from the sweet yield of their trees. Since the juice sours quickly, whatever is not drunk is cooked immediately (usually over clay ovens hollowed in the earth) to a thick dark treacle or a somewhat lighter brown syrup; this syrup may be stored for long periods of time in jars and vats in the house. When needed, the syrup is mixed with water to make a sweet sugar drink. Consumed several times daily, often in place of any solid food, this drink is the normal sustenance of both the Rotinese and Savunese populations when no fresh palm juice is available. The syrup may also be crystallized in thick squares to form a brown rock sugar, or fermented to make a kind of beer. As a further product, the Rotinese (but not the Savunese) use this fermented beer as a mash from which they distill a fine sweet gin.

A young Rotinese in the crown of a lontar palm.

The lontar is among the most efficient of the world's sugar-producing plants. There is as yet no systematic study of the differential yield of lontar during a single season. Yields are, however, extremely high. They depend on the number of inflorescences tapped on each palm. Measurements indicate that a palm with five productive inflorescences will yield over 6.7 liters of juice in a day, or 47 liters in a week, while a palm at the end of its tapping period with only a single productive inflorescence will rarely yield less than 2.25 liters, or well over 15 liters a week.[22] The length of time a lontar will continue to produce depends mainly on the skill with which it is tapped and slivered.

At a minimum, a single palm can produce for three to five months, although on both Roti and Savu intensive palm-tapping is concentrated in a period of two months during the dry season. The conversion rate of juice to syrup depends on the cooking process. The Savunese, for example, cook the juice longer than the Rotinese and produce a thicker, darker syrup. The conversion of juice to sugar for Rotinese cooking is at a rate of approximately 15 percent. Ten liters of juice will thus yield 1.5 liters of cooked syrup. If one uses a conservative figure of only 3.5 liters per day for a two-month period, one palm would still yield 210 liters of juice, which would produce 31.5 liters of syrup. This would corroborate the frequent contention that any family on Roti or Savu can support itself from one or two palms that produce through an entire season. Most Rotinese and Savunese claim to be able to tap 20 to 30 trees; such claims ignore the fact that cooking, not tapping, is generally the limiting factor on syrup production. Rarely, in my experience, does anyone tap more than 10 to 15 trees at any one time, but the yield from even 10 trees, in two months, could be 315 liters of syrup.

The lontar supplies more than a source of subsistence for these islands.[23] The lontar, and to a lesser extent the gewang, provide in a bewildering number of ways the necessities of daily life. The full fan leaf of the lontar palm is used for thatching the house, which appears from the outside to be nothing more than an immense stack of lontar leaves; it is used also to make a native form of umbrella; it may be bent, shaped, and tied to create various sizes of bucket-like containers that are used for dozens of purposes from collecting palm juice, to carrying water, or—when punched with holes—to sprinkling in small gardens. The full leaf of the lontar is also shaped to form a near-hemispherical sounding board, into which a stringed bamboo tube is inserted. This is the *sesandu,* the unique musical instrument of the Rotinese. Separate strips of lontar leaf are plaited to make baskets, sacks, saddlebags, mats, fans, or are fashioned into hats (distinctive marks of Rotinese identification), belts, knife-sheaths, children's playthings, simple kinds of sandals, and even—when rasped thin—into a coarse cigarette paper. The outer layers of the spiked leaf of the gewang are peeled away and thin strips of the inner leaf extracted; these strips may be twined and tied and then woven, in the same way as thread, to make a rough-textured, durable burlap-like clothing. On Roti, this clothing no longer competes with cotton clothing, but it was once widespread and is still frequently worn by men and women engaged in heavy labor. Until the early years of this century, the Rotinese used this heavy gewang cloth to make durable sails for their boats and sold a quantity of these sailcloths to other native sailing people who visited the island. The long fibrous leafstalks of the gewang and the lontar (the former is superior) may be sliced, whittled, or twined to make ropes, bindings, straps, harnesses, and bridles. Whole, these same leafstalks are interlaced to make fences or bound together to make walls and partitions of a house. Old lontar leafstalks are the firewood for the cooking ovens. The wood of both tree trunks makes a much used but inferior plank for building, while the hollowed trunk of either tree is made into feeding troughs or cooling vats for stills. Finally, most Rotinese are buried in a lontar coffin, most Savunese wrapped in cloth in a lontar mat. After a Rotinese has died, a lontar leaf is split, folded, and knotted to form a three-pronged fork-like object called a *maik* or *ola.* This lontar leaf represents his spirit and is added to a cluster of

A Rotinese trimming lontar leaves.

similar leaves inside the house. Other maik that represent the power of these ancestors are hung wherever there is need of their protection—near cooking fires, in ripening fields, beside animal corrals. Thus it can be literally said of the Rotinese and Savunese that they are fed, equipped, attired, buried, and remembered after their decease by the products of their palms.

Tapping and the pruning of trees for their leaves and leafstalks is done during the dry months, April to November. Tapping may be done throughout this interval but there are two peak periods, one at the beginning of the dry season in April and May, the other toward its end in September and October. This second period is one of near-ceaseless activity, and cooking continues most of the day and often until late at night. The syrup of the first period is for sale, for export to the district capital or for making gin; in the second, more intensive tapping period each household produces most of its annual reserve. This second period follows the harvest and according to the success of the harvest, each household may gauge its needs for the rest of the year. The result is a considerable flexibility in the Rotinese and Savunese economies. There is a shift to greater lontar use during drier years, and a shift to lesser use in years of better rainfall. The lontars have never failed and in a mere two months, the slack months of the year in eastern Indonesia, the Rotinese and Savunese obtain the major part of their subsistence needs. This secure reliance on palms provides these populations with greater leisure during the rest of the year but, more importantly, with the time and opportunity to undertake and pursue other economic activities, at times at a greater risk than other neighboring groups who must depend on their often precarious swidden agriculture.

Palm utilization is only the nucleus of a complex interrelated economy. One immediate advantage of additional free time in the dry season is the opportunity for both men and women to engage in regular offshore fishing. A brief period of fishing forms part of the daily round of a large number of Rotinese. No one lives out of walking distance from the sea. The tides are classified in a monthly cycle according to the time and extent of their ebb. Stone fish walls, built at strategic locations all along the shoreline, are used as weirs to trap fish in the ebb tide. Following this ebb cycle, Rotinese fish at different times during the day and by torch light at night. Any Rotinese can tell the tide of the day, and anyone with a free hour or two can adjourn to the fish walls to catch fish. Net, line, and trap fishing are also utilized, but not on a daily basis.

Almost as important as fishing is the gathering of seaweed. Whether or not a day's tide fishing proves successful, it is usually possible to gather a leaf-bucket or two of raw seaweed. On islands where there is a distinct lack of vegetable foods, this seaweed appears to provide an important supplement to the daily diet.[24] It is not unusual on Roti to come upon an entire family dining regally from the contents of a couple of lontar buckets, one containing five or six liters of sweet palm juice, the other brimfull of salty, slimy, slightly sour strands of green seaweed. This particular combination of sweet and sour may not appeal to everyone, but those accustomed to it certainly enjoy it with considerable relish. The Savunese and Ndaonese add a further culinary treat: a small "seaworm" known as the *nyale,* which appears with annual regularity and in great quantities on the southern coasts of these islands. Pickled in lontar vinegar, these nyale also make an excellent food.[25]

Two other closely related activities in this palm economy are semi-intensive pig-rearing and large-scale honey-gathering. Pigs may occasionally be fed the fruit of the female lontar; they are frequently fed fresh lontar juice and always receive the residue and spill from the syrup-cooking process; often, but not regularly, they are fed surplus syrup mixed with water. Syrup feeding is done more regularly on Savu than on Roti, where it is the gewang, rather than the lontar, that provides pig feed. These palms are felled, cut into cylinder-block wheels, and rolled home where they are chopped and allowed to soak in water. The resultant hard sago-mash makes a starchy pig feed. Each household owns at least a few pigs, which spend their days scavenging beneath and around the house. Rarely will a household's pigs, however, number more than seven or eight, and a system exists for farming out extra pigs. There are no occasions for the massive slaughter of these animals, although they are consumed liberally at all feasts. Nor are they exported in large numbers. They contribute, instead, a stable protein supplement to the diet.

With tens of thousands of palms dripping a sugary juice from their crowns, the bee populations of Roti and Savu are considerable. The Rotinese, by long tradition, allot one day a week for the bees to drink undisturbed. The only checks on these populations are the occasional tropical cyclones that lash the islands and scatter the bees to sea. Since these islands already have an abundant supply of sugar foods, neither Rotinese nor Savunese prize honey as a special delicacy. Instead, since the earliest days of the Dutch East India Company, honey has served as a valuable export commodity.

The Ndaonese are lontar-tappers like the Rotinese and Savunese, but they have developed their own unique complement to this economy. All of the men of Ndao are goldsmiths and silversmiths, and they leave their island at the beginning of each dry season to fashion jewelry for the peoples of the Timor area. They also sell finished jewelry and woven cloths and willingly take advances on orders for work to be completed by the following season. Their payments are in the foodstuffs of the new harvest and in small livestock. When they have completed their work and been given their payments, most men return in time to tap their lontar palms during the peak production period.

FORMS OF CULTIVATION AND ANIMAL HUSBANDRY

The Rotinese and Savunese are gatherers in that they "harvest" their palms for the great majority of their needs. They are also cultivators on extremely poor land. Unlike the Timorese or Sumbanese, they have ceased to rely for their livelihood on swidden agriculture: their various fields are generally of a more permanent nature. What is more, in any reasonably good year, they can expect better yields from relatively small gardens near their houses than many Timorese can hope to obtain from their extensive clearings of scrub and secondary forest, often located at a distance from their settlements. Part of the answer to this seeming paradox is again the lontar palm.

While Rotinese and Savunese settlement patterns differ, they have in common the requirement of proximity to a source of water and a sizable number of palms. Since palms abound, this second requirement poses little difficulty. Most settlements are located in and about stands of lontar palm. By the end of the dry season when tapping has begun to decrease, these settlements are strewn with the debris of the palms. Leaves and parts of leaves lie scattered everywhere and, if someone has rethatched a house, the old leaf-thatching also remains stacked up somewhere. These leaves are not wasted. They are gathered and laid down as a thick leaf-carpet over each garden. And just before the rains are expected, they are burned to provide what is, in effect, an excellent fertilizer.[26] In addition to this soil restorative, animal manures are gathered and laid on specially selected gardens, usually separate tobacco gardens. In this way gardens may be used from year to year.

Through the use of lontar leaves and animal manures the Rotinese and Savunese have solved, to a limited extent, the problem of soil fertility that constrains Timorese and Sumbanese agriculture. They have also surmounted in various ways the difficulties involved in cultivating land, while at the same time maintaining herds of grazing animals. Instead of a single solution to these difficulties, it is necessary to examine the various solutions that have been developed separately on the two islands. The subsidiary agricultural activities of the Rotinese and Savunese do differ. Conditions are by no means identical on the two islands, and the crops that are planted vary somewhat. The major differences are not so much in the techniques used, the foods that are grown, or the animals that are kept, but rather in their relative importance, proportion, and organization in a total system. Thus, there are notable variations in this total system in different areas of Roti.

A major difference between Roti and Savu is that there exist on Roti a few well-located sources of natural spring water, mainly in central and eastern Roti.[27] These permit the limited development of wet-rice agriculture. On Savu, though some sources of water do exist, they are extremely limited and poorly located. There are one or two lakes in southwestern Roti that can be dammed and a number of small rivers in northwestern Roti that can be diverted, but in general west Roti resembles Savu in its limitations on wet-rice agriculture. The Rotinese themselves recognize this obliquely and attribute

The burning of lontar leaves fertilizes a garden. This adaptation of a swidden technique is the means by which the Rotinese have been able to move from slash-and-burn agriculture to semipermanent gardening. Above, a Rotinese woman carpets a garden with lontar leaves before burning; below, the leaves are burned in preparation for planting the garden.

the resemblances to ancient Savunese influence in these areas. It is possible with equal justification to attribute these resemblances, in part, to the systematic developments inherent in lontar palm exploitation.

Fencing (or, more precisely, fence construction) is crucial to agricultural undertakings throughout the islands of the outer arc and has important economic consequences. For the Timorese, the most common type of fence is a stout barricade of felled tree trunks interwoven with heavy branches. This kind of fence comes to nearly the height of a man and must be annually repaired and reinforced to prevent grazing cattle from entering the fields. Ormeling, summarizing the research of various agricultural extension officers, reports that the Timorese, in their defense against livestock, must expend from one-fourth to one-third of their total labor input on crop protection; despite this enormous effort, the fencing provides insufficient protection against animals, both large and small.[28]

A further apparent difficulty that faces the Timorese cultivator is the lack of any large, relatively stable social grouping that might direct communal labor in the arduous tasks of clearing, fencing, and turning the soil. According to Schulte Nordholt, it is generally three or four individuals, a small core of agnates, joined in some instances by their affines, who cooperate in working the fields. When necessary, they must call on others for assistance and must provide these laborers with a communal meal, which is itself part of a sacrifice to the powers of the earth. In recent years, as the Timorese clearly admit, this traditional system has begun to break down—or rather, it has begun to develop into a system based on a mutual exchange of labor.[29]

Fencing on Roti and Savu contrasts sharply with that on Timor. Most Rotinese fences are constructed of a readily available material: the leafstalks primarily of the gewang and secondarily of the lontar palm. The stalks are about five feet long and can be interwoven quickly between supporting poles driven into the ground. This type of fence can be easily constructed, easily reinforced where necessary, and easily repaired from year to year. For more permanent fencing, Rotinese use another available material: large chunks of the coral limestone with which Roti abounds. Savunese fencing seems to be even better adapted, and more labor-saving as well. Although leafstalk fences and finely constructed rock walls can be found on Savu, the Savunese prefer what they call "living fences." One kind of living fence consists of a low mound of earth planted with cacti. Within a few years, these cacti form a barrier virtually impenetrable to all animal intrusion. The other kind of preferred fence is itself a wall of living trees. Savunese stake out their fields by planting, at close intervals, branches of the *kahi* tree (*Lannea grandis* Engl.). When these branches have taken root and grown, it is a simple task to close the gaps between them with other branches or leafstalks to make an effective form of fence. Unlike Timor, where trees are felled and destroyed as part of the clearing process of the fields and to provide fence materials, Savunese actually restore trees to the land with their fences.[30]

There is a further form of fencing on Savu for which there is no equivalent on Roti. On Roti, palms grow nearly everywhere and are rarely planted.[31] A few individuals have planted lontar for themselves but these cases (as yet) hardly constitute common practice. For most Rotinese, the need for more lontar palms has not arisen. This is not the case on Savu, where there are found what may best be described as lontar enclosures. An enclosure consists of anywhere from 50 to 100 or more palms that have been specially planted in a dense cluster. These enclosures are well fenced to protect the trees in their early stages of growth; once the trees have grown to a safe height, the fencing is allowed to fall into disrepair. These enclosures can be observed in Liae in the southern part of Savu, and according to various informants are also to be found in Mesara to the west. More significantly still, such enclosures are said to be a recent phenomenon, one that has apparently occurred

A Savunese lontar garden in a fenced enclosure in Liae. The special planting of a cluster of palms marks a further stage in lontar utilization on Savu.

within living memory. They constitute a conscious attempt to increase the number of lontar and concentrate them for purposes of tapping. The fact that the fencing and planting of lontar palms has now begun in certain areas of Savu suggests a potential new dimension for palm utilization in the islands. Under the pressure of increasing population, a system of intensive gathering has begun to develop into an even more efficient system of gathering based on cultivation of the prime sources of supply.

In this connection, the social organization of the labor on Roti and Savu is as important as the techniques, materials, and rationale of fencing itself. On Roti, there exist permanent fencing corporations known as *lala*. These lala have memberships that may vary from 10 persons to 50 or more, depending on the nature of the field. All plots within a lala are individually owned, planted, and harvested, but each member is obliged to maintain a portion of the common fence. Failure to do so deprives a member of the right to plant his field for a period of one to three years, or may result in permanent loss of a field in the case of complete neglect.

Membership in these corporations is open to anyone who inherits, purchases, or is given a field within the complex or who extends the fence at its periphery to include an additional cleared piece of land. In the case of irrigated land (either wet-rice fields or irrigated orchard gardens), members share a common source of water. All sources of water are "owned" by specific clans. This ownership is a ritual entitlement to appoint a person to perform sacrifices for the lala watered by the same spring or river diversion. The members themselves appoint persons from among their membership to one or two titled positions in the lala (*manake:* "the cutter"—that is, "the decision-maker," and *manakila-oe:* "the distributor of water"); these individuals make all decisions affecting the lala, issue orders for labor, and apportion water to fields. Once the fields have been planted, the lala is closed to all members except these titled officers, and they alone determine when the lala may be opened for harvesting or, in the case of an orchard, for picking.

In the case of the dry fields that are still to be found on the island, essentially the same structure is maintained, but it is organized around the single figure of a manake. The island has reached a stage where little land remains to be cleared of primary forest. The shifting that occurs is from one dry-field lala to another and as far as possible (in a minimal seven- or eight-year cycle) the former lala membership is reconvened to clear scrub brush from their fields and to restore their communal fence. The extent to which this has stabilized is indicated by the fact that dry fields have individual names like wet-rice fields. As this form of dry-field cultivation has declined, it has been replaced by semipermanent, fertilized household gardens. These smaller gardens are owned and fenced by each individual household. Since they are near at hand, they can be carefully tended and are less subject to destruction by livestock.

The scale of the social organization of agricultural labor on Savu far exceeds that of Roti. To this day, each of the traditional states of Savu is a ritually constituted organization directed toward the communal conduct of agricultural and tapping activities. Each state has its own complex priesthood and ceremonial system based on a lunar calendar, and although their rituals may resemble one another in essential features, each state conducts its own activities in a phased cycle over the calendar year.[32] The named months of the calendar demarcate various seasonal pursuits, and the priests of state, with their attendants and functionaries, determine and oversee cooperative agricultural efforts. Each state is divided into residential and cultivable land and, until recently, few Savunese have ventured to live outside the precincts of their village. As on Roti, individual plots of land are owned, worked, and harvested by households—but the time for planting, working, and harvesting these fields is regulated by the priesthood. One can almost describe the state apparatus of Savu as the equivalent of an elaborate, all-embracing lala.

Besides the organization of labor in communal activities, all the islands of the outer arc need to balance the requirements of cultivation with those of animal husbandry. Fencing is a major factor in this equation, but the control of the animals is equally important. As in the case of cultivation, there are important differences between Roti and Savu, on the one hand, and Timor (and, to a lesser extent, Sumba) on the other.

Among both the Timorese and Sumbanese, the traditionally important livestock have been water buffalo and pigs. The goat, which archaeological excavation indicates to be an ancient animal in this area, was and is of relatively minor importance. Horses were introduced to these islands, probably via Java, well before the arrival of the first Europeans. In the nineteenth century, horse herds on Sumba increased because of the stimulation of export trade. In the twentieth century, cattle were introduced to both islands for the purpose of eventual export; their numbers have expanded enormously, although more so on Timor than on Sumba. The increase in the number of cattle on Timor, with the resulting decrease in the number of water buffalo, and the combined increase of horses and cattle on Sumba have created the present conflict between shifting cultivation for subsistence and livestock-raising for export.[33]

On Roti and Savu, the situation is different. First, there is intensive pig-rearing, for which there is no equivalent among the Sumbanese or Timorese. Secondly, smaller livestock are of considerable importance—not only goats

but also sheep. Unlike goats, which are free-ranging animals, sheep must
be tended. In economies like those of the Sumbanese and Timorese, where
animals are allowed to graze freely and labor is allocated to the protection of shifting fields, sheep present a problem. In the outer arc, only Rotinese and Savunese keep herds of sheep to the extent that their very presence
is a recognized distinguishing characteristic of these populations. Finally,
the Dutch scheme that introduced Bali cattle first to Timor and later to
Sumba failed on Roti and Savu. The water buffalo has not been displaced.

A number of factors are undoubtedly responsible for the retention of the
water buffalo on Roti and Savu. Its status as a medium of bridewealth exchange taken alone is insufficient explanation. In east Roti, for example,
bridewealth is indeed reckoned in female water buffalo, whereas in west
Roti it can also be reckoned in equivalent native units of gold (*oma*).
Throughout Roti, however, it is possible to pay bridewealth in goats or
sheep. The same would seem to be true of Savu, where the buffalo is an
important but not an exclusive medium of exchange.

Another factor in the predominance of the water buffalo is its capacity to
withstand the heat and desiccation of the long dry season on Roti and Savu.
Despite its name, the water buffalo on both islands must go without water
to wallow in for several months of the year. In the dry season, these animals
can be seen standing for most of the day under the shade of a few trees. They
graze only early in the morning, late in the afternoon, or at night. Their
weight loss is considerable, and invariably by the end of the season, some
water buffalo simply collapse and have to be killed. But most survive and
seem to regain their weight within a month or two of the first rains. Under
these same conditions, it is said that most of the lightly built Bali cattle
introduced by the Dutch died out. In fact, however, a few roaming head of
these cattle remain and are hunted by the descendants of the lords to whom
they were originally given.

Water buffalo are also retained because they are considered indispensable
to wet-rice cultivation on both islands. After the rains have soaked the earth,
water buffalo are driven in circles through the sodden fields, treading them
to several feet of mire. Dikes and irrigation canals are laboriously rebuilt,
and rice is sown by broadcasting it or is planted by hand after having first
been grown in seedbeds. This use of the water buffalo, not as a plow animal,
but as the plow itself, is a further factor in the failure of the Dutch cattle
scheme.[34]

The distribution of the buffalo on Roti confirms its use in agriculture and
provides the first of several indicators of a contrast in the local economies of
the eastern and western portions of the island. On the basis of available,

relatively reliable animal distribution figures (which date, however, from the colonial period),[35] the northern and eastern domains of Roti, which have the greatest potential for wet-rice cultivation (Baä, Termanu, Korbaffo, Diu, and Bilba) and which comprise 33 percent of the total area of the island, had 29 percent of the population, a mere 20 percent of all pigs, but 53 percent of all water buffalo. The more intensive lontar areas in the west, with higher population densities (Lelain, Dengka, Thie, Oenale, and Delha), which comprise a nearly comparable 31 percent of land area, had 44 percent of the population, only 25 percent of all buffalo, but 65 percent of all pigs. Other livestock were more equally distributed. The same five eastern domains had 33 percent of the goat and sheep herds; the western domains, 45 percent. Extending this comparison, the Savu group of islands, with somewhat more than half of Roti's population (56 percent) and with approximately 61 percent of its surface area,[36] at the time these figures were compiled had more pigs than the entire island of Roti.

The pattern of animal husbandry on these islands does not permit indiscriminant grazing. The general pattern during the growing season is to tie, tend, or herd livestock during the day and to pen or corral them at night. In parts of Savu, this has developed to the point where certain areas are entirely closed to grazing animals and the fields within these areas no longer require fences. Generally, however, goats, sheep, and pigs are kept in pens beneath or beside their owner's house; all the buffalo of a village area are confined in a communal corral. The heat of the dry season restrains water buffalo and restricts them to areas of shade and, where possible, pools of water in riverbeds. But as the growing season continues, the Rotinese, for example, recognize the need for buffalo to graze at night despite the risk of their intruding into fields. This constitutes a calculated risk, a trade-off, on which Rotinese court law is explicit. Any animal that intrudes into a lala may be shot, provided one fires from outside the fence. As long as this intrusion is not the result of defects in fencing, the court will award the meat of the animal, half to the owner and half to be divided among those whose fields suffered damage. Even when permitted to range freely, buffalo herds tend to graze in a confined area and their droppings, great brown flatcakes baked in the sun, may easily be gathered for fertilizer by the children of the area. Finally, after the harvest, animals are purposely penned in fields to graze on the stubble and further manure them.

Critical variables in the native economies of the islands of the outer arc include both fencing and herding. At one extreme, there is the situation on Timor: notorious overgrazing by cattle and enormous expenditure of time-consuming labor, organized by small groups of kin, in the fencing of frequently shifted fields. At the other extreme is Savu, where the fencing of fields has been greatly simplified or in places actually eliminated, where livestock are penned or corralled during the growing season, and where communal labor is directed by an indigenous priesthood. Roti lies between these extremes and is able to exploit various possibilities. Fencing is done by strictly regulated corporations. Most fencing is relatively permanent and labor is mainly expended on fence restoration. Animals at times are penned or corralled, but are given a greater freedom to graze than on Savu. On both Roti and Savu, an accommodation between cultivation and animal husbandry has taken place precisely where there is a conflict between these activities on Timor.

The differences between the palm-centered economies of Roti and Savu and the swidden economies of the neighboring islands, particularly Timor, are considerable. This contrast can be summarized and displayed as a related complex of elements, shown in Table 1.

Whereas the Rotinese and Savunese economies consist in a number of positively interrelated elements that are efficiently adapted to the exploitation of their ecological situation, the Timorese economy seems locked in a negative and increasingly nonadaptive system. The economy of the east Sumbanese shares many of the features of the Timorese economy, but the low density of the east Sumbanese population makes their situation less critical.

Having developed this contrast in some detail, it is necessary that we make further fine distinctions among the populations who rely upon palms before proceeding to examine the direct clash of their economies with those based on swidden agriculture.

INTERRELATIONS AMONG MEN AND LIVESTOCK

The basic contrast between a lontar economy, as found on Roti, Ndao, and Savu, and a swidden economy, as practiced on Timor (and Sumba), is evident. Judged as a general system, the Timorese economy seems, to an exceptional degree, to be a single structured system. In adapting to their environment—climatic conditions, lessening soil fertility, widespread erosion, and the pressure of a larger population—the Timorese have been forced, owing to the nonavailability of other modes of production, to rely even more heavily on swidden. This investment of time and labor merely maintains a system for which there is no future and—at present—no alternative. The introduction of cattle, in an attempt to diversify this economy, had the converse

TABLE 1   Contrasting characteristics of the palm-centered economies of Roti and Savu and of the swidden economies of the nearby islands (typified by Timor).

Roti and Savu	Timor
1. Intensive palm utilization.	1. Deteriorating swidden agriculture.
2. Extensive honey-gathering.	2. Limited honey-gathering.
3. Semi-intensive animal husbandry centering on pigs and water buffalo. Sheep and goats very important.	3. Replacement of water buffalo by cattle. Nonintensive husbandry and indiscriminate grazing. No sheep and few goats.
4. Extensive offshore fishing, and gathering of raw seaweed.	4. No fishing.
5. A shift from swidden agriculture to semipermanent gardening and, where possible, development of wet-rice cultivation.	5. Either: (a) lengthening of the fallow cycle and increased shifting of fields, with the need for larger fields to compensate for decreasing productivity; or (b) shortening of the fallow cycle and a decline in livestock.
6. Elimination of field fencing or corporate construction of durable fences. Trend toward penning and corralling of animals.	6. Increasing expenditure of time and labor on more extensive, strong (but never permanent) fencing to guard against intrusive cattle.
7. Permanent organization of communal labor beyond the level of the kin group.	7. Organization of labor by small groups of kin and affines, with additional labor obtained either by feasting or mutual exchange.
8. Use of lontar leaves and animal manures as fertilizer on small gardens.	8. No use of manures. Fertilization only from field burning.
9. Free time to engage in other activities.	9. Slack periods, largely spent guarding dry fields; ''ordinary hunger season'' annually.

effect. Cattle benefited their owners, as well as the merchants and middle-men, while they restricted the majority of swidden farmers.

A lontar economy, by contrast, is unusual not only because of its special mode of production but because of its diversity. Most Rotinese and Savunese are simultaneously tappers, farmers, fishermen, and herders, while Ndao-nese are tappers and goldsmiths. The lontar is the pivot. Without it, subsistence would probably be as precarious as on Timor. But lontar production provides (a) time to engage in a variety of activities, (b) the ability to alter, at some risk, other aspects of the economy and, with this ability, (c) the means to adapt these subsystems, in a reasonably short time, to changing conditions. Rather than some monolithic whole, a lontar economy comprises a series of related but relatively independent subsystems, any of which may be modified or developed provided that the pivotal lontar production is not altered. This is, in fact, the case on the islands of the outer arc. Roti, Ndao, and Savu have developed different subsystems of their lontar economies. The same is true of the various states of Roti (shown in Map 3). The states accord varying emphases to their economies, and individuals may, to a certain extent, gauge their pursuits to meet their needs by choosing from a range of subsistence activities. This diversity, though difficult to summarize, is the key to Rotinese and Savunese adaptiveness.

Amid this diversity, it would be useful to scale these islands or their local areas by means of some set of independent indexes whose significance can be related to palm utilization. To do this, it is possible to examine the systems of livestock-raising found in association with the lontar economies in the different areas. This examination can be posed in terms of three sets of variables: land, people, and animals. The animals, for purposes of this comparison, are pigs, water buffalo, and the combined population of goats and sheep. The object is to relate the human populations to their corresponding animal populations. The immediate difficulty with this analysis derives from the problem of diversity. Both human and animal populations are distributed over widely differing areas. Relative land area therefore is a factor that must be taken into consideration. A possible solution might be to treat all these populations in terms of their density per square kilometer. This would provide a crude but serviceable means of limited comparison. The initial comparisons, for example, of the carrying capacity or human population density per square kilometer of the lontar and the swidden regions in the outer arc have already provided one such measure. At this stage, my aim is to develop and refine further measures.

By means of a series of stepwise regressions using the available figures,[37] summarized in Table 2, the various populations—human and animal—can be related to land area and then, with these correlations, can also be related

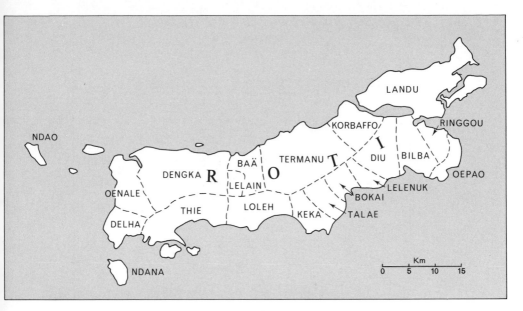

MAP 3 The island of Roti showing its various states.

to one another with the effect of land area removed. (The statistical procedures involved in this analysis are discussed separately in Appendix B.) Interpretation of the results of this analysis corroborates certain common native observations about the different local emphases of the palm economies of Roti and Savu. In other words, it provides quantitative measures of general observations.

In a lontar economy, pigs are a prime means of converting palm stuffs to protein. Throughout most of the tapping season pigs, like people, drink a daily diet of lontar juice.[38] At the height of the tapping season, they receive most of the froth from the cooking pots, while during the rainy season they are frequently given syrup and water. In addition, throughout the year (on Roti in particular) pigs are regularly fed the soaked, pulpy core of the gewang palm. Pigs and palms go together, and one can view pigs as a reasonable indicator of palm utilization.

Water buffalo, on the other hand, are required in wet-rice cultivation. After the earth has been soaked by the rains or initially irrigated, herds of these immense animals are required to tread the soft earth to deep mud. Nowhere in wet-rice growing regions of any of the islands of the outer arc have cattle supplanted water buffalo. Besides being a mark of prestige and wealth, water buffalo are a source of protein and the main means of working the land. One can view water buffalo as an indicator of wet-rice cultivation.[39]

For the purposes of this analysis goats and sheep have been grouped

TABLE 2   Populations of men and livestock on Roti, Ndao, and Savu.

State or island	Land area (sq km)	Human population	Buffalo population	Pig population	Goat population	Sheep population	Combined goat-sheep population
Landu	169	1,481	229	122	502	917	1,419
Ringgou/Oepao	57	3,171	283	64	256	43	299
Bilba	59	2,942	363	64	221	822	1,043
Diu	61	1,356	205	64	152	739	891
Korbaffo	60	2,466	430	246	391	772	1,163
Lelenuk/Bokai	52	598	94	46	63	98	161
Termanu	177	4,586	857	125	341	435	776
Baä	48	2,663	667	246	503	688	1,191
Talae	33	974	115	71	153	105	258
Keka	42	1,148	83	46	171	281	452
Loleh	77	3,928	175	102	231	170	401
Dengka/Lelain	178	7,390	625	1,135	1,775	1,937	3,712
Thie	93	7,911	484	676	574	1,342	1,916
Oenale	64	2,394	85	284	87	594	681
Delha	44	1,333	41	341	85	625	710
Ndao	9	1,686	11	123	151	190	341
Savu	747	27,311	3,880	4,010	1,180	4,595	5,775

together, in part because the native classification groups them together. On Roti, they are both *bii,* and on Savu, *kii.* Goats are considered the "real" or "native" animal (*bii-hik/kii hawu*) and sheep have been assimilated to this category (*bii-lopo/kii djawa*). Sheep have little wool and in appearance actually resemble goats. Both are raised for their meat. Goats and sheep need pasture, but they need not have—and in fact do not have—choice pasture. These animals graze on the poorest of denuded rock-strewn land. Sheep must be tended. Goats wander more freely, though when they have grown large, male goats are often hobbled. Both goats and sheep graze widely, often not far from each other on the same land, and they tend not to congregate (as do water buffalo) near sources of water. Thus there is firm justification for the native view that goats and sheep graze where nothing much can grow and where no other animals can survive. The designation of an area or a stretch of land as "goat-sheep land" usually indicates that it is fit for little else. On such land, there is only a limited possibility of cultivation, and there are usually too few palms to make tapping worthwhile. One can thus interpret goats and sheep as a kind of indicator of sparse, relatively poor pasture land. One would, therefore, expect a gross correlation between states with the largest land areas and the largest goat-sheep populations, but once the factor of area has been removed, this indicator may reveal a further aspect to the possible economic emphases found in these island economies.

A Rotinese herder tending a flock of sheep. These scrawny animals graze on the eroded scrub land that covers much of Roti.

In examining the makeup of the animal populations associated with lontar economies, one can both differentiate these economies in terms of their possible subsystems and highlight the contrast between the lontar economies and those of the swidden areas. The Timorese possess large numbers of cattle, fewer water buffalo, goats, and pigs; the Rotinese and Savunese keep water buffalo, no cattle, sheep in larger numbers than goats, and sizable populations of pigs.

One would expect the variables in this analysis—people, buffalo, pigs, goats, and sheep—to show some correlation with land, their supporting base. As it turns out, buffalo show a higher relation to land than does the combined total of the goat and sheep populations. The human population shows less correlation than goats and sheep, while pigs show the least. The correlation coefficients are as follows:

Buffalo	0.85
Goats and sheep	0.73
Humans	0.71
Goats	0.66
Sheep	0.63
Pigs	0.62

Removing the effect of land area on these animal and human populations and then correlating them with one another, the most significant relation to emerge is that between pigs and people. Figure 1 locates the various states in terms of the regression line of pigs on the human population. Dengka and Thie, the states of west Roti, identified by their intensive lontar economy and higher density of population, along with Savu and Ndao, the islands to the west that conform to this same intensive palm utilization and dense population pattern, are the major pig-raising areas. Delha in west Roti, although it has a low population, fits with this same group. At the midpoint and on the line of regression is Baä, followed by Korbaffo and Oenale, while Loleh with all the states of east Roti appear as relatively low pig-raising areas. Although not a perfect diagrammatic representation, since Loleh groups with east Roti, and Korbaffo and Oenale strike a balance between east and west Rotinese patterns, nonetheless the pig-raising dimension in Figure 1 gives an approximate geographic plot of the states of Roti and of the islands of Ndao and Savu as one moves from east to west.

Another significant correlation to emerge[40] is that between the pig population and the combined goat and sheep population. Examined separately, there is a closer correlation of pigs with sheep than with goats. This suggests that in the areas of more intensive pig-raising there is a progressive shift

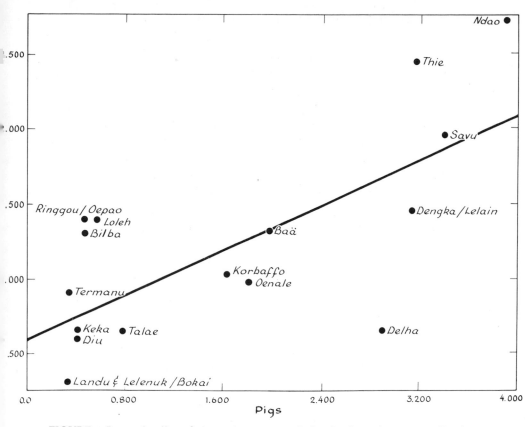

FIGURE 1 Regression line of pigs on human population for the various states of Roti and the islands of Ndao and Savu with the factor of land area removed.

from goats to sheep. In other words, there appears to be a tendency toward greater specialization, which emerges as a gradual shift from a system of husbandry that permits limited free grazing for goats to one that concentrates on increased herding of sheep. Since, however, this analysis is based on a limited number of observational units, it is best to be somewhat cautious in the interpretation of the data.

It is possible, however, to relate the various forms of animal husbandry found on Roti, Ndao, and Savu to one another as coherent, comparable economic strategies. Taking the ratios of all animal populations within each area and dividing them by the sums of the ratios of buffalo, pigs, and goats plus sheep provides an estimate of the ratio of each of the animal populations to the total livestock of that area. By means of this standardization, again with the effect of land area removed, one can examine the pattern by which each area (state or island) apportions its livestock.[41]

The picture that emerges is indeed striking. All of the states and islands in this analysis have lontar-centered economies, but only the states of west Roti, Ndao, and Savu are lontar-intensive. These are the areas of highest population density and, as we have seen, the areas of most intensive pig-raising. They are also, not surprisingly, the areas where pigs represent the highest proportion of the total livestock. These areas are Delha, Ndao, Savu, Oenale, Dengka/Lelain, and Thie, in that order. In the states of east Roti that require buffalo not only for meat but also to tread the rice fields, buffalo represent the highest proportion of the total livestock. Ringgou/Oepao, Termanu, Baä, Bilba, Lelenuk/Bokai, and Talae rank highest according to this criterion. Korbaffo and Loleh have the most even balance in livestock. But both states have a higher proportion of buffalo than of pigs and therefore are still weighted to the eastern Rotinese pattern. Diu has almost the same proportion of buffalo as Korbaffo and Loleh, but instead of pigs its livestock includes a high proportion of goats and sheep. Landu and Keka, the two states with the last remaining forest, and Diu, with the largest stretches of grassland savannah on Roti, are the three states with goat-sheep-oriented economies.

Figure 2, a barycentric representation, provides a graphic illustration of these economic strategies.[42] All the states are located by triangular coordinates that represent the three kinds of animal populations. Each of these coordinates has a scale from 1 to 100, reading from the base to the tip of each angle. One angle represents water buffalo; the second, pigs; and the third, goats and sheep. The proportional mean for all these lontar economies is an almost-perfect balance of the three kinds of livestock: 0.35, buffalo; 0.34, pigs; 0.31, goats/sheep. This point is plotted near the center of the figure, and it can easily be seen how the various states diverge from this mean strategy. The states of west Roti, Ndao, and Savu cluster to one side of the triangle; those of east Roti to the other side. Underlying the diversity of local economic strategies are certain clear tendencies in the palm economies of the area. It is the implications of these tendencies that we shall consider next.

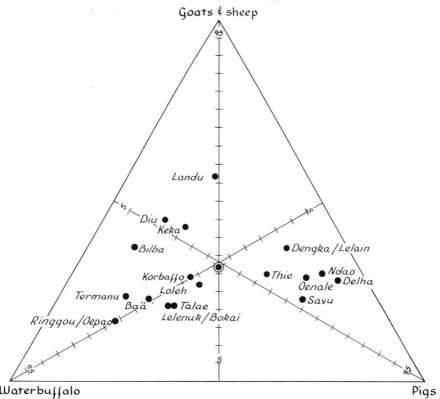

FIGURE 2 Barycentric representation of the proportions of water buffalo, pigs, and goats and sheep in the various states of Roti and on the islands of Ndao and Savu, showing how each state or island diverges from a theoretical balance of the three types of livestock. For a full explanation of the derivation of this figure, consult Appendix B.

CHAPTER TWO

The Clash
of Economies

TO TAKE INTO account the results of the previous analysis and to integrate them into the general structure of the argument, a brief recapitulation is in order. Simple population density figures for the outer arc of the Lesser Sundas revealed a significant difference between the islands of Savu and Roti and their affiliates, Raijua and Ndao, on the one hand, and the two larger islands to the east and west, Timor and Sumba. The difference was seen to lie, in part, in the economies of the islands.

The economies of east Sumba and much of west Timor are heavily dependent on swidden agriculture, which is characterized by a lengthy cycle of field rotation, burning as a method of land-clearing, and extensive fencing to protect crops from free-ranging animals. Originally, both Sumba and Timor had more or less the same sorts of animals. Then each began raising animals for export to bolster their traditional economies: horses in the early nineteenth century on Sumba, and cattle in the early twentieth century on Timor and later on Sumba. The structure of the societies on these islands, the very methods by which the animals were introduced, and the way in which this export trade was conducted fostered the development of native states controlled by wealthy, powerful elites, without radically altering the subsistence base. Instead, the animals raised for export further burdened and constrained the sectors of subsistence agriculture.

By contrast, the smaller islands are even drier, more wind-swept, and more eroded than the larger islands. Their main reliance is on palm utilization, around which a mixed economy has been created: some wet-rice cultivation, some dry-field cultivation, gardening, herding, fishing, and a variety of other gathering activities. In this diversified economy, the swidden cycle of field rotation has almost entirely ceased. It has been replaced by permanent or semipermanent fields and gardens, fenced with readily available palm leafstalks, as on Roti, or by means of living fences as on Savu. Or, as is beginning to occur on Roti and is already fully developed in parts of Savu, fields are left unfenced and animals are penned and corralled. In either case, animals are no longer allowed to graze freely at all times as they do on Sumba and Timor. The shift to semipermanent gardens is made possible by the use, as fertilizer, of lontar leaves and easily gathered animal manure.

Herding is important, but livestock are not raised chiefly for export. Attempts to seed these islands with Bali cattle have failed miserably. Cattle have not displaced water buffalo, and these animals continue to provide the

Savunese about to feed their pigs beneath the lontars. The syrup and fruit of these trees constitute the primary food for pigs. Pigs in turn are a principal means by which Savu's palm economy is able to support its dense population.

means of preparing fields for wet-rice cultivation. Sheep have been introduced, and indeed have become vital to the economy; scrawny, nearly woolless, and not unlike goats with which they are associated, they are raised exclusively for their meat. In palm economies, pigs take on a special significance because they can be fed on palm products. They in fact constitute a reliable index of palm utilization, and hence there is a high correlation between pigs and people. The more highly populated areas on these islands are the chief pig-raisers and the more intensive palm-users.

The key to these economies is twofold: a dependence on palms, and a versatility of peripheral pursuits. Within the same general framework, it can be shown that the economic strategies of different areas on these islands vary considerably. This flexibility is crucial. A system that consists in a variety of interrelated, though not wholly dependent, subsystems is more responsive and adaptive to changing conditions than any system that is committed to a limited number of such subsystems. In any one year and in any one local area, the various subsystems of the economy may make proportionally different contributions to the subsistence of the population.

On the other hand, in these economies, a discernible trend toward greater specialization has appeared in association with population increase. Lontar-tapping is a labor-intensive activity, and as long as there are sufficient palms, these economies are capable of absorbing new labor. It is significant that where population densities are among the highest, as in Liae on Savu, and palms have become less available for tapping, a new form of specialization is beginning to occur: the planting of lontars in walled enclosures, which in turn permits increased efficiency in tapping. Although the demographic histories of these islands reflect a number of disruptive factors, the evidence suggests that there has been a mutual interrelation between population and specialization. This specialization, based on palm utilization, involves more than mere palm-tapping.

Increasing the number of palms that are tapped and pruned should, to some extent, increase the amount of leaf-fertilizer available for gardens.[1] Greater palm utilization also leads to intensification in the rearing of pigs. Increased pig-raising appears to be correlated with further specialization in the herding of small livestock, particularly in the tending of sheep. This specialization itself is not directly correlated with population growth, but involves various indirect changes in the forms of cultivation and in the general pattern of the relation between cultivation and animal husbandry—a trend toward small, semipermanent gardens and away from the uninhibited grazing of larger animals.

Specialization also involves the factor of time. The most productive phase of lontar-tapping is concentrated in a two- or three-month period. Since most fishing activities and most of the tasks of gardening as well as pig-rearing are left to women while herding falls to the very young or very old men, a majority of the adult male population has considerable free time at regular intervals; they are able to engage in a variety of activities and can even, from time to time, leave their islands for several months of the year.

Finally, there is the important factor of the social organization of labor. Historically, all the islands of the outer arc have been divided into petty states of varying size. In the heyday of the sandalwood trade and prior to the arrival of Europeans, Timor in particular possessed large kingdoms. These kingdoms, like the lesser states on neighboring islands, seem to have been primarily based upon the ritual amalgamation and hierarchical determination of local kin groups. Whereas the effects of the disintegration or perpetuation of these political traditions are important to a historical analysis, they should not be allowed to mask the possible emergence of other forms of social integration based on principles other than those of strict kinship. Apart from the communal labor owed to local rulers, the subsistence activities of the majority of the peoples of Sumba and Timor appear to be (and probably have always been) organized on the basis of cooperation among a small number of kinsmen and their affines. This is no less true for a great deal of the everyday labor of the Rotinese and Savunese. Lontar-tapping, the most crucial of all subsistence activities, is still almost exclusively limited to the cooperation of one or two households. Yet on Roti and Savu there have developed, in very different forms, social institutions for the organization of labor beyond the level of the kin group. The lala (or fencing corporations) of the Rotinese usually include a core of related individuals. But by the rules of membership, these lala can and almost always do include nonkinsmen. Similarly, the Savunese priesthood is determined by clan membership, but the agricultural regulations laid down and the duties assigned by these priests affect all individuals in a state, regardless of their kinship affiliation. Despite evident cultural differences, the densely populated islands of Roti and Savu resemble each other not only in terms of their palm economies but in the degree and complexity of their social institutions.

To this point, discussion has centered on developing the contrast between the palm economies of Savu and Roti and the swidden economies of Sumba and Timor—the one type efficient, flexible and adaptive, the other ineffective, deleterious, and increasingly nonadaptive. One key factor remains to be introduced, and it is this factor that converts a contrast of economies to a clash of economies. The simple fact is that the collapse of one type of economy provides the basis for the other: in the outer arc, the deterioration of swidden agriculture has given rise to palm savannahs. Credit for the recognition of this crucial factor must go to the geographer F. J. Ormeling. In his discussion of the effects of human activity in the reduction of Timor's forests, he noted that lontar and gewang palms were among the first trees to appear on overworked swidden. "Owing to their fire-resistancy," he wrote, "both palms are pioneers on regularly burned land."[2] Thus these palms are not confined merely to Roti and Savu. At lower altitudes on the alluvial plains and hilly limestone stretches of the dry coastal regions of Sumba and Timor, they are almost as abundant as on the small islands. It is to these niches in west Timor and east Sumba that Rotinese and Savunese have migrated. As potential competitors for what is essentially the same kind of ecological niche, the Savunese have tended to migrate to Sumba, the Rotinese to Timor. On both islands these populations have settled in areas of palm savannah, sometimes in the very midst of swidden cultivators. From these secured enclaves they have expanded to pursue their various other activities. On Sumba and Timor, palm economies directly confront swidden economies.

In this situation a curious reversal seems to have occurred. It is reasonable to assume that the climatic conditions now generally felt throughout the outer arc had their first effects on the small, low-lying, unprotected islands of Roti and Savu. Abundant evidence in their own legends indicates that the Rotinese and Savunese were once swidden cultivators like the Timorese or Sumbanese. As their agriculture grew more precarious, it must have produced in its wake the palm savannah necessary for a new form of economy. Since the Rotinese and Savunese were the first to experience these changes, they had the earliest opportunities to develop an intensive palm economy. Their position of initial disadvantage provided them with new advantages.

The simple technology required for tapping lontar palms is virtually identical throughout a wide area of eastern Indonesia and beyond. Knowledge of tapping techniques could have reached the islands at an early period by a variety of ways. Native legends generally attribute their discovery to independent invention, almost always by individual ancestors who came from the west.[3] From a variety of such traditions, it is possible to construct a chain of connections that attribute the spread of the techniques of lontar-tapping from Raijua to Savu, from Savu to Ndao, and from Ndao to Roti. The essential point is that on each island the transition from a swidden to a palm economy was undoubtedly a gradual one. Since the development of this palm economy is still in process, no historical point can be designated to mark the change from one form to the other. By their relative isolation and unimportance to the outside world, the peoples of these islands were able to make the transition without major interference.

As inhabitants of small islands, the Rotinese and Savunese probably also were constrained to adapt to new conditions by the lack of land when their swidden began to fail. On the large islands of Timor and Sumba, indications are that the first reaction of the swidden cultivators was to abandon the palm lands wherever possible in favor of agricultural land, whatever its quality. On Timor, but apparently not on Sumba, the population has increased to the point where productive land is becoming increasingly scarce.[4]

In east Sumba and most of west Timor, however, the transition to a palm economy has been precluded by the immigration of Rotinese and Savunese. The present situation of the populations of the outer arc suggests a historical development that has involved processes of ecological replacement. The small populous islands of Roti and Savu, with their efficient palm economies, have managed to hive off a portion of their populations to the larger neighboring islands of Sumba and Timor. Since palms follow swidden climax, and the Rotinese and Savunese were the first peoples forced to adapt to such a change, they had an advantage over their neighbors when these populations began to experience similar effects of adverse ecological conditions. But these neighboring populations had neither the time nor the opportunity to adapt as the Rotinese and Savunese had on their separate islands. As a result, they gradually relinquished the palm savannahs of their coastal regions to incoming Rotinese and Savunese, who were better able to exploit them.[5] In these areas, where two hundred years ago there were Timorese or Sumbanese, today there are Rotinese and Savunese. In absolute numbers, the indigenous populations of the larger islands have always outnumbered the intruders, but the settlement density of the incoming peoples has provided them protection against the more widely scattered local inhabitants.[6] Despite occasional outbursts of sharp hostility, the evidence indicates an all-over pattern of retreat by both Timorese and Sumbanese—a pattern less of open conflict and more of indifferent recognition of respective spheres of activity. Moreover, there has occurred no blanket-like total replacement of one population by another, but rather a motley patchwork interpenetration that finds palm-tappers surrounded by hill-dwelling agriculturalists, or swidden peoples swamped by tappers. The process of replacement is still continuing.

Using simple ecological analogies to explain complex historical changes can obscure as well as clarify what has happened on these islands. Without a doubt, some process of ecological replacement has occurred and can be documented in terms of the historical record. Possessed of similar advantages and therefore competitors for the same type of ecological niche, Rotinese and Savunese have, it would seem, avoided competition by directing their migrations mainly to different islands. But it is clear that the historical factors that led to and facilitated the migrations of these peoples also created new niches—new forms of employment—particularly in the town of Kupang, which became the locus of a governmental bureaucracy and a center for trade. In Kupang, at an elite level, Rotinese and Savunese compete but they also cooperate. To speak of ecological replacement in Kupang overstrains a simple analogy. The historical events that gave rise to Kupang have created new opportunities to which to adapt. This process too is a continuous one. Palm-tappers need no longer rely exclusively on their palms nor swidden farmers on their dry fields. A host of new factors intervene.

CULTURE AND ECONOMY

A major element in the development of the present situation in the outer arc was the arrival of Europeans in the sixteenth and seventeenth centuries and the gradual incorporation of the islands into a colonial empire. This foreign intervention, while profoundly affecting the situation, has provided an invaluable record of the developments of the past three hundred years. Although this historical record can never answer all of the questions one would like to pose, it provides sufficient information for a rough chronicle of these islands' histories and their interrelations. Instead of speculations on the basis of an ecological model, it is possible to consider a fuller range of factors that have contributed to the present situation.

The second part of this study consists in this chronicle of three centuries of ethnic relations. The starting point is the mid-seventeenth century and the first concern is to outline the agricultural, political, and social situation of the islands at the time of the arrival of the Dutch. For a number of reasons, the focus throughout is clearly on the Rotinese and Savunese. The first reason pertains to my own personal acquaintance with the Rotinese and Savunese and the insights this acquaintance affords me in interpreting the historical records about them. A more important factor is that early documents deal primarily, and in great detail, with the Rotinese and Savunese; until the nineteenth and twentieth centuries, there is relatively little equivalent information on the Timorese and Sumbanese. Perhaps most important is the fact that the historical documents are themselves an aspect of the problem to be studied. They present a picture of mutual social and economic stereotyping that has contributed to the conditions they are intended to describe.

To appreciate this, one must delve in matters that are as difficult as they are important to pose. As one examines the historical documents, it is clear that there has arisen over the centuries the notion that the bulk of the Timorese and Sumbanese populations are marked by a closed, passive, taciturn impenetrability. Their rulers or other intermediaries have always acted on their behalf. Toward their rulers, Timorese and Sumbanese generally show elaborate deference and respect. The Savunese and Rotinese, on the other hand, according to numerous observers, are typified by a brash, seemingly provocative, and at times unbearable insolence. Both Savunese and Rotinese avoid elaborate courtesy behavior and in fact have traditions that ridicule what they consider unnecessary deference. Neither their leaders nor the colonial administration have been able to exert full control over these willfully evasive individuals. Via their relations with the Dutch, Rotinese and Savunese developed the image of themselves that has affected their dealings with the other populations of the region. Both peoples, with evident justification, came to regard themselves as "progressive" in contrast to either the Timorese or the Sumbanese.

A more cautious appraisal might view these popular labels as at least partially the product of the colonial period. This is not to underestimate the cultural differences among these various populations but merely to recognize that Dutch relations were built upon these differences and hence tended to develop them further. Such an appraisal must also recognize that some of the evident differences among the peoples of the outer arc can be attributed to the different nature of the economies of the region. A diversified palm economy may well provide its participants with a different outlook from that provided by a precarious swidden economy. Certainly their similar economies have given both Rotinese and Savunese a capacity for expansion and may therefore have contributed to their common stereotype as progressive and industrious peoples. As an illustration of these differences, one need only examine attitudes toward crop failure and famine.

On Timor, in particular, it is usually expected as a kind of annual inevitability that there will be a hunger period of a month or more as food supplies dwindle before the next harvest. If in the previous year crops have failed to any great extent, the hunger period becomes a famine. Given the nature of their economy, there is little—save husbanding of all food resources—that a Timorese can do to stave off this famine. It is difficult, in this instance, to attribute Timorese passivity simply to some deep cultural tradition.

But on the island of Roti, for example, one frequently hears the repeated Indonesian phrase, *Makanan tidak putus:* "There is no break in food supplies." This is not a claim that crops never fail. It is exactly the opposite. It is an expectation that every year some crops *will* fail and some foods will be unavailable. Calculations are always made for these failures, but on the assumption that with a varied food supply there can be no total failure. There is also the assurance that the palms will never fail, coupled with the belief that, if they—the Rotinese and Savunese—were deprived of their other food sources, as they were during the Japanese occupation, they would still have their supply of lontar juice and syrup. With a variety of foods, there can always be something with which to carry on. In lean years living may not be good, but it is possible.

These same attitudes seem to characterize individuals' responses to failure. Failures, when they occur, are inevitable but temporary conditions. In Rotinese, the closest approximation to the word "failure" is *singok:* "deviation, missing the mark, straying on a side path," and the most recurrent theme in Rotinese rituals is a kind of melancholy insistence that life, though modeled on the order of the heavens and especially of the sun and moon, never attains this perfect order. Man's life is not harmonious. *Tema ta nai dae bafak; tetu ta nai batu poi:* "Perfection is not of this earth; order is not of this world." Yet one rarely meets a Rotinese who, in the midst of adversity, is not planning (usually out loud) his next venture. Savunese response to failure is more stolid and perhaps even more stoic, yet not unlike that of the Rotinese. Risk-taking—since there is a basis for it—is permitted, even encouraged, often after some particular failure. Men to the age of 30 or 40 are allowed to wander and travel, gaining "experience," and involving themselves in a variety of catch-as-catch-can activities. The attractiveness of these ventures seems to lie not in any one certainty of success, but in the variety of possible successes.

Some of these attitudes, particularly on the part of the Rotinese and Savunese, are indicated quite early in the Dutch documents of the seventeenth and eighteenth centuries. These attitudes came to be regarded as general cultural indicators and were taken as the basis for local Dutch policy decisions that set the colonial framework of the region. But in themselves they are only part of a more complex equation.

At a general level, there is an evident linguistic and cultural line that divides the peoples of the outer arc. This line of cultural demarcation passes between Ndao and Roti. The Savunese and Ndaonese are linguistically more closely related to the peoples of Sumba, just as the Rotinese are linguistically more closely related to the Helong peoples and to the Timorese. In almost all respects except basic economy—in language, culture, social structure, political traditions, religious organization, ceremonial life, and by myths of migration—the Savunese must be grouped with the Sumbanese and the Rotinese with the Timorese. By these same criteria, the Rotinese and Savunese stand poles apart. The more one comes to know them, the more apparent these cultural differences become.

Thus the first part of this study has attempted to outline the contrast between the palm economies of Roti and Savu and the swidden economies of east Sumba and west Timor. The second part is based on a different set of contrasts: the cultural and social constrasts between the Rotinese and Savunese that are evident in the differing histories of the two islands. What is remarkable is the complex combination of economic similarities and cultural differences that have helped to shape the relations of the Savunese and the Rotinese with the Dutch, their attitudes toward Christianity and education, their particular demographic histories, the patterning and timing of their migrations, their solidarity and divisiveness, and even the modern forms of employment to which each has tended to gravitate. The question is not simply what economic and social changes have occurred over a three-hundred-year period, but how various cultural attitudes have influenced these changes.

Seen from the present, the inclination is to emphasize a common pattern of expansion and development for both island peoples; seen in historical perspective, it becomes apparent that very different events have led to a similar end. It is, therefore, important to recognize different levels of interpretation. At one level, it can be argued that the Rotinese and Savunese have moved to occupy a separate set of favorable ecological niches; at another level, that they have merely retraced the routes of their ancestors to assume a place with their closest cultural coheirs. The historical record provides sufficient information for a multilevel interpretation of the past.

PART TWO

The History
of Island Relations

CHAPTER THREE

The Intricate Background
of Island Relations

TO BEGIN THE historical inquiry into island relations of the past three hundred years, certain background information is essential. We must first consider what drew Europeans to this area, the nature of their involvement with one another and with native rulers, the conditions they encountered, and the agricultural transformation they initiated. And we must also examine in some detail the social and cultural differences among the populations, particularly the Rotinese and Savunese, on whom the Dutch relied—initially to maintain their position and eventually to further their goals for the region.

EARLY EUROPEAN RELATIONS IN THE LESSER SUNDAS

The resource that for centuries attracted traders to the Timor area was high-quality white sandalwood (*Santalum album* L.). The island of Timor was the center of this early trade. Sumba, dubbed the "Sandalwood Island" by European mapmakers, actually had only an inferior supply of this wood and never attracted the trade that Timor did. By the seventh century, Timor was already renowned for its fine sandalwood.[1] Indonesians from other islands and Chinese both traded directly with the rulers of Timor, who controlled sandalwood-felling in the interior. A Chinese document of 1436 reports that on Timor there were "twelve ports or mercantile establishments, each under a chief."[2]

To propagate their faith and to gain a share in this trade, the Portuguese —after their conquest of Malacca in 1511—gravitated toward Timor and the

MAP 4 An early Dutch sailing chart of the Timor area (*Algemeen Rijksarchief, Leupe 453*). Although this map bears no date, archivists have attributed it to the seventeenth century.

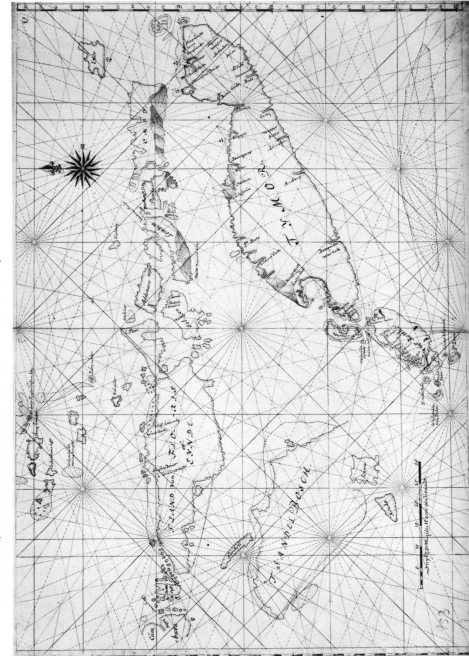

Lesser Sundas. As a base for their trading activities, they settled on the island of Solor, directly to the north of Timor. In 1566, to protect local converts from Moslem sea-raiders, the Dominicans erected a fortress on Solor. This fortress settlement introduced a new element to the area. Native converts and Portuguese soldiers, sailors, and interpreters intermarried; and these Portuguese-speaking, mestizo Christians eventually became an independent force, known later as the Topasses or "Black Portuguese."

The Dutch, under the command of one Apollonius Scotte, appeared in the area in 1613 (see Map 4 for one of their early sailing charts) and, after three months' siege, managed to capture the fortress of Solor, but not before a thousand of its inhabitants had transferred themselves to Larantuka at the northeastern corner of the nearby island of Flores. The history of the next fifty years is as confusing as its records are intermittent. The Dutch were unable to take Larantuka, which remained the seat of the Black Portuguese (or, as they were referred to in some Portuguese mission documents, "our Christians of Larantuka"). To maintain their position, the Dutch had to garrison the Solorese fortress, which they renamed Fort Henricus. Twice, in 1625 and 1629, a Dutch commander of the Solorese garrison deserted to Larantuka. For a time Fort Henricus was abandoned by the Dutch and reoccupied by the Portuguese, who were able to withstand a Dutch siege in 1636. In turn, the Portuguese abandoned the fort and the Dutch returned briefly, only to transfer their garrison in 1653 to Kupang on Timor.[3]

The extent of early Portuguese relations with the indigenous population of the outer arc is difficult to assess. There were brief Dominican missions to both Roti and Savu before 1621,[4] and there are hints in later Dutch records of an alliance between the Black Portuguese and the ruler of Melolo in east Sumba. Most Portuguese efforts were directed toward Timor. Control of Timor at this time was exerted from the interior of the island by what native tradition identifies as the loosely federated, jointly located empire of the Atoni and Belu peoples. Some of Timor's coastal rulers who owed tribute to either Sonba'i or Wehale began to convert to Christianity in order to ally themselves with the Portuguese. In accordance with a fairly standard pattern for the period, the ruler of Wehale in the interior of Timor demonstrated his opposition to the Portuguese by claiming conversion to Islam. In 1641, in response to Portuguese activities on Timor, the Moslem ruler of Tallo (near Macassar in the Celebes), a staunch opponent of the Portuguese, raided three coastal settlements on Timor. In 1642, as retaliation, the Portuguese launched their only expedition into Timor. They converted the ruler of Sonba'i, who submitted without struggle, and ravished the lands of the ruler of Wehale, who offered resistance. The fall of Wehale marked a sudden, symbolic end to the old Atoni-Belu empire; the rulers of its loosely allied territories are reported to have turned to the Portuguese and to have accepted Christianity.

The Dutch East India Company continued to increase its hold on trade in the East Indies. When in 1641 the Dutch took Malacca from the Portuguese, the direct control that the Viceroy of Goa could exert over the Portuguese-speaking groups of the Timor area seriously declined. Although designated as Portuguese, the Topasses were a separate force in the area. Of mixed origins, including the descendants of Dutch deserters, they had settled on the islands, had intermarried with the local population, spoke native languages, and could deal effectively with the traditional rulers of Timor and Flores. From Larantuka, via their enclaves on the north central coast of Timor, the Black Portuguese were able to exercise undisputed influence in the interior to obtain for themselves the major share of the sandalwood trade.

In 1656, after three years' struggle to maintain their fort at Kupang, the Dutch Company sent a large expedition to Timor to crush the power of these Black Portuguese. The Company called upon one of its most illustrious military commanders, Arnold de Vlaming van Oudshoorn, to make quick work of the Black Portuguese and their Timorese allies. Instead, in Amarasi, a Topass-led army of Timorese routed the Dutch. Subsequent to this Dutch defeat, for a hundred years, a precarious stalemate prevailed between these two forces. The Dutch could not be driven from Kupang, nor could the Topasses be thwarted in the interior. The Company's outpost on Timor, it seems, was intended not so much to earn a profit as to prevent the Portuguese from gaining a monopoly in this, the poorest region of the Indies. Finally in 1749, the Topasses assembled a large native army to destroy Kupang. By this time, in addition to the Dutch, Kupang was defended by a native free soldiery and a conglomeration of Timorese, Solorese, Rotinese, and Savunese soldiers. In a chaotic battle at Penfui, near Kupang, the Topasses were defeated. This blow to the influence of the Black Portuguese by no means ended their power, but it did dramatically reverse the hundred-year-old relationship that gave the Dutch no more than a toehold on Timor. The balance of power in west Timor gradually shifted to the Dutch.

Lifao, a small settlement on the north coast of Timor within the territory of the native state of Ambenu, served as the Black Portuguese shipping port for the sandalwood trade. The initial policy of the Portuguese Viceroy in Goa was to acknowledge whoever controlled the forces of the Topasses as the official ''Captain Major of Timor.'' At irregular intervals beginning as early as 1695, the Viceroy attempted to appoint a Portuguese official as Governor at Lifao. Each successive appointee was either rudely expelled, besieged, or overthrown by the Topasses and their allies. At the time of the battle of Penfui, the Portuguese Governor was himself besieged at Lifao. He regarded the defeat of the Black Portuguese at the hands of the Dutch as just punishment for their deeds.

After their victory, the Dutch pressed their advantage over the Topasses, signing contracts with local rulers, most of whom—in the interior of the island and along the north coast—had formerly been allied with the Portuguese. In 1761, after providing refuge in Kupang to the Portuguese Governor, the Company's chief officer, an energetic German by the name of Hans Albert von Pluskow, was murdered by the Black Portuguese leaders in Lifao, where he had gone in hopes of reinstating the Governor and concluding a treaty with the Topasses. The Company's response was expressly to disassociate itself from Pluskow's personal diplomacy and once again to reaffirm its long-standing policy of avoiding unnecessary involvement in what, to officials in Batavia, seemed a never-ending and profitless succession of tortuous political disputes in the Timor area. The Dutch in effect retreated to the environs of Kupang, where they exercised nominal sway over many of the local rulers of west Timor.

In 1769, another Portuguese Governor, beleaguered in Lifao by the Topasses, finally removed his garrison and the entire populace of Lifao to Dili, a site on the northeastern coast of Timor, far removed from the region the Topasses controlled. Gradually, from this new capital, Portuguese control was extended over the eastern side of the island; the Topasses and their descendants were left with undisputed influence in the central coastal regions. By this time, however, the sandalwood trade had seriously declined and much of what remained passed into the hands of Chinese merchants, who were permitted by the Company to export sandalwood from Kupang on a commission basis and from Atapupu without close scrutiny.

Eventually, in the latter half of the nineteenth century and the early part of the twentieth, diplomatic negotiations between Portugal and the Netherlands fixed the present boundaries on Timor. The western half of the island became part of the Netherlands East Indies, to be later incorporated into the Republic of Indonesia. The eastern half of the island became an overseas territory of Portugal, but included with it was the enclave of Oekussi on the western half of Timor's northern coast. This remnant territory of the Topasses went to Portugal as, earlier, the Topass territories on Flores had gone to the Dutch. The events of the seventeenth and eighteenth centuries resulted in a partitioning of Timor into political spheres that has affected relations in the outer arc to the present day.

THE FOUNDATION OF DUTCH RELATIONS IN THE TIMOR AREA

The Dutch claim to a position on Timor dated from 1613, the time of Apollonius Scotte's initial visit to the island. The Lord of Kupang, the ruler of the Helong, was as receptive to the Dutch as he had been to the Portuguese. Scotte writes that he "offers his land for the construction of a fort and expresses his willingness to have himself christened, together with all his subjects, as he promised the Portuguese before our arrival."[5] The Dutch, however, did not return to Kupang for over forty years. Finally in 1647 a Dominican friar, Antonio de Sao Jacinto, accepted the Kupangese offer and built a stone wall and palisade fortification at Kupang. After a quarrel among themselves, the Portuguese left this fortification in neglect. It was only after their stronghold on Solor, Fort Henricus, was damaged by an earthquake that the Dutch, in search of a new strategic location, returned to Kupang and settled there, taking what remained of the Portuguese fortification in 1653 without firing a shot.

The Dutch United East India Company was, by charter, a trading enterprise. In theory, its officers were concerned with establishing advantageous relations with local rulers in the interest of trade. In practice, the thrust of Dutch concern was to obtain a total control of trade. Because of the specific conditions of the Timor area in the middle of the seventeenth century, the Company was forced to adopt various expedients. The Dutch had arrived after the breakup of the Atoni-Belu empire. There was no longer a single ruler with whom they could sign a treaty or contract an agreement of trade. Instead, on their arrival they were faced with literally dozens of claimants to local power, not only on Timor but on other islands as well. Many of these claimants were already allied with the Black Portuguese, an independent, ill-defined, but securely vested force, itself divided into rival factions, which neither the Dutch nor the Portuguese could comprehend or control. In the three-cornered struggle for power and influence among the local peoples, alliance with one claimant usually meant alienation of other personages who could join one of the opposing sides. For over a hundred years, from 1653 to 1769, a complicated struggle ensued until a tacit accommodation was reached by which each opposing force was allowed its separate sphere of influence.

Timor was the focus of this struggle, but it carried over to other islands. The Topasses, like the Dutch, were a maritime power. They were based on Timor and at Larantuka on Flores, but were able to form brief alliances with some of the rulers of Roti and apparently even contracted an alliance with a ruler on Sumba. More often, for the Dutch, it was not actual alliance so much as the threat of alliance that prompted them to action. Any local revolt could be interpreted, legitimately or ingeniously, as a Topass-inspired provocation. To this the Dutch would respond with armed retaliation.

In the early years after the establishment of the Company fort, Concordia, at Kupang, there were seven linguistically separate groups who maintained relations with the Dutch. These were the Savunese, Ndaonese, Rotinese, Kupangese (or Helong), Timorese (or Atoni), and Solorese. Contracts with Sumbanese rulers were not concluded until the Great Contract of Paravicini in 1756. Even after this contract, relations with Sumba continued to be minimal through the middle of the nineteenth century. In the seventeenth and early eighteenth centuries, the majority of Timorese along the north coast and in the interior, as well as the congeries of Tetun-speaking Belu groups, were allied with the Black Portuguese. Only with the signing of the Contract of Paravicini were some of these peoples brought into nominal relations with the Dutch.

Relations with Solor predated establishment of the fort at Kupang. The Solorese were Moslem supporters of the Dutch against the Portuguese and Black Portuguese, whom they had helped drive from their island. Although they protested the removal of the Dutch garrison from Fort Henricus, some Solorese joined the Dutch and settled on a strip of beach in Kupang not far from the fort itself.[6]

The first major Dutch contracts of the period were signed between 1654 and 1655 with the rulers of the five small states of the northwest coast of Timor that ring the bay of Kupang: Kupang, Sonba'i, Amabi, Taebenu, and Amfoan. Since these were the first states to join the Dutch, they were often referred to as the "five loyal allies" of the Company on Timor.

Among the five Timorese allies, the ruler of Kupang was entitled to precedence. His realm was the first to offer an alliance with the Dutch; his subjects, already a remnant population linguistically and culturally distinct from the other Timorese, probably suffered the most disastrous consequences of this alliance. In the first years their unprotected villages near Fort Concordia suffered devastating reprisals from the Topasses and hostile Timorese. Later in the eighteenth century the ruler of Kupang, still under pressure of attack, moved his subjects to the island of Semau in the Bay of Kupang where, in the next century, their settlements began to be swamped by an influx of Rotinese.

A difficulty with the early contracts is that it is unclear precisely who signed them on behalf of the local populations. This affects the historian who attempts to interpret them, as it did the Dutch who claimed to be acting in accordance with the contracts. A common cultural feature of many of the political systems of the Timor area is a dual sovereignty—a division between a person endowed with spiritual authority and one or more persons who exercise political power on behalf of this spiritual authority. Undoubtedly the old Belu-Atoni empire was based on these principles. In the signing of treaties, therefore, it was often the executive figures of the various territories who obtained the recognition of the Dutch as rulers and legitimate representatives of their states. Not infrequently these recognized rulers did not have the authority to command the recognition of inhabitants of their own territories, who either opposed them or recognized some higher traditional figure. Local legends to this day abound with stories about this kind of confusion over legitimate rule.

Often, too, claimants from rival descent lines would vie for Dutch recognition of their rights. Any decision, one way or another, might eventually precipitate a split among factions in the local territory. Instances of "local unrest," which at first the Dutch interpreted as instigated by the Portuguese, were usually a result of these internal disputes over rule. The unstated premise of the contracts was that the Company, and later the Dutch government, had the right to intervene and to act as external arbitrator in local political disputes. The Dutch would act to end hostilities between warring states, to return "conquered" territories, and to restore "legitimate" rulers. The arrest and exile of vexatious rulers or irreconcilable opponents was common.

On a number of occasions, the involvement of Company officers in a local dispute was contrary to Company directives from Batavia. Since one side usually had a stake in involving the Dutch, there was no simple way of avoiding entanglement. Policy and practice were by no means coincident, and Company officers were forced by the situation to commit themselves far more than the Company allowed. When (as happened more than once) a Company officer was killed for his involvement in this type of dispute, the Company refused to retaliate, recognizing that the officer or officers involved had overstepped Company authority.

Ultimately, all of a chief officer's decisions had to be submitted to the Governor General in Batavia for his approval. Decisions therefore were contingent, but they often had to be taken immediately and in the name of the Governor General himself. Since Kupang was isolated and, in comparison with other Company factories, dependent upon the relatively infrequent sailing of ships, it could take from four to six months for approval and ratification of a particular course of action. This time gap left considerable leeway for confusion and manipulation.

It must also be recognized that the caliber of officers who were dispatched to an embattled outpost like Kupang was not always the same as that of officers sent to profitable and prestigious "factories" (that is, trading posts) elsewhere. It is apparent from various investigations of officers in Kupang that they did not at times report as fully as was required on the nature of their activities. Early on, Kupang gained a reputation for the unruliness of its garrison. In a 1665 report the entire garrison, from top to bottom, was described as "leading a very foul, slovenly, and unruly life, [spent] as much with drunken drinking as with whoring."[7] It was not just collusion, but also cohabitation with members of the local population, that led to a particular officer's involvement in political affairs. In their early dealings with the local population, the Dutch tended to follow a similar, though less permanent, course than the Black Portuguese. In the native view, this "wife-taking" implied obligations to the "wife-givers."

The case of Sonba'i, one of the five loyal allies, presents a good illustration of some of the complications that could arise in Dutch-Timorese relations. Although not all the details of the case are clear, enough have been ferreted out to provide a general outline.[8] The original "Sonba'i" was a ruler who represented the spiritual authority of the Atoni half of the old Belu-Atoni empire, known as Liurai-Sonba'i. This ruler submitted to the Portuguese when they overran his territory in 1642. Later when the establishment of the Topasses on Timor threatened his rule, a Sonba'i ruler fled to Kupang, where he was signatory to a contract with the Dutch in 1655. In 1659, the rulers of Kupang, Sonba'i, and Amabi were taken on a visit to Batavia to be impressed with the power of the Company. In the meantime, in the mountainous area of his realm, the Topasses replaced the Sonba'i ruler with his former executive minister who, however, continued to acknowledge the Sonba'i's authority and kept him informed of Topass activities. His subjects in the mountains continued to send him tribute in Kupang.

This state of affairs was maintained even after the defeat of the Topasses at Penfui, although amicable relations with the Dutch began to cool. In 1771, an executive ruler in the mountain territory of Sonba'i was exiled to Cape Town for ordering the massacre of a gold-prospecting expedition within his territory. In 1775, when the old ruler of Sonba'i died in Kupang, his young son and successor was brought up in the household of the Company's chief officer, W. A. van Este. Another executive ruler in Sonba'i, himself of Sonba'i descent and therefore a potential claimant to supreme authority, attempted to persuade van Este to murder the child. The boy overheard a conversation to this effect and fled to the place of Sonba'i's old residency in a territory known as Molo. There he reestablished his rule and maintained a fierce opposition to the Dutch, while another Sonba'i descendant replaced him in Kupang and continued to reside there. This gave rise to territorial distinction between the realms of the Great Sonba'i in the interior and the Little or Lesser Sonba'i near Kupang. Gradually, as the Dutch pressed campaigns into the interior during the nineteenth century, the realm of the Great Sonba'i disintegrated into the states of Molo, Fatule'u, and Miomafo.[9]

Initially, there were certain advantages to signing treaties with as many specific rulers or claimants to rule as came forward with promises of loyalty. The fragmentation of opposing forces gradually rendered them powerless. The Dutch in the Timor area were a small force. The garrison at Kupang rarely numbered more than a handful of Europeans. At full strength, Kupang might have a couple of dozen Europeans, not all of Dutch origin.[10] At the decisive battle of Penfui, for example, the total European force comprised a commanding officer, one sergeant, two corporals, and twenty common soldiers.

In a situation of such understaffing, a further advantage of signing treaties with numerous petty states was that one state could be turned against another. One requirement of the contracts was the obligation on the part of loyal states to supply a levy of armed men to serve in the Company's military campaigns, usually directed against disloyal states. Although this requirement was not always written into the early contracts, it was well understood. Only the Contract of Paravicini set out in detail the required levies from each state. In the early period, the levy was all the men that a state could muster.

The Company used these native forces with ruthless effectiveness. Their expeditions pitted not only one state against another, but the forces of one island against another. Soldiers of the five loyal allies on Timor were used to crush local insurrections on Roti and Savu and, in turn, Rotinese and Savunese soldiers were used to defend Kupang and extend Dutch rule on Timor. Most men returned after each expedition. Still, as a result of these forays, two settlements of musketed, free native soldiers called *mardijkers* had arisen in Kupang by the early years of the eighteenth century. One settlement was a heterogenous collection of Dutch adherents, many of them the descendants of emancipated slaves from islands outside the Timor area; the other settlement seems to have been comprised of a high proportion of Savunese and Rotinese soldiers. At Penfui the Europeans were assisted by 130 mardijkers, 240 Savunese, 60 Solorese, 30 Rotinese, and a large number of Timorese. (Of these only the Europeans, mardijkers, and Savunese are credited with holding their ground in battle.) Toward the end of the eighteenth century, possibly in the early nineteenth century, another native element was added to this motley military force. The so-called *Papangers* were descendants of an original force of Philippine soldiers who had been enlisted by the Spanish and were later transferred to the Dutch. Contingents of Papangers served in many areas of Indonesia, and eventually one group settled in Kupang. As with other native soldiers, the Papangers were granted land in the immediate vicinity of Kupang.

Given all of the obligations demanded by the Company, the early contracts were remarkably simple documents. One may take as a typical example the contract signed on 2 July 1655 by Jacob Verscheijden [Verheijden] and the "great and mighty kings on Timor," Ammassie [probably Amarasi, who later revolted], Sonnebayer [Sonba'i], and Coromeno Ammaber [Amabi]. The contract consists of seven articles, phrased in the names of the Timorese rulers. The first article ends forever the state of war between the Timorese and the Dutch. In the second, the Timorese rulers promise the obedience of their lands and peoples to the Company and a willingness to be faithful to the "uttermost need." They vow to withhold alliances from those who are enemies of the Company and to pursue hostilities against them, granting the Company their help as need would demand. In the third article, they promise to bear what burdens the Governor General, in all reasonableness, imposes upon them, with the obedience and faithfulness of all their subjects, like "upright confederates" of the Dutch. In the fourth article, they promise to drive all enemies of the Company from their lands and shores and deny them trade in any of their products, such as gold, silver, metal, turtle shells, and slaves. They grant the Governor General the right to build anywhere in their district any fortification as strong as he wishes without objections from themselves or their descendants, and they bind themselves to assist in the building of these fortifications. In the fifth article, they agree to render good treatment to all Dutchmen who are subject to the Company, to trade without deceit and in accordance with the customs of their land the trees, livestock, and fruits of the earth, and to sell these in all sincerity. The next article requires full quotation: "Whereas all states, lands, and peoples under God's singular governance are fully changeable, should it happen that the Honourable Company makes peace with the Portuguese, we desire to be freed of this contract and always to remain so, for we are not disposed to endure that nation in our land." This article is of particular interest because of the fact that the Dutch had entered into an uneasy and short-lived truce with the Portuguese from 1644 to 1652. The calculated inclusion of this clause provided assurance that, were another such Dutch-Portuguese truce reached, the states on Timor that were friendly to the Dutch would continue to oppose the Portuguese. The final article reaffirms the other six as unbreakable, adding, with flourish, that the contract was concluded with the drinking of one another's mingled blood.[11]

The simplicity and all-inclusiveness of these one-sided commitments allowed the Dutch considerable latitude in their dealings with native states. As various states revolted and then returned to Dutch allegiance, as new states arose from the fragments of former states, or as states ended hostilities among themselves, the Dutch concluded new contracts with them. Virtually all of these featured general promises of total loyalty and specific details of the local peace settlement. Only the Contract of Paravicini in 1756—a lengthy document of many pages, some thirty articles, and numerous clauses —elaborated on mutual obligations. Its first article, however, renewed and reaffirmed all previous contracts, pacts, accords, and agreements, in general and in their specifics, that rulers had concluded with the Company. The representatives of 48 native states on Solor, Timor, Roti, Savu, Ndao, and Sumba signed the Contract of Paravicini, with the Belu ruler of "Waiwiku Bahale" signing on behalf of 27 named dependent territories. This was the last contract signed by the Company in the Timor area. Thereafter as new states emerged or others disappeared in a continuing process of political ferment, the relations agreed to by the Dutch were given a less formal status.

From the end of the eighteenth century, when the Dutch government assumed the obligations of the bankrupt East India Company, to the end of the nineteenth and beginning of the twentieth century, when the Dutch East Indies government began to intensify and rationalize its rule in the outer islands, the legal status of all these small self-governing states remained without precise clarification but also without challenge. Whatever governance there was—based theoretically on a policy of noninterference— it involved as many unwritten traditions as written ones. Few rulers possessed copies of any of the documents their ancestors had signed, and those who did guarded them from scrutiny as sacred heirlooms. The oral traditions of these states preserve rich memories of the exploits of their rulers, but few of these memories extend to such things as articles of contract. As for the Dutch in Kupang, it seems unlikely that they had a complete record of former contracts and agreements. To have obtained these would have required enormous research in the archives of the old Company. Administrators' reports in the nineteenth century belie a comprehension of relations in the previous centuries.

Clearly, however, a major reason for the relative disinterest of the Company and later of the Dutch government in the Timor area was the lack of exploitable resources and of potential for profit. The Company was lured to the area to prevent a Portuguese take-over. It had hopes of gaining a share of the sandalwood trade, but this trade had already begun to decline. For a while the Company was sustained by hopes of finding gold in Timor, but after the murder of a gold-prospecting expedition in the interior, further plans were dropped. Slaving could be profitable,[12] but it met with native resistance and in the Timor area native allegiance was necessary in the struggle against the Portuguese and the Topasses.

Each year, as a form of mutual recognition, gifts were exchanged by the Governor General and the rulers of the area. Most Company trade was in fact carried out at this elite level. Although forced for strategic reasons to sustain the costs of its officers in Kupang, the Company was rarely able to return a profit. The single continuing theme that runs from the time of the foundation of the first Dutch outpost on Timor to the present day is the repetitive statement of the area's deficiency in natural resources. Recent government documents speak of the Timor area as a *daerah minus,* a "deprived region" just as, over three hundred years ago, in 1656, a Governor General could confidentially conclude that "in the Solor and Timor area there is little for us to do in the future, virtually no sandalwood to negotiate, and more costs than profits to be gained for the Company."[13] The defining features of the Timor area have been its poverty and ecological inadequacies.

THE AGRICULTURAL TRANSFORMATION OF THE TIMOR AREA

Special attention must be given to a historical examination of the paucity of those resources upon which the people of the Timor area have been dependent. Within a century of the arrival of the first Portuguese traders, the supply of sandalwood from Timor had been so depleted that this trade offered little attraction to the Dutch Company. In their early estimation of the supply, the Dutch were perhaps too pessimistic because, for the better part of the eighteenth century, sandalwood trade continued to afford the Black Portuguese and a number of Chinese traders a lucrative income. By the nineteenth and early twentieth centuries, however, there can be no doubt that the major resources of sandalwood had been irreversibly diminished. The delicate ecological balance upon which the tree depends seems to have been permanently affected. Attempts at reforestation have not proved successful. Sandalwood thus became a symbol of Timor's past rather than its future.

More profound changes had occurred, however, than the destruction of Timor's sandalwood. It must be recognized that the "traditional" agriculture of the present day—especially in the swidden areas of Sumba and Timor —is in large measure the creation of the period following the arrival of the Dutch. The gradual agricultural transformation of the Timor area that has occurred over the past three hundred years has resulted from the introduction of new food sources. The most prominent has been maize; of lesser importance were sweet potato and cassava, and along with these, squash, onions, garlic, eggplant, and—in the last decade—tomato.

The spread of maize, above all, has affected the agriculture of the entire area. Now the chief source of subsistence for the bulk of the people of east Sumba and west Timor, it has displaced earlier food crops and, in the process, altered the nature of cultivation on these islands. To comprehend this process it is necessary to enumerate the more important of the earlier food crops and to examine the agricultural system on which they were based. A few pockets on the large islands and large areas of the small islands, where for ecological reasons maize has not spread, retain evidence of this previous agricultural system.

Agriculturally, the Timor area has generally been seen as a meeting ground, a region of convergence of two cultural influences: the first identified with the mainstream of the "Indonesian" peoples, having economies based chiefly on cereal agriculture; the second identified as a "Melanesian" or mixed "Melanesian-Papuan" culture, with economies dependent on root crops.[14] The introduction of new crops has further complicated the picture without obscuring this earlier contrast. In many ways the area is a veritable museum that reflects its agricultural past.[15] Although pushed aside, no food crop seems to have been totally displaced everywhere; and consistently, new food crops have been assimilated to previous native categories. Maize has usually been assimilated to the category of sorghum and Job's tears; sweet potatoes and cassava to the earliest category of tuber, which focused on yams; and new forms of "taro" to the older category of taro.[16] In a few places one can find all these crops grown by the same population under the rubric of a few general terms.

With the use of both archival sources and native evidences, it is possible to make a reasonable list of the main crops grown in the Timor area prior to European arrival.[17] The seven most important ones were rice, millet, sorghum, Job's tears, green gram, pigeon pea, and sesame. Indigenous names for these plants can be found on all the islands near Timor—even on those islands where the least important of these are no longer grown.[18]

The first two of these crops, rice (*Oryza sativa*) and millet (*Setaria italica*), should occasion no surprise. Rice ranks first in the native order of prestige foods. But it also forms part of the daily diet of only a small fraction of the total population—mainly high nobles, the wealthy, or those supplied by the government bureaucracy. For the majority, rice is primarily reserved for feasting. In fact, for some islands like Timor and Roti, rice and millet are the only traditionally permissible foods that may be served with meat at a feast. The ritual significance of these prestige cereals should not be equated with their contribution to subsistence.

There are today dozens of varieties of rice that are named in native classification according to size of panicle, length of growing season, color, origin, or some other distinguishing feature. There is considerable popular willingness to try new varieties, including (to take a recent example) forms of "miracle" rice that have begun to be distributed in the islands. Everywhere varieties of rice with short growing times are said to be replacing older varieties with longer growing periods. Rice cultivation is encouraged, at all levels, by local and national government officials, even in regions where other crops would seem to be more suitable. In years with good rain, these policies have some success; in years of poor rain, they can be disastrous. What is happening to millet is the very opposite of what is happening to rice. The cultivation of millet has declined radically and is continuing to decline. Whatever its previous status and economic importance, this crop has now dwindled to insignificance.

Sorghum (*Andropogon sorghum* Brot.), like millet, requires little rain and therefore can be grown in the dry areas where other forms of cultivation are difficult or impossible. Because it is drought-resistant, it has retained its importance in all of the driest parts of the Timor area. This sorghum grows to a height of two to three meters, and a growing field, especially at a distance, resembles a field of maize. It seems that the early Portuguese sailors, on first seeing these tall stalked plants, identified them as maize. Similarly, on encountering maize for the first time, many of the indigenous groups of the Timor area classified it with their sorghum. In the Dutch literature sorghum is referred to as "cafir corn" (*kafferkorn*) or as "great millet," while on both Roti and Savu it is referred to as "true" or "indigenous" corn (Roti: *pela hik;* Savu: *terae hawu*) as opposed to maize (Roti: *pela* or *pela sina:* "Chinese corn;" Savu: *terae djawa:* "foreign corn"). In the Indonesian dialect spoken in the Timor area, this sorghum is called *jagung Rote:* "Rotinese corn." Curiously, the Atoni name for sorghum is *pena kase:* "foreign corn," implying some more recent outside origin.

Classed as a kind of sorghum (Rotinese: *pela hik dele nggeok*) and still mentioned as one of the cereals grown on Roti, particularly in east Roti in the nineteenth century, are Job's tears (*Coix lachryma jobi* L.). At present, Job's tears are of little significance, but this plant may have been one of the earliest food crops on Timor. I. C. Glover, in excavations in east Timor, discovered a seed of this cereal pierced for use apparently as an ornament at an excavation level that dates back 5,000 years.[19]

The green gram (*Phaseolus aureus* Roxb.), also known as the mung bean or the golden gram,[20] the pigeon pea (*Cajanus cajan* L.), and sesame (*Sesamum orientale* L.) are three of the earliest crops of the Timor area, although now their distribution and importance vary in different regions and on different islands. All are hardy, drought-resistant plants. Of the three, the green gram is the most important. High in protein and rich in vitamin B, it is one of the oldest cultivated leguminous plants in the Indonesian archipelago. The green gram is still a major food crop on Savu and Ndao, where it is usually intercropped with sorghum and constitutes a dietary staple. It is also a valuable crop in the Belu regions of Timor, where it is grown, not for local consumption, but primarily for sale to Chinese merchants who export it to Java via the port of Atapupu.[21] On Roti and in the Atoni regions of Timor, the green gram has all but disappeared; and on Sumba, its distribution is spotty. In recent years the government agricultural service has attempted to stimulate the replanting of green grams on all the islands of the outer arc.

A precise date for the introduction of maize is difficult to determine. The Spanish are usually credited with bringing it to Indonesia, but early references to this crop, expecially by the Portuguese, are misleading because they often seem to have confused maize and sorghum. The earliest Dutch references to maize, with respect to Timor, can be found in one of the General Missives of the Governor General of the East India Company for the year 1672.[22] In this directive it was urged, as part of a general attempt to improve native cultivation, that maize (*"sjagon, Spaense ofte Turckse taruw"*) be planted and spread on Timor. This would imply that maize had not yet reached Timor and that the Company was committing itself to promote this crop. Timor thus appears to have been the first island of the outer arc on which maize was planted and became well established. Its spread on the island seems to have been extremely rapid, since W. Dampier, who visited Timor in 1699, roughly a quarter of a century after the Company directive, reports that maize had already become a common food.[23] From Timor maize spread to neighboring islands, but it was not adopted as rapidly or as completely as on Timor.

What is significant about the earlier food crops is that, with the possible exception of rice, all of these plants can be intercropped in the same field or garden. On Roti, for example, it is still possible to find some gardens that include millet, sorghum, pigeon peas, sesame, cucumber (*Cucumis sativus* L.—another early food plant of the Timor area), along with more recent crops such as squash.

The introduction of maize precludes this kind of intercropping and requires new forms of planting. The older mix of crops could be successfully interspersed in the same fields and harvested at different times, the strategy being to obtain a mean harvest of the whole. Since maize is less successfully intercropped with other plants, it usually requires a field to itself and is often planted on land after a first or second harvest of dry rice. As it spread throughout the islands, it displaced millet and, to a limited extent, sorghum. This displacement seems to have radically affected the old multiple intercrop system. The cultivation of green grams and millet declined, while rice and maize came to predominate as the two main dry-field staples.

A remarkable variety of localized patterns of planting have arisen on the various islands. In exclusively swidden areas, rice is planted on more fertile ground, especially in the first two seasons after a field has been cleared; maize is grown on drier ground or in fields that have already yielded their harvest of rice. Sorghum is reserved for the driest areas. In east Sumba, where maize has spread, it has not been able to replace sorghum in the extremely dry regions; on the other hand, in the swidden areas occupied by the Atoni, sorghum appears to be a foreign crop and may have been of lesser importance.[24] Roti is variable. East Roti, where millet was once a major crop, has developed maize gardens; west Roti has similar kinds of household gardens, but in them sorghum is the main crop. Various plants, including millet but not green grams, are intercropped with sorghum. On Ndao and Savu, however, sorghum and green grams constitute the major crops. Maize is of no importance on Ndao and of relatively little importance on Savu.

Where water is available for irrigation, there are further planting traditions involving wet rice. In Savu, for example, where sources of water are very limited, rice is still grown exclusively by irrigation. This has always been the practice in Savu; there is no dry rice. On Roti, most rice is grown in fields that are in some way irrigated, although some rice is grown on depressions of land where rainwater can accumulate. According to native traditions and some nineteenth-century descriptions of the island, genuine dry cultivation of rice once occurred there. On both Timor and east Sumba, dry rice predominates, even though wet rice is also cultivated in riverbeds.

The picture, while by no means simple, shows the effects of the spread of maize. Only Ndao, Savu, and west Roti, in different ways, retain an approximation of the older intercrop system. To a large extent, this is probably a result of the dryness of these areas. In most of west Timor and east Sumba, intercropping has given way to a more exclusive maize cultivation. Thus it is not swidden agriculture per se that accounts for the precarious subsistence base of the peoples of Timor and Sumba, but the historical creation of a monolithic form of swidden overly dependent on maize. The initial gains achieved by the use of maize are now threatened through the inflexibility of the system that has resulted.

This contrasts with the small islands, where the spread of maize was either very limited or largely confined to a system of gardens whose development had already begun to render swidden obsolete. Ecological conditions are partially responsible for these constraints on maize cultivation. Historically, another significant factor is that maize reached the islands after the initial development of their lontar economies. Thus maize could only be accommodated within a system of cultivation that no longer provided the primary means of subsistence.

Evidence from the seventeenth and eighteenth centuries on the lontar economies of these islands is explicit and incontrovertible. One eighteenth-century description of lontar utilization on Savu is, as we shall see, among the most detailed ever written on this mode of production. Reports from as early as 1660 describe Roti as covered by a ''great quantity of tapping trees'' (*groote quantiteijt tijfferboomen*)[25] and in fact, the earliest account of the Indonesian lontar singles out Roti, among the islands of the East Indies, expressly for the degree to which its population had already become dependent upon a daily diet of lontar juice and syrup. The first volume of G. E. Rumphius' monumental study, *Het Amboinsche Kruydboek*, written in the second half of the seventeenth century (though not published until 1741), gives an accurate summary of the uses of the lontar on Roti. Although Timor is also mentioned, the full account makes it clear that Rumphius' reference has to do specifically with Roti. A part of this classic description, translated from a somewhat archaic Dutch, deserves quotation:

> The inhabitants of Java, Baly, Timor and Rotthe use the tapped *Sura* [lontar juice] more for sugar than for drink, first cooking from it a syrup (called Gula) which is thereafter left to dry in small baskets and tiny saucers; however, on Timor and Rotthe, it is much used to drink (this they call *Tua*) and there they are much attached to it, saying that it serves both as food and drink; for daily use, they mix it with a certain quantity of water and grow healthy and fat from it; they keep it in containers which they make from the leaves of the *Sariboe;* these they hang in their houses and anyone who comes there may freely drink of this and so satisfy his thirst, even before he has greeted anyone, this being an act of politeness and custom in that land.[26]

Already by the mid-seventeenth century, Roti had begun to gain the reputation that so intrigued Batavus Drystubble. Although more exclusively dependent upon the lontar, Savu never attained Roti's literary fame. Yet for the Dutch Company officers and later colonial administrators who had to deal with the populations of these islands, the lontar palm became symbolic of their common economic identity. As a symbol for the way of life of both the Rotinese and Savunese, it succeeded in masking radical differences between the two populations.

THE SOCIAL BACKGROUND OF ROTINESE AND SAVUNESE
RELATIONS WITH THE DUTCH

Any account that compares Rotinese and Savunese involvement with the European powers must, from its start, note some of the remarkable social differences between these two island populations. Some of these differences are the product of the islands' long history of relations with the Dutch East India Company. Most, however, result from other factors. Both Rotinese and Savunese have achieved remarkably similar ecological adaptations, to the point that their economies can be viewed as variants of the same form. Yet in other fundamental respects, the Rotinese and Savunese differ considerably. In language and culture, in social organization, in political institutions, and in religious practice, the Rotinese and Savunese present a series of contrasts.[27] A single difference in strategic location is one factor to be considered as background to a discussion of the other more significant social contrasts.

Roti is located off the western tip of Timor and is clearly visible from its shores. Savu, on the other hand, lies some hundred miles from Timor in the midst of a sea that even today is regarded as notoriously hazardous for sailing craft, particularly during the west monsoon. In the seventeenth century, by virtue of its location alone, Roti could not but be drawn into the contest for the Timor area and there were areas on Roti that were subjected to devastating attacks and reprisals in the early contact period. Savu's relative isolation, however, made it of little strategic significance to outside contending forces. As a valueless little island, it could be safely ignored.

Except for manpower and some food supplies, neither Roti nor Savu had resources for trade to attract the Dutch East India Company. Small, already deforested, and relatively populous islands, neither had defensible "interior" regions, as on Timor, into which a dissident population could retreat when threatened. Both islands were essentially open to the sea and could hardly resist for long a full-scale assault from the outside. Despite this fact, Roti's history from the middle of the seventeenth to the middle of the eighteenth century is checkered with sporadic, unsuccessful attempts at resistance to Dutch interference. For Savu, Dutch interference was so minimal that there was apparently no need for concerted resistance; for the comparable period, there appears to be no record of Savunese opposition to the Dutch.

This initial involvement with the Dutch established varying internal patterns on the two islands. Always ready to act on the assumption that any sign of resistance was inspired by the Portuguese, the Dutch quickly and effectively ended local hostilities on Roti. By the middle of the eighteenth century they had imposed on the various small states of the island a relatively effective peace. After 1756, although disputes over territory persisted, there was no open warfare and only occasional brief bursts of hostility ensued among the local states. For Savu, the opposite was true. Local warfare persisted throughout most of the nineteenth century, and only in the twentieth century were open hostilities successfully suppressed.

This differing Dutch involvement also contributed to the division of the island of Roti and, to a certain extent, to the unification of the island of Savu. Through a complicated and by no means intentional process, which began in the seventeenth and continued through the nineteenth century, the Dutch divided Roti into 18 separate, semiautonomous petty states. Later attempts in the twentieth century to provide the island with some semblance of unity proved largely futile. The older divisions, sanctioned by long tradition, had become too firmly established to be swept away by a process of bureaucratic rationalization. Even today, these 18 divisions remain primary for any Rotinese's personal identity. On Savu, the question of unity was settled by internal warfare and feuding; by the late nineteenth century one state, that of Seba, favored by its strategic port on the north coast and by its special association with the Dutch, had expanded to encompass within its borders nearly half the territory of the island. When, in the nineteenth century, the ruler of Seba was declared by the Dutch as the Raja of Savu, his accession was accepted by most Savunese.

It would be extremely misleading, however, to conceive of the location of these two islands as the only important factor to influence Dutch involvement. The pattern was also affected by the different social and cultural conditions found on the islands. To understand better the outline of this involvement, it is necessary to extend the contrast between the Rotinese and Savunese.

In the outer arc the linguistic line of demarcation that separates the two major linguistic subfamilies of Austronesian falls just off the western coast of Roti. The language of Savu, and with it that of Ndao,[28] belongs to the Sumba-Bima grouping of languages, whereas Rotinese belongs to the Timor-Ambon grouping. In line with these linguistic differences, social and cultural patterns together with local legends of origin suggest historical derivation from different areas of Indonesia. The languages and traditions of Savu point toward western Indonesia; those of Roti to the Moluccas and other islands in the east. From what little is known of the islands and is at least suggested by native legend, it is not unreasonable to speculate that the present

Savunese may derive mainly from one or another chance landing of peoples coming from Sumba and beyond; the evidence on Roti, on the other hand, suggests a far more complex migration of various separate but linguistically related peoples coming from Timor. Local cultural differences and, in particular, linguistic divergence on Roti is now too considerable not to have predated European arrival in the area. One can only conclude that the diversity that the Dutch encountered and fostered by their policies on Roti was already far greater than that of Savu and was itself an important factor in early Dutch relations.

It is more, however, than just a difference of language that distinguishes Rotinese from Savunese. Just as important is the way language is used on the two islands. The patterns and evaluation of speaking are indicative of major cultural contrasts. To begin with, on Savu and Raijua there is one language, and variation in speech from one area to another is relatively slight. On Roti, however, dialects vary considerably and are critically important in the culture. A precise determination of dialects on Roti, given a situation of continuous variation, would be somewhat arbitrary. Based on a variety of phonological, syntactic, and semantic features, various classificatory schemes can be constructed. By one account adopted by the Dutch linguist, J. C. G. Jonker, there are nine dialects on the island.[29] Among the Rotinese, however, it is common to hear the assertion that each of the island's 18 states has its own distinctive "language" or dialect.

The fact is that the Rotinese pride themselves on their differences. They rely on their distinctive ways of speaking just as they rely on styles of traditional dress, nuances of customary law, and details of ritual, to emphasize minor peculiarities and thereby affirm their social and political separateness. This attitude seems to reflect a difference in cultural assumptions between Rotinese and Savunese. Among themselves, Rotinese tend to assert their differences and to exaggerate them; Savunese seem to assume a basic similarity in their way of life and are genuinely surprised to discover the degree to which there is indeed local variation on the island. Historically, Savunese from different parts of the island have tended to overlook their minor differences and have been able to cooperate in mutual endeavors. On the other hand, Rotinese efforts at cooperation among themselves all too often have ended in petty factious quarreling.

For Rotinese, talk is the very spice of life and arguing its most pleasurable form. This cultural focus is not something of recent occurrence among Rotinese. To judge from a long list of Dutch comments going back to the seventeenth century, talkativeness and litigiousness are the outstanding characteristics of the Rotinese that have struck even casual visitors to the island. In

1891, for example, the naturalist Herman ten Kate, on a tour of the eastern islands, visited Roti briefly and observed: "Nearly everywhere we went on Roti, there was a dispute over this or that. The native, to wit the Rotinese, can ramble on over trivia like an old Dutch granny. I believe that his loquaciousness is partially to blame for this, for each dispute naturally provides abundant material for talk."[30]

This Rotinese attitude toward language and skill in speaking is reflected, in various ways, in the island's political structure. One of the earliest Dutch reports on Roti, for the year 1656, already mentions a number of local territories, all of which were later to emerge and to become formally recognized by the Company as self-governing states under particular dynastic lines. It is apparent from subsequent records that the Dutch, at the time of their arrival, encountered local leaders with some traditional powers of dispute settlement whom they could designate as "regents" and later as "rajas." It is possible to trace the political development of these states both in Rotinese oral traditions and in specific Dutch accounts.[31]

Nevertheless, from a Rotinese point of view the essential feature of these states is a court. Traditionally, it was presided over by a ruler and attended by representatives of each clan of the state and by noted elders. In Rotinese, court and state are synonymous and are referred to by the same term, *nusak*. Each of the 18 separate states on Roti is distinguished not just by its peculiar dialect but by a slightly variant form of customary law. Possessed of its own law, each court can claim to be unique. Moreover, each court provides a forum for speaking, for in litigation a Rotinese can display nearly the full range of his speaking abilities. As a result, the history of the Rotinese seems at times to be an endless succession of court cases.

In his early missives to Kupang, the Governor General in Batavia constantly had to warn Company officers not to become involved in the interminable squabbles of the Rotinese. Yet this proved almost impossible. A large portion of the reports on Roti for the eighteenth century that are to be found in the Company's annual *Timor Book* consist in lengthy accounts of Rotinese legal disputes. It appears that the Rotinese were quickly able to draw the Dutch into the web of their own island politics and were, in fact, able to seize upon the new modes of adjudication that the Dutch offered in order to promote their own ends. By the late nineteenth and early twentieth century, the Dutch colonial service, by informal tradition, had established Roti as a testing post. If a young administrator could weather the storms of the litigious Rotinese, he was duly promoted. The Rotinese, in turn, obliged the Dutch by reviving all old litigation to welcome each new incoming administrator. Unwittingly, Dutch policy seems to have allowed the Rotinese to indulge their love of speaking by creating, or at least by sustaining, the means of continuous factiousness.

Whatever precarious sense of island-wide identity exists among the Rotinese derives, in part, from their ritual language. Originally, in fact, the only genuine native name for the island was in this ritual language; the name "Roti" (or "Rote") was an outside imposition given the island by either the Portuguese or the Dutch.[32] Ritual language is a distinct and immediately recognizable form of speaking used in all situations of formal interaction— in ceremonial occasions, in negotiations, in greetings and farewells, in chants, songs, and dance. Essentially, it is a form of oral poetry based on principles of semantic parallelism.[33] For the creation of its word pairs, it relies heavily on the use of different dialect terms for the same object or concept. Although there is some local variation, it is far less marked than that of everyday speech. And since it utilizes dialect variants as a resource for its composition, this language achieves a unity based upon diversity. It should be noted, however, that the Dutch introduction of Malay presented the Rotinese with another linguistic vehicle similar to, and in many ways more flexible and more widely applicable than, their own ritual language. Malay was, therefore, readily accepted as an additional "ritual language" for dealing with foreigners, for coping with Christianity, and even for dealings among themselves and with other native populations. It is by no means unusual for Rotinese to resort to Malay when speaking among themselves rather than discourse in separate dialects of their own language.

On Savu, language is not a divisive force nor is it the focus of the same obsessive attention as on Roti. Unlike Roti, courts and litigation are of little concern. The Savunese lack of interest in what the Dutch deemed to be important "political" matters led to serious misapprehensions. In 1914, for example, in the midst of the radical, uncontested reorganization of Savu's political structure, a Dutch officer on the island provoked a near war, the destruction of a school, a church, and a schoolteacher's house in the territory of Mesara by attempting to forbid the staging, on a Sunday, of a ritually required cockfight.

A confusion over political and religious affairs dogged the entire history of Dutch relations with the Savunese. From their earliest encounter, the Dutch were able to conclude contracts with local leaders on Roti and thereby establish relations of trade and alliance with their incipient states. On Savu, however, the Dutch encountered difficulties in concluding any kind of formal treaty. At best, they could recognize territories, but they could not determine who "ruled" them. From 1648, when regular contact was begun by the Dutch, until 1756, no formal contracts were signed with the Savunese.

Even after the appointment of titled rulers for the island's territories, the Dutch-imposed political system was retained only with difficulty.

In fact, the problem was more one of "containing" than of retaining the system. The title of "Raja," instead of being reserved for a sign of rule, the way the Dutch intended it, permeated the island. Just over a century after the formal contract establishing the Rajas for Savu, the first missionary to reside on the island, a man named Teffer, could report that "there are on Savu more rajas than there are houses . . . for frequently one finds different rajas in one house."[34] By 1918, the system of territorial Rajas was dissolved without protest and a single ruler appointed for the island.[35] This dissolution was quite unlike what was happening on Roti during the same period. There it proved impossible to abrogate the judicial power of the local rulers, and although for a time there existed an appointed Raja of Roti, each local ruler retained his native title and continued to maintain his court. The Savunese, however, seem to have evidenced no compulsion to retain their local rulers. The one major effect of the Dutch system of rule was to concentrate power and wealth in support of the ruler of Seba who was inevitably elevated, apparently without opposition, as Raja of Savu.

On Roti, the Dutch encountered a system of local rule whose petty politics were at times exasperating. Yet the tradition of rule it presented was reasonably intelligible to foreigners and remarkably open to outside involvement. On Savu, the Dutch were met with a system that was effectively closed to them—one that remained, throughout the history of their mutual relations, basically incomprehensible. Thus with Roti, the Dutch became involved in the local politics of the island's separate parts, whereas with Savu, through lack of understanding, they tended to deal only with the island as a whole despite the fact that the divisions of the island were fundamental.

On Savu what is of overriding importance is the maintenance of a complex lunar ceremonial cycle presided over by various independent priestly hierarchies. Savu's territories are not identified in terms of their rulers, but in terms of the differential phasing of this total ceremonial system. Each territory or state has its own calendar; the months of these calendars name specific seasonal events or activities in that particular state. The occurrence of essentially the same natural phenomena at slightly different intervals, the staggering of similar activities, and the use of an intercalary month to correct gross discrepancies keep the separate calendars in phased conjunction. These separate lunar calendars are unified within a larger ceremonial cycle by means of sacrifices that are carried out at specified annual intervals in the various states. The entire cycle culminates, after 81 years, in what is called the *Kelila Rai Ae*, "The Great Island *Kelila*."[36]

Nothing could present a more striking contrast to Roti than this extraordinarily complex ceremonial cycle. Roti has no lunar calendar, and religious organization on the island has never gone beyond the level of the clan, whose only major ritual was an annual harvest ceremony known as the *hus* or *limba.* In some states these separate clan ceremonies were organized to occur in a sequence that could last for approximately one month after the harvest. This month of feasting was the only public manifestation within a state and was unrelated to whatever might be happening in neighboring states. States were organized in terms of the structure of their court, not in terms of an annual cycle of ritual performances. Furthermore, the Rotinese have no priesthood. Clans were represented by their titled court official and by the elders of the clan's lineage segments. Nowadays most clan rituals are no longer performed and other rituals are reduced to elaborate recitations and to verbal dueling. Although there are oral poets who may be rewarded for their special services, these *manahelo* (or "chanters"), as they are called, are not priests and may not make offerings or sacrifices. Traditionally each individual household made its own offerings to the ancestral spirits, so that on Roti, religion has had a far more individualized expression than on Savu.

At the time of the Dutch arrival, there were seven ritual territories or states on Savu, including Raijua. By the nineteenth century, primarily because of the expansion of Seba, there were five. Each state has its own priestly hierarchy, which is responsible for the conduct of its monthly ceremonies. The highest rank in this hierarchy belongs to the *Deo Rai,* "Lord of the Earth;" second in rank is the *Apu Lodo,* "Descendant of the Sun." Thereafter, in the separate hierarchies, there is a variable structure of religious offices and attendant functionaries. Succession to all of these offices is strictly determined within specific clans; however, the persons selected for the offices do not perform rituals for their own clans, but on behalf of the entire state. Their duties are set forth in terms of the calendar. Each of the main priestly offices is represented by its own large hemispherical stone, which serves both as the priest's seat for certain rituals and as a sacrificial altar. For all necessary rituals the priests have the right to demand appropriate sacrificial animals from the entire populace.

The main priests of Savu in their activities and in their person are intimately associated with the agricultural and tapping cycle of the year. In the ritual division of labor in Seba, for example, the Deo Rai is identified with the green gram or mung bean, whose growth cycle determines the course of the calendar; the Apu Lodo is identified with rice, and another priest with sorghum. In Liae, a state on the south coast of the island, the Deo Rai is identified with the entire agricultural season and the Apu Lodo with the lontar-tapping season.

Throughout Savu, the physical person of the Deo Rai and, to a lesser ex-

tent, that of the Apu Lodo, is subject to strict priestly injunctions. The Deo Rai, for example, must abstain from sexual intercourse from the moment of his selection. Since continuity of the priestly line is essential, one of the oldest members of the appropriate lineage is always selected. More importantly, from the time of first planting to the time of harvest, the Deo Rai and the Apu Lodo may not leave the vicinity of their houses. Actual inspection of the growing crops is delegated to an "overseer," who reports what is happening and acts in the name of the priests.

Owing to the numerous ritual restraints on the Deo Rai, it was apparently impossible for the Dutch to appoint him as ruler or regent. In fact, it is questionable whether they were, at first, aware of his existence. According to Savunese legends, the Deo Rai was invariably unable even to meet the Dutch on their arrival. When the Dutch finally recognized rulers for Savu, they seem instead to have chosen the Apu Lodo as their representative in each of the states on the island. Overlooking the ritually superior and therefore supposedly "religious" figure in the society in order to appoint a lesser "secular" figure as ruler was a pattern, if not a policy, that the Dutch followed on a number of islands in eastern Indonesia.[37] On Savu this proved not to be entirely successful because the offices of Apu Lodo and of Raja were soon regarded as ritually incompatible. As a result, in each state in the course of a generation or two these offices became separated although they were generally retained within the same clan. In popular sentiment, in all but Seba, the office of Raja diminished by contrast to that of the Apu Lodo. Rather than effecting an alteration in the priestly hierarchy, the Dutch managed, at best, to bolster a few political positions almost entirely separated from it.

If a society's rituals can be seen as an expression of underlying cultural values, then the ceremonial performances on Roti and Savu are further manifestations of fundamental differences between these island populations. By any standard, the Rotinese are indifferent ritualists. They can talk a good ceremony but they are rarely concerned with actually performing one; rituals provide yet another opportunity for oration. By contrast, Savunese rituals are dramatic performances that require little verbal accompaniment, and certain of the major rites are actually performed without speaking.

Facing page: The *Deo Rai* (Lord of the Earth) of Seba. The highest priest of the largest state on Savu stands inside his house holding a ceremonial short-sword.

Whereas Rotinese rituals involve verbal dueling, Savunese rituals empha-size physical confrontation. During each of the three months of the high ceremonial season, this takes the form of cockfighting. The male members of an entire ceremonial territory—its villages, clans, and lineages—divide into two opposing groups that confront each other. Cocks embody men, but men represent their lineages, which are in turn identified with particular classes of spirits. At the end of the lunar year, this confrontation becomes more direct in some states. Men confront one another on opposing sides in intense rock-throwing battles. These ceremonies epitomize Savunese ideals. Whereas on Roti, resort to physical violence to settle disputes is taken as a shocking sign of a person's lack of speaking ability, on Savu, where litigation and debate are neither institutionalized nor elaborated, physical confronta-tion is admired and certainly not avoided. Not surprisingly, therefore, early Dutch records repeatedly praised the Savunese for their martial prowess. In

Two Savunese holding cocks just before they are loosed to fight. Cockfighting is one of the central rituals of Savunese ceremonial life: the outcome of each contest is in-terpreted to indicate the fortunes of the coming year.

the decisive battle for the town of Kupang in 1749, for example, of all the native participants on both sides, only the Savunese held their ground. Beginning in the seventeenth century, the Dutch actively recruited Savunese, but always in limited numbers because they were wary of having too many Savunese stationed together in one place.

If in language and culture, political and religious organization, the Rotinese and Savunese differ, the same is no less true of their basic social organization. Despite late Dutch attempts to treat the island as if it had villages, settlement on Roti is scattered. The members of the clans that constitute any particular state live interspersed with one another. More importantly, there is no overarching structure of relations to unite the clans in one state with those in another. Clanship ends at the border of each state. Since the movement of individuals among states was once a common feature of Rotinese life, there are specific lineages or descent lines within most clans that are known to be derived from ancestors who came as "clients" from other states. While these origins may be tacitly acknowledged, they do not give rise to any formal relations. Membership within one clan precludes attachments to another. To this day, between 90 and 95 percent of all marriages occur within the state, so that each state is largely an endogamous unit. The only formal relations among states were those contracted through marriages among the states' rulers. There were, however, no permanent marriage alliances between particular states; these alliances shifted from generation to generation.

While the basic and essential political principles of clan structure are similar throughout the island, there is considerable local variation below this clan level. In most of central and eastern Roti, named lineages exist, and specific relations among these lineages affect but do not determine marriage patterns. In southern Roti, named lineages are rare, and a moiety structure governs marriage relations among clans. In some instances, therefore, it is the clan and in other instances it is the lineage that becomes the exogamous unit. In all of Roti, the house or household is the prime property-holding unit. Clans and lineages claim rights to ceremonies and ritual rights to water, but not to land or property. Genealogical reckoning is based on a line of male names, although in the case of client lineages a single female name is permitted to serve as a link between male names and is eventually treated as if it were a male name. On the other hand, individuals recognize three to four generations of a maternal line of origin. This line, while recognized by the obligatory exchange of gifts and ritual service, does not constitute a lineage, since it varies in each generation for every set of full siblings. Rotinese customary law allows polygamy, which has always been confined to nobles and wealthy individuals, but at the same time exerts influence against divorce.

Social organization on Savu presents a check list of differences from that of Roti. Descent groups or "clans" are called *udu* in Savunese. They are based on a long succession of male names, not unlike the names that order the clans or *leo* on Roti. Each udu recognizes a common village of origin. Some are further divided into component lineages known as *kerogo,* occasionally of "client" origin. The leading kerogo of a clan always occupies the village of origin while other kerogo occupy subsidiary villages that maintain ritual ties to the original one. Although individuals may reside outside their proper village, a village is usually synonymous with a descent group both in theory and in practice. The name of a village may often be the same as that of a particular udu or may be used as a common alternate designation for it. Therefore, unlike Roti, settlement is localized in named villages. Clansmen do not live intermingled with one another, and common residence implies adherence to and participation in a specific set of rituals that contribute to the organization of the total ceremonial system.

In addition to these discrete localized "male" groups, the Savunese have two nonlocalized "female" moieties: *Hubi Ae,* "The Greater Blossom," and *Hubi Iki,* "The Lesser Blossom." The hubi are further divided into named *wini,* or "seeds." Membership in one of the two hubi is reckoned exclusively through the mother. Thus every Savunese belongs to an udu and to a hubi. The hubi are island-wide institutions, and their existence and importance tend to overcome the narrow allegiances of the udu. Although, as on Roti, there is a strong tendency to marry within one's territory, the stated preference is for marriage within the same hubi. No obstacles are posed by social structure to marriage with a member of another territory. The religious functions of the udu are primarily involved with maintaining the ceremonial system, whereas the hubi are important in arranging the rituals of the individual life cycle. Unlike Rotinese law, Savunese custom sanctions only monogamy; adultery causes ritual pollution; divorce, however, is permitted and frequent. Relations between men and women before marriage or between marriages are relatively uninhibited. The first Dutch missionaries to reside on Savu were shocked at the number of what they considered to be illegitimate children—what Savunese call "children of play." For the Savunese, however, this has never posed a problem. Hubi membership is of prime importance for the individual and is in all cases indisputable. Udu membership involves residence, and it would seem that it has never been difficult to assimilate the children of clanswomen into the local group. By contrast, the lineage membership on Roti is ultimately determined by the payment of bridewealth and is a subject fraught with legal complexities.

Despite similar modes of livelihood, the marked differences between Rotinese and Savunese are implied by linguistic separation and evidenced in religious, social, and cultural organization. The list of differences could be greatly expanded. But by emphasizing some of the more fundamental dissimilarities and by examining those features of each society alluded to in the early documents, it is possible to suggest the broad outlines of these societies at the time of the arrival of the Dutch. The differing reactions to the Dutch on the part of these two island populations become somewhat more intelligible. And it becomes possible to discern the historical developments in each society that are the product of some three hundred years of mutual relations. It also becomes possible to perceive the interaction of specific cultural traditions, colonial policy, economic opportunity, and ecological constraints in the outer arc of the Lesser Sundas.

CHAPTER FOUR

Roti, Savu, and the
Dutch East India Company

FROM THE MIDDLE of the seventeenth century until the time of its dissolution at the end of the eighteenth century, the Dutch East India Company maintained a dominant position in relation to the small islands of Roti and Savu. Although specific relations and the degree of Dutch involvement differed radically for the two islands, this century and a half marks a distinct historical period. For the Rotinese in particular, this was a formative period of considerable cultural significance.

DUTCH RELATIONS WITH ROTI IN THE SEVENTEENTH CENTURY

At the time relations were established between the Dutch and the Rotinese, the Dutch position on Timor was particularly precarious. The occupation in 1653 of the deserted Portuguese fortifications in Kupang afforded the Dutch a mere toehold on an island that was largely controlled by native states allied with the independent Black Portuguese. After the rout in 1656 of Arnold de Vlaming's military expedition into Amarasi, the Dutch expected a full-scale attack on their meager stronghold in Kupang. A resolution was therefore taken to abandon both the fortress of Henricus on Solor and the fortress of Concordia on Timor and gradually to transfer all fortifications to the island of Roti. It was argued that Roti was "fruitful, well-peopled, for the most part already under our control and well positioned against the trouble and damage of the Portuguese." The plan was to build a fort "big enough to accommodate 60 to 70 men so as to gain some footing in the area and to keep an eye on the doings of the Portuguese, and to resume the sandalwood trade if a better opportunity presented itself.''[1] This fort was presumably to be built on the north central coast of the state of Termanu at a place with a wide semiprotected harbor called Namo Dale. This was the port of call for all official Dutch visits to the island and later became the site of a *pagar*, or minor Dutch fortification. The initial resolution to transfer to Roti, however, was never implemented. The Company's *Opperhoofd* Hendrik ter Horst resolved to remain another year in Kupang, ostensibly to oversee an imminent transfer of the fortifications from the island. In the end, the Dutch hung on in Kupang from year to year. The final Portuguese push to drive them from the island never materialized, and in the course of a century they were able to reverse the situation and came to dominate most of western Timor.

During the early years of this period of military insecurity, Roti retained its potential as an island for retreat, an area to fall back to in case of a shattering defeat on Timor. (Map 5 shows de Vlaming's sketch of the area.) Roti therefore had to be secured and isolated from all possible Portuguese interference. This explains, in part, the ruthlessness with which the Dutch in these early years dealt with even the rumor of Portuguese-inspired insurrection.

Several serious and indeed disastrous incidents marked early Dutch relations with the various states of Roti. It is difficult, however, to determine the precise causes of the Dutch military actions on the island. Prior to the arrival of the Dutch, the Rotinese had maintained some form of contact with the Portuguese. The Dominicans and Jesuits seem to have vied with each other between 1620 and 1630 in the attempt to establish a mission on the island. By all accounts, this kind of Portuguese involvement was short-lived and unsuccessful.[2] The Black Portuguese, whom the Rotinese called *Sina Nggeo*, or ''Black Chinese,'' seem also to have had contact with the Rotinese. But the island had no sandalwood and therefore was peripheral to Black Portuguese commercial interests. To this day, the Black Portuguese are best remembered for their attempts to capture slaves.[3] After the arrival of the Dutch, they did try to foment or at least to offer support to local uprisings on the island. The best evidence for this comes from some of the eastern parts of Roti, particularly the states of Bilba and Ringgou. Certainly it is clear that Portuguese plans for driving the Dutch from the area included forcing them from the island of Roti as well. None of these plans came to fruition. Yet there are good indications that many local Rotinese rulers attempted to involve the Dutch to their own political advantage, on the pretext that other states or local communities were plotting with the Portuguese or were in other ways openly disloyal to the Company.

Mutual manipulation is the best way to characterize Dutch-Rotinese relations throughout their history. Evidence of this pattern emerges from the

MAP 5 Arnold de Vlaming's sketch map of islands in the Timor area, 1656 (*Algemeen Rijksarchief, Leupe 1288*).

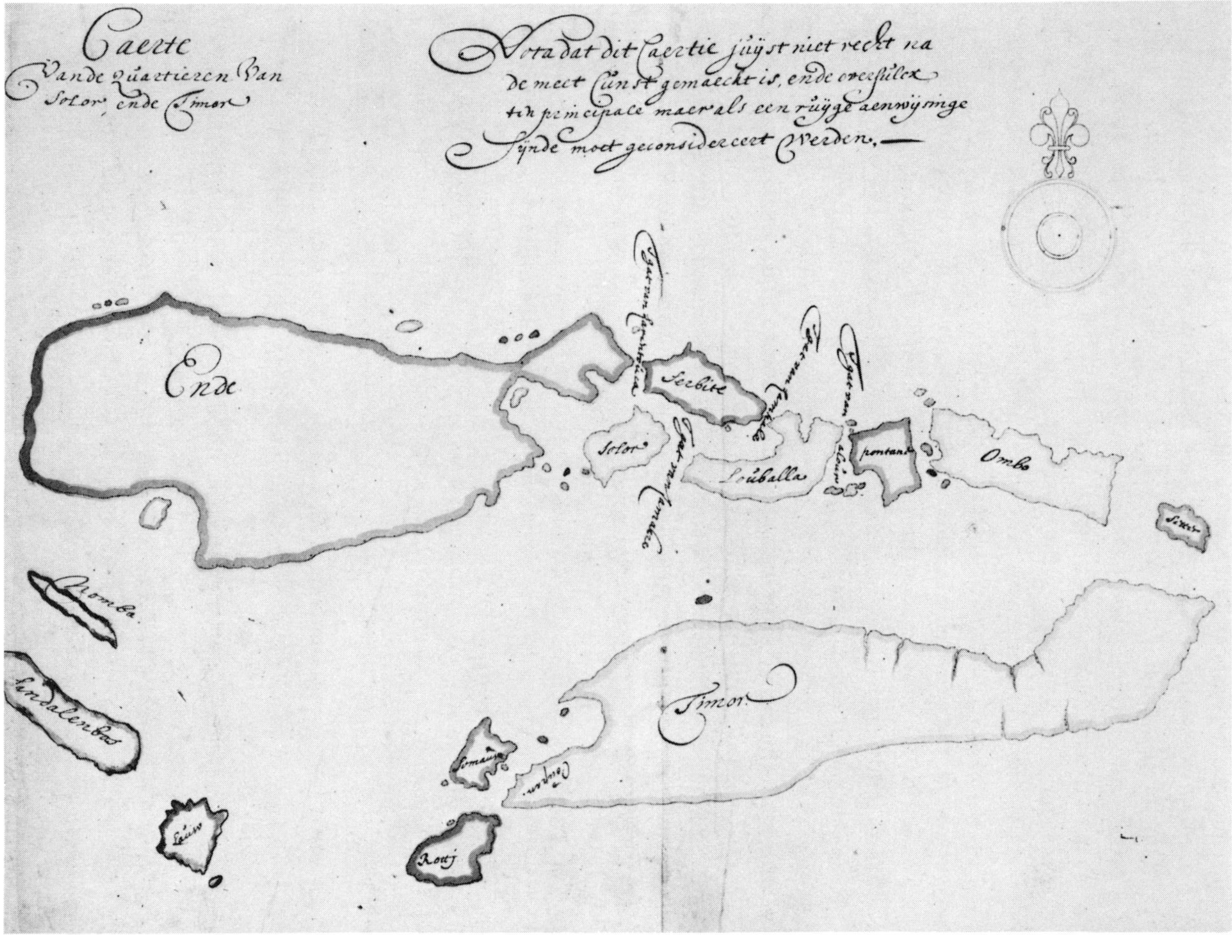

first missives on Roti and recurs consistently in all documents to the period
of independence. From the outset of contact, Company officers became involved in the jealous and hostile rivalries of Roti's many rulers. Initially for
the Dutch, whose forces were limited, there was an advantage in dealing
with many small states—none of which were capable on their own of mounting any serious opposition. Unfortunately for the Rotinese, the Dutch at first
were unwilling or unaccustomed to tolerating the kind of machinations they
encountered; they relied on sheer force to achieve their ends. Only gradually, as they were repeatedly forced to take sides in complex disputes, did
Company officers develop alternative means to sort out contrary claims to
rule and territory.

A brief review of the more serious of these incidents is sufficient to indicate the nature of the early relations. Certain Rotinese rulers sought alliance
with the Dutch as soon as they had established themselves in Kupang. In
1653, the rulers of the four easternmost states (Landu, Oepao, Ringgou, and
Bilba) swore allegiance to Opperhoofd ter Horst. In the following year, ter
Horst led the first armed expedition to Roti "to strengthen his allies there
against their enemies." The expedition attacked and devastated the eastern
state of Korbaffo, which was reported to have been allied with the Portuguese.[4]

In recommending the transfer to Roti, Arnold de Vlaming himself wrote
one of the earliest reports on the island. This report dates from 1656.[5] In it
he divided the states of Roti into two groups: those allied with the Dutch
and those allied with the Portuguese. Of the 12 Dutch allies, 10 name states
in eastern or southern Roti that are recognizable to this day. One names a
territory that became part of the state of Diu. Only the last name is obscure
and difficult to determine. Of the states said to be allied with the Portuguese, de Vlaming listed Dengka, Baä, Loleh, and Pau Dale, probably Bau
Dale, a territory eventually incorporated within the western borders of Termanu. (Reports by ter Horst covering approximately the same period refer to
"five old rebels," centering on Dengka, Baä, Loleh, and variously named
minor territories.) But de Vlaming ventured to add an element of caution to
his account: he questioned whether the division he had described was based
on actual allegiance to the Portuguese and Dutch or whether it reflected a
local hostility in which the Dutch had joined and thereby forced the ad-
versary into formal opposition. This astute observation is almost certainly
well-founded; for with the exception of Thie and Oenale, the division of
states that de Vlaming described coincides with the oldest traditional division of territories on the island—the division between *Lamak-anan* and

Henak-anan or, as it is also phrased, between the "sunrise" and "sunset."

De Vlaming's expressions of caution went unheeded. Although it is difficult to construct the course of events in these early years, it is clear that those states opposed to the Dutch suffered repeated attack. Apparently at some time between 1656 and 1658, Dengka, Loleh, Baä, and Pau Dale were overrun and forced to pay a fine in gold to the Company. In a letter dated 3 October 1658, ter Horst reports that these same states had begun again to raid their neighbors to gain the means to pay the fine that had been levied upon them.[6] In the following year a cyclone struck the island, leaving the rebellious states open to attack by a combined force of all the allied states. A report for 1660 describes the five old rebel states as "burnt," "devastated," and "decimated."[7] Dengka, the leading rebel state, was ordered to render a further payment to the Company of 133 slaves. When Dengka delivered only 33 of the required number of slaves, and Loleh, whose ruler was obliged to assist in the indemnification payments, declared its continuing opposition to the Company, another show of force was required.

On 19 October 1661, the new Opperhoofd in Kupang, Cuylemburg, with a force of over nine hundred soldiers, sailors, and allied Timorese, swept through Loleh and killed an estimated five hundred persons in a single day. Overwhelmed by this military action, the ruler of Dengka hastily assembled the required number of slaves and delivered them in person to Cuylemburg in Kupang, However, while this ruler was absent from the island, his son gathered other local rulers together, swore to destroy Baä, Thie, Termanu, and Landu, and began by attacking the neighboring state of Thie. At the same time, complaints began reaching Cuylemburg concerning Bilba's actions in east Roti. It is apparent from the way in which Cuylemburg described the attempts on the part of Bilba's neighbors to make that state appear "odious to the Company" that there was a dawning awareness among the Dutch about the state of relations among rulers on the island.[8] Phrases about how the Rotinese were a people "who were not to be trusted too much" had already begun to appear in earlier reports.[9] The stage was set for a new approach in dealing with the Rotinese. In the following year, 1662, Cuylemburg sailed for Roti to sign the first formal contract with the island's rulers.

The Contract of 1662 consisted of seven articles and the only rulers mentioned by name in it were those of Dengka, Termanu, Korbaffo, and Bilba. It was not a contract based on general principles but one that dealt mainly with points of concern in Dutch-Rotinese relations. The first article called for an end to all disputes among signatories to the contract. The next two articles were intended to restrict trade to that allowed by the Company: the

Rotinese were to trade neither with the Portuguese nor with any other native trading people such as the Solorese, Bimanese, or Makassarese without Dutch permission, nor were the Rotinese permitted to sail to those parts of Timor or Solor where the population was hostile to the Company. The fourth article called for a return of all runaway slaves to their respective owners in the different states. The fifth article urged the rulers to confer among themselves to settle all disputes over stolen livestock. The sixth article required the rulers of Dengka, Termanu, and Korbaffo to report any attempts by unauthorized persons to demand livestock in the name of the Opperhoofd. The final article instructed the ruler of Bilba to return captured prisoners to the territory of Bokai.[10]

This simple contract by no means ended all strife on Roti. On the contrary, disputes among the states seem to have continued unabated. But there was less need for armed intervention by the Dutch. By strategically enlisting the support of the rulers of the major states of eastern, western, and central Roti, the Dutch succeeded in overcoming some of the sharpest traditional cleavages on the island. Yet control of native trade remained an issue of concern. Already in 1664, Cuylemburg was informed that the ruler of Dengka was secretly trading with ships from Lamakera on Solor.[11] This kind of trade continued to be a problem for over ten years until 1676 when another expedition was launched against Dengka, Loleh, and their allies. The strongholds of these states were once more ''destroyed'' and a combined fine of 100 slaves was imposed, ''so that they would never more harbor any Makassarese under their jurisdiction nor, even less, take part in or intrigue in anything to the disadvantage of the Honorable Company and her allies.''[12]

The bloodiest incident in Rotinese history took place five years later. This massacre and destruction is less attributable to Dutch intention than it is to a lack of control over native troops. In 1681 Thie, Dengka, and Oenale threatened to attack Lelain and Termanu. This was interpreted as a direct threat to the Company, since over the years Termanu had become the Company's most consistent ally. Therefore an expedition of 26 Dutch soldiers together with 500 or 600 Timorese from the states of Kupang, Amabi, and Sonba'i were sent in several ships to Termanu, where they joined an undisclosed number of Rotinese in an attack on the three rebellious states. Although accounts vary, it is clear that Roti had never experienced such slaughter. The native troops went on a rampage. There was indiscriminate head-taking of men, women, and children. Those attacked seem to have offered no resistance; instead, they fled to rocks and caves where they died in droves during attempts to smoke them from their shelters. The ships that returned to Kupang brought with them 96 men, 158 women, and 184 children as prisoners to be sold into slavery. In addition, Dengka was condemned to pay a fine of 70 more slaves and 10 *kati* of gold, and Thie, 100 slaves and 8 kati of gold. Because Oenale had lost two-thirds of its population, this state was relieved of any further payments to the Company.[13]

When word of this expedition reached Batavia, the Governor General sent a stern letter of rebuke to the Timorese rulers who were judged to be mainly responsible for the killing and destruction. They were instructed that such "killing of defenseless old men and of women and children was not done for it was against the custom of the Dutch." Henceforth they were "not to take the heads of defenseless men or women and children but were to deliver them as prisoners to the head of the army." They were also told that "the Company seeks no one's ruin and harm but wishes only that all should live in peace and quiet."[14]

This proved to be the last serious invasion of the island by Dutch-led forces, but for the succeeding half-century Roti continued to pay a high price in slaves—not only as fines owed the Company, but for other reasons as well. Instead of the power of the death penalty, the recognized rulers of Roti had the power to condemn persons into slavery for serious crimes. Such condemned prisoners were handed over to the Company as part of each state's tribute. This power could be and indeed was used by rulers against those who opposed them. It served to underscore a major contradiction in Dutch policy.

Every one of the 18 states that were eventually recognized by the Dutch were mentioned by name in one or another of the reports on Roti written in the first few years of contact. Yet for many of these states, it took a century or more to achieve formal recognition by the Company. With recognition came the right to a considerable degree of autonomy over a roughly specified territory; the right to maintain a separate court with all that this implied; and the legitimization of a hereditary line of rulers. Recognition, for the Rotinese, was no mean political prize. But it must be realized that in addition to those states that we know obtained recognition, there were also named in the early records quite a number of territories that never succeeded in attaining this status. Recognition required local agitation for autonomy and separation from some larger, already recognized state. Such agitation, when it began, was invariably branded as a form of sedition against the Company's legitimate rulers. Leaders who were successful, however, became rulers; those who failed were labeled as rebels and not infrequently hunted down and sold into slavery.

In seeking allies and conferring recognition upon them, the Company started a process of fragmentation that was difficult to check. Had the Com-

pany not intervened in Rotinese affairs, questions of territorial sovereignty
would have been settled either by warfare or through the more complex processes of dynastic succession in states whose ruling families were allied and
had intermarried. Rotinese oral traditions suggest that prior to the arrival of
the Dutch, a succession of rulers in the central state of Termanu had already
laid claim to or conquered most of the area between Bilba in the east and
Dengka in the west. By preventing warfare and by overseeing a strict succession within each separate state, the Dutch were forced by the dynamics of
the situation into conceding recognition to ever-smaller territories based on a
kind of popular local acclamation. Ironically, Termanu, the state that remained the most steadfast of the Company's allies, lost more of its former
territory than any other. But even Termanu, with Dutch assistance, was able
to resist some of the attempts at separation within its borders. As a background to political developments during the period of the Company's sur-
veillance of Roti, there can be seen this tension between two conflicting
principles of legitimacy. It resulted in an intermittent struggle between
those who had achieved recognition and those who were contending to obtain it.

Technically, the Contract of 1662 recognized only Dengka, Termanu,
Korbaffo, and Bilba. In actuality, the Dutch consistently dealt with a number of other states as if they had this same formal recognition. A contract
signed in 1690-1691 rectified this oversight by renewing the articles of the
previous contract. It added as well a number of specific articles to end disputes between particular states, plus one important article requiring that future disputes between states be settled at court in Kupang. Besides those
already recognized, the Contract of 1690 formally recognized the states of
Landu, Ringgou, Oepao, Baä, Lelain (referred to as Ossipoka), Thie, Loleh,
and Oenale. This brought to 12 the total number of legitimate states.[15]

In response to continuing unrest in Ringgou, Bilba, and Oepao (supposedly prompted by the Black Portuguese), another military expedition was
sent to Roti in 1700. Significantly, in contrast to previous expeditions, the
captain of this expedition was able to settle hostilities by "mediation" (*met
tussenspreecken*). Another peace treaty was signed. One article was of special
signficance in that it divided the disputed territory of Diu between Korbaffo
and Termanu.[16]

The most important contract signed with the rulers of Roti, as well as with
all of the rulers of the Timor area firmly within the Dutch sphere of control,
was the Contract of Paravicini signed in 1756. This contract or treaty established Diu as an independent state and assigned to Bokai a line of rule that
made it a recognized state. While this brought to 14 the number of states on

the island, it certainly did not end the process of subdivision. A few years after 1756, Lelenuk arose out of a division of Bokai. Two territories, Talae and Keka, bordering Bokai but under the control of Termanu, began agitating for autonomy on the basis of the precedent set by Lelenuk. In 1772, both these states were acknowledged. Delha, which arose out of a division of Oenale, was the last state to be recognized. The date of acknowledgment is not clear; it may have occurred either in the last years of the eighteenth century or in the early years of the nineteenth century.[17] Thereafter the Dutch realized only too clearly the implications of their previous policy and stoutly resisted any further recognition of new states. In the face of continuing pressure for local autonomy, they were obliged to adopt new procedures to meet the situation.

There was a further reason for Roti's critical importance to the Dutch. At Fort Concordia in Kupang, they commanded a strategic harbor. But most of the territory of Timor was beyond their control. Indeed, in the early years they controlled only a few miles of coast and were allied with a few Timorese rulers whose states were under constant attack. Moreover, the Dutch were over five hundred miles from any other Company outpost. Since sailing followed the monsoon winds, there were long intervals between the arrival of ships. Provisioning the settlement at Kupang was at times an acute problem. Given the irregularity of seasonal rains, the limited potential for agriculture in the northwestern corner of Timor, and the continuous raiding that went on, the Timorese were themselves often dependent upon the Dutch, who were in no position to deny their allies in time of need. It was natural therefore that Roti was seen as a secure source of food for Kupang and its surrounding area. Roti's potential was immediately recognized, especially when the Dutch had decided to retain their position at Kupang. Thus in a letter to the Governor General in 1659, Opperhoofd ter Horst promised that the Dutch enemies on Roti would soon be vanquished and that the Company would thereby gain "a good larder" (*een goede spijscamer*).[18]

Ter Horst's promise quickly became a reality. The General Missives for 1666 report that Roti was already providing "the food provisions for Kupang."[19] This also included the Timorese allies. The year 1680 was a famine year on Timor, and the Dutch licensed representatives of their allies from Sonba'i to sail to Roti in search of food provisions for themselves.[20] Although there are numerous references to boats being licensed to sail to Roti for supplies there is scant information from these early years on what foods Roti was supplying and in what quantities. Only toward the turn of the century were these supplies recorded on a regular, ledger-like basis.

Entries in the *Timor Book* indicate that both Roti and Ndao were able to carry on a trade in surplus lontar syrup. Other entries reveal that Roti was regularly supplying Kupang with both rice and millet in addition to its annual gifts of tribute to the Company of large quantities of bees' wax. These early payments of wax varied, for example, from 1,013 Dutch pounds in 1699 to 2,735 pounds in 1725.[21] In every year they greatly exceeded the wax supplied by the five loyal allies of the Dutch on Timor. More surprising and less immediately explicable is the fact that in 1711, Roti also began paying tribute in green grams or mung beans (Indonesian: *kacang ijo*), a crop that now is hardly grown on the island.

For some thirty years, despite occasional poor harvests, these payments in green grams increased gradually; then suddenly, a precipitous rise in tribute occurred. The tribute rose to 28,500 Dutch pounds in 1751; 47,000 pounds in 1755; 66,000 in 1758; to a high of over 135,000 pounds in 1769. In a single decade, the production of green grams doubled and then doubled again. This spectacular response of Rotinese agriculture to persistent Dutch prompting is an indication that a new stage in Dutch-Rotinese relations had been reached. The production is itself a clue to the profound change in those relations during the first half of the eighteenth century.

THE INTRODUCTION OF CHRISTIANITY AND EDUCATION TO ROTI IN THE EIGHTEENTH CENTURY

The year 1700 can appropriately be seen as marking a new phase in Dutch-Rotinese relations. For just under fifty years the Dutch and Rotinese had been groping toward some mutually acceptable accommodation. In 1700 a major dispute, of the kind that previously had provoked brutal Dutch intervention, was settled by mediation. All the elements that were to provide the means for politically stable relations and for future communications had been established and were beginning to operate by the turn of the century. As a result, in the first half of the eighteenth century, a momentous cultural transformation took place on the island of Roti.

The means of accommodation and communication were several. To begin with, an official interpreter was stationed on Roti. The information that the Dutch in Kupang received about affairs on the island became more substantial and more reliable. In turn, the Rotinese were given a clearer understanding of what was expected of them in their alliance with the Dutch. Secondly, all of the recognized rulers of Roti had agreed, by prior contract, to refer their disputes to the Council of Rajas in Kupang. This council, comprised of all of the rulers of the Timor area, was presided over by the Opperhoofd himself.

The Rotinese were particularly prone to rely upon this form of settlement. It is interesting to note that while the loyal Timorese rulers played a prominent part in the early years of the council, few of the council's court traditions were adopted by the Timorese themselves. The Rotinese, however, appear to have had their own indigenous tradition of dispute settlement by a kind of court within each individual state or *nusak*. These nusak courts were comprised of all heads of clans within the state and were presided over by the ruler himself. The similarities between these courts and the Council of Rajas suggests that the council may even have served as a model for the development of nusak courts during the eighteenth century.

Besides the council, there were other means of formal communication between the Dutch and the Rotinese. Already in the seventeenth century, the rulers of Timor would on occasion address a letter to the Governor General in Batavia and would receive a reply. Several times they were joined in their letter by one or another of the rulers of Roti. In the eighteenth century, this exchange of letters became an annual practice and the Rotinese rulers soon began to send their own separate letter. This missive would usually recount important events during the previous year, express grievances if there were any, acknowledge receipt of past gifts, and request specific new ones. To the letter was affixed a precise reckoning of the tribute, in the form of wax, foodstuffs, and slaves, that was to be sent to Batavia from each particular state. The gifts of the Governor General were usually muskets, fine cloth (particularly *patola* cloths from Gujarat), gold and silver batons (*tong-kat*), and—until the Rotinese learned to distill their own liquor from lontar syrup—large quantities of Dutch gin.

In cases heard by the Council of Rajas and the Opperhoofd, decisions were made in the name of the Governor General and had to await his final approval. This made the Governor General the source of final appeal for parties involved in disputes. It therefore became a practice among Rotinese rulers who were at odds with one another to send separate letters to the Governor General setting forth, in some detail, their side in a dispute. These letters are among the most revealing documents in the *Timor Book*. They provide the best evidence of a change in the quality of communication between the Dutch and the Rotinese. Instead of vague rumors of uncertain involvements by the rulers of Roti, these letters pour forth the reasons, arguments, and issues of the complicated many-sided disputes in which these rulers were involved. By midcentury, somewhat to the consternation of officials in Batavia, the documentation on what appeared at a distance to be a few trivial cases, had escalated to hundreds of pages in the *Timor Book*.

Despite a clear improvement in communication, there were certain aspects of relations with the Dutch that were, it would seem, unacceptable to

A Rotinese in a lontar hut tending his gin still. The Rotinese learned the technique of distilling from the Dutch in the eighteenth century, when the Company each year would give several barrels of gin to the island's rulers. By learning to distill lontar syrup, the Rotinese developed their own substitute for Dutch gin. The syrup is fermented to make a mash, which is cooked in a clay pot capped with the pulpy flesh of the lontar fruit. The distillate is then cooled as it passes through a pipe inserted in a section of a hollowed lontar trunk that has been filled with water.

the Rotinese. The Governor General was held in awe and respect, for he was the distant embodiment of authority. However, this same awe was not extended to officers of the Company in Kupang. In spite of an emphasis on hierarchy, the Rotinese have traditionally prided themselves on being able to deal with their rulers directly and without a great show of deference. Rotinese rulers seem to have treated the Opperhoofd and other officers in much the same manner as their subjects treated them. This would often turn into open confrontation in council and in one case led to the killing of an Opperhoofd. (In 1746, several Rotinese rulers were responsible for firing upon and killing a visiting Opperhoofd who had grossly violated Rotinese custom. They defended their actions to the Governor General. A commission was sent to investigate and, remarkably enough, the chief perpetrators were merely admonished for their crime.)

Nevertheless, there was a decided gulf between the Dutch and the Rotinese. The Portuguese, whose civilizing mission depended upon intermarriage with the native elites of Timor and Flores, were willing to share both their language and their religion with their allies. That a mere handful of Portuguese could succeed so well and for so long against as efficient and systematic an organization as the Dutch East India Company was, in large part, a result of this openness of relations that their descendants continued. In contrast to the Portuguese, Company officers were shifted every few years, so that there were few opportunities to form permanent attachments. Brief liaisons were not uncommon, but these were not condoned by the Company. Moreover, the Dutch retained a separation in language and religion: Malay, not Dutch, was the language of communication. And in the early years of the Company, religion even more than language appears to have served as the banner of formal separation between the Dutch and the native peoples of the Timor area. To judge from several diaries that date from this period, attendance of officers at religious services occupied a portion of each day's official activities. The primary task of the ministers who were sent to Kupang was to promote the betterment of morals among officers. Although there was no outright Company policy that discouraged the preaching of Christianity to native peoples, very little was done to encourage it. The Dutch Reformed faith, under the aegis of the Company, did not take the form of an evangelizing Christianity.

Yet conversion to Christianity carried with it distinct advantages. It provided a certain elevation in social status. It also provided a change in legal status, as native Christians were not strictly subject to the local adat law that applied to different native communities. There also existed a widespread native assumption, by no means always confirmed, that Christians were favored in disputes with pagans. More importantly, Christians could not be condemned into slavery. And what held for individuals was equally appropriate for states; the Dutch had no right to demand a tribute of slaves from a "Christian state."

In the Timor area, the Rotinese were the first—and, for the Company period, virtually the only—people to grasp the implications of Dutch local practice. This was to affect their relations not only with the Dutch but with other native peoples of the area. Changes came about gradually, but there was one incident, seemingly trivial at the time yet in retrospect of singular importance in establishing a new cultural precedent. This incident involved a Rotinese by the name of Baa Mai.

Baa Mai was a clan lord in Termanu who objected to and, in fact, openly contravened the authority of Termanu's Lord, Ndaomanu. In 1724, after repeated provocations including vilification of the Lord's ancestry, Ndao-manu with his court of other clan lords condemned Baa Mai to death. The imposition of the death penalty by a native court meant, in effect, that Baa Mai had to be surrendered to the Company to be sold into slavery and sent to Batavia. Therefore the Lords of Dengka and Loleh and the Company's interpreter, William Abrahams, intervened, took custody of Baa Mai, and had him transported to Kupang. Ndaomanu was particularly insistent that Baa Mai be immediately condemned and put on a ship for Batavia. Instead, probably because of his relations with the other nobility of Roti and Timor, Baa Mai was freed in Kupang. To make matters worse, a small native boat was sent secretly to Termanu to rescue Baa Mai's wife, children, and sister. All of them were granted protection by the five Timorese rulers. To compli-cate affairs even further, the Opperhoofd in Kupang, Balthazar d'Mouch-eron, took Baa Mai's sister as his mistress and she bore him a son. And as a consequence of her new status, she and her son were allowed to become Christians.

Ndaomanu had no choice but to appeal directly to the Governor General in Batavia. In a letter dated 18 August 1728, he argued for the return of all Baa Mai's family. He further stated that he had given no permission for the sister to be baptized, but that if she were returned, he would bestow her upon a Christian who lived in his state. To counter Ndaomanu's letter, the five rulers of Timor sent their own letter, dated 23 August 1728, defending their actions in the case. In the end their letter, which had the implicit back-ing of the Opperhoofd, settled the case in favor of Baa Mai and his family, but it also publicly established a new precedent. A short extract from their letter, written in the tortuous style of the period, gives a good indication of their argument:

> that the forementioned female person, namely the sister of Baa Mai, having been sought from us, five regents, by the Company's *Opper-hoofd* Balthazar d'Moucheron as his householder, therein did we fully agree, which afterwards a little son having been procreated by these same persons, so have we jointly as regents, for these reasons, given per-mission to this sister of Baa Mai along with her little son to receive holy baptism this year, since she was disposed with her whole heart to seek the Lord our God, having obtained a child of Christian blood and in-deed not only of Dutch blood, but sprouted from the blood of a Com-pany's *Opperhoofd* who has been, for us, like a father and lord.[22]

The case of Baa Mai was a complicated one that took almost five years to be resolved. Baa Mai's relation to Ndaomanu is never made clear in the documents, but his protection in Kupang certainly resulted from his connections with the other high nobles of the area and had nothing to do with Christianity. The case came to focus on Baa Mai's sister and Ndaomanu's demand that she be returned. The decision of the Governor General to refuse was based not on her connections with the Opperhoofd but on the grounds that she was a Christian and therefore no longer subject to Ndaomanu's authority. While there were already some Christians on Roti at this time, they were not numerous and their status had not previously become an issue before the law. The precedent set in the case was therefore of critical importance and its significance was certainly not missed by other Rotinese, especially since Ndaomanu was the most powerful and influential ruler on Roti.

In the same year that the Governor General delivered his decision in the case of Baa Mai's sister, the first Rotinese ruler became a Christian. In 1729, the Lord of Thie and his entire family were baptized. Poura Messa's motives for converting can never be known. His baptism occurred during a smallpox epidemic on Roti, and the old ruler died shortly after his baptism. His son, Benjamin Messa, the first Rotinese ruler to use a Christian name, succeeded to the lordship of Thie.

Christianity interjected a new element into native politics. In 1730 the southern and central states of Thie, Loleh, Lelain, and Baä were threatened by Oenale and Dengka to the west and Termanu and Korbaffo to the east. (Delha was still part of Oenale, just as Keka and Talae were still integral parts of Termanu.) From year to year there were shifts in alliance. Termanu and Korbaffo were also involved in hostilities with Bilba over the territories of Diu, Lelenuk, and Bokai. Almost every year, however, the south central states were raided from one side or the other.

Benjamin Messa's first request as a "Christian king" was for a schoolmaster. The first individual sent to Thie was a local Christian from Kupang named Johannes Senghadje. Although the sources at this point are not precise, Benjamin Messa and Johannes Senghadje, in company with the Lord of Bilba, apparently attempted to form some kind of new state. For this, Senghadje was dismissed and Messa was apprehended but pardoned. Once reinstated, Messa renewed his earlier request and in 1735 the Company acquiesced and appointed an Ambonese Christian, Hendrik Hendriks, as schoolmaster in Thie.

The primary purpose of a schoolmaster was to give instruction in Christianity. With the prestige of a schoolmaster, Thie became the center of an alliance of "Christian states" in south central Roti. When Thie was raided, Messa was quick to claim that his Christian subjects ought not be captured by pagans from other states. When, on behalf of his father, Ndaomanu's

The blind Raja of Thie, Jeremias Messakh, holding the staff of office that in 1726 was given by the Dutch East India Company (V.O.C., or *Vereenigde Oostindische Compagnie*) to Messakh's ancestor, Poura Messa. The inset shows the inscription on the silver head of the staff.

son attacked Kuli in Loleh, the survivors fled to Thie. It was at this time, while in Thie, that the ruler of Loleh asked permission to be baptized.

To understand the extraordinary nature of this request under the circumstances of the period, one must realize that this request from the ruler of Loleh had to be forwarded to the Church Council of Batavia and from there to the Synod in Amsterdam. It is mentioned in a letter sent by the Council in Batavia on 26 February 1740 to the Synod in Amsterdam: "On Roti, the Church Council asks for a minister immediately, especially since the Regent of Soly [Loleh] and his subjects seek to be baptized in the name of Christ."[23] In another letter, dated 16 October 1741, the Church Council sent a further report on Roti to Amsterdam. In the district of Thie, there were 4 church members, 964 ordinary unconfirmed Christians, and 182 persons waiting to be baptized. For Roti, a minister was urgently requested "especially since the Regent of Soli [Loleh], along with the families of his *temukung* [clan lords] who number well over 700 requested baptism."[24] The minister who was eventually dispatched to Roti arrived in time to baptize not only the ruler of Loleh but two other rulers who were being drawn into Thie's confederation.

In 1741 or 1742, Baä and Lelain [Ossipoka] ceased paying the tribute demanded by Termanu and joined Thie and Loleh in open resistance. In 1743, the combined forces of Termanu, Korbaffo, Dengka, and Oenale besieged the central village of Baä, eventually forcing the Lord of that state, and with him the Lord of Lelain, to flee for protection to Thie. The details of the events leading to this flight are described in a long letter to the Governor General from Tou Dekalilo, Lord of Baä, and Bako Dale, Lord of Lelain, dated 14 October 1743. The final paragraph of the letter records their conversion to Christianity and their requests for schoolmasters.

> In May 1743, Dengka, Termanu, Oenale and Korbaffo came to blockade our territory so that the people of Baä up until the 6th of June were neither able nor allowed, by night or by day, to come out; thus unable to withstand [?] their hunger, they broke and fled to the territory of Thie [whereupon] Dengka, Termanu, Oenale, and Korbaffo burnt the whole territory [of Baä]; now we of Baä and Ossipoka [Lelain] have met the *predikant*, Hermanus Sanders Zijlsma in Thie, who, following our request, has baptized us by the grace of God and have also met the two present schoolmasters who are in Thie to instruct the children; so we of Baä and Ossipoka have need of the *predikant* and a schoolmaster to instruct our children, though still we find ourselves under the protection of the King of Thie; and we, being Christians, request of [your] high Lordships that we be permitted to return to our territories.[25]

The coming of Christianity did not put an end to disputes on the island. If anything, it added a new dimension that heightened continuing rivalries. The unending disputes only confirmed the Dutch in their view that the Rotinese were simply a "quarrel-seeking" people. From the first, Company officers in Kupang were wary of Benjamin Messa who, to judge from the letters and documents of the period, must have been a cultural innovator of the first order. His rivals in Termanu, Ndaomanu Sinlae with his brothers and their sons, seem to have been archtraditionalists who chafed at any Dutch interference in their affairs.

One of the chief contentions between Thie and Termanu was over Christianity and slavery. The particular dispute dated from a raid that Termanu made on Thie during the reign of Poura Messa. A number of people from Thie were taken prisoner, including a noblewoman whom Ndaomanu gave to a clan lord in Dengka. For years Benjamin Messa attempted to get these people returned. Some of them apparently wished to become Christians, and Messa managed to take a predikant to Dengka, where he baptized the woman from Thie and her family. After a series of further complications and various attempts to reach agreement on exchanging prisoners, it was decided by the Opperhoofd that in return for his "Christians," Benjamin Messa was to give nine men to Termanu and two to Dengka. In his own separate letter of 26 June 1743 to the Governor General, Messa asked to be excused from his part of the exchange on the grounds that "we have now become Christians and are disposed to follow the manners of Christians."[26]

At the outset, the first request of a Christian king was usually for a schoolmaster to teach the Malay Bible. This request, made initially by Benjamin Messa, was followed by similar requests from the ruler of Loleh, Zakarias Dihoea [Ndi'i Hu'a]; the ruler of Baä, Toedeka Lilo [Toudenga Lilo]; and the ruler of Lelain, Naho Dali [Nau Dale?]. The presence of a schoolmaster contributed to the legitimacy of the claim to being a Christian state. Further, it increased the general prestige of certain states on the island and, in Rotinese eyes, appeared to give them a greater advantage in dealing with the Dutch. This created almost immediately a new form of rivalry among the rulers of the states of Roti. Some rulers followed the example of Benjamin Messa and converted to Christianity, thereby claiming the right to a schoolmaster; but even states with non-Christian rulers demanded to have their own schoolmasters, no matter what the cost. The first schoolmasters were sent to Roti without any apparent specification of return payment. When nearly all of the rulers of Roti began demanding schoolmasters, the Company officers had no choice but to specify a price for each schoolmaster. The escalating demand for schoolmasters and the Company's willingness to supply them spurred the boom in green gram production that occurred during the middle of the eighteenth century.

In agreeing to supply the island with schoolmasters, the Company stipulated an annual payment of either 6,000 Dutch pounds of green grams or two slaves to cover the cost of each teacher sent to the island. Prior to this time, there was no fixed standard for determining the level of tribute. The amount of tribute was left to each state's ruler and was, in theory, freely given by these rulers to the Company. The quantity of tribute, however, determined the quality of the return gift sent in the following year to each ruler. Major gifts of valuable objects naturally went to the more powerful rulers of Roti.

Before the establishment of fixed payments in green grams, tribute was irregularly given and consisted of various products. Slaves, bees' wax and, occasionally, rice and millet were sent to Kupang as tribute. The amount of green grams given as tribute was initially minimal but gradually increased in quantity. In 1711, green gram tribute amounted to no more than 2,942 pounds; in 1733, this tribute had increased to 15,667 pounds; and in 1751 —the year the Company made its decision on the price of a schoolmaster— tribute stood at 28,500 pounds.[27] After this date, the *Timor Book* shows a two-column ledger for Roti: the amount of green grams delivered and the amount needed to reach the required level. By 1755, tribute in green grams had jumped to 47,000 pounds and by 1758 had reached 66,000 pounds.

There was, however, an unmistakable irony in this situation. Originally the small, beleaguered states of south central Roti had sought Christianity as a form of protection against their larger neighbors. The requests for schoolmasters were part of this protection, but when the Company put the price of a schoolmaster at either 6,000 pounds of green grams or two slaves (which, of course, the Christian states refused to render), the balance heavily favored the large non-Christian states of the island. For many of the smaller states, the Company's quotas were impossible to reach. Thus by 1754, there were reported to be over 3,000 children in six schools on the island. These schools were in Oenale, Dengka, Termanu, Bilba, Ringgou, and Landu, all—with the exception of Ringgou—states without Christian rulers. The states of Thie, Loleh, Baä, and Lelain, which had been the first to request schoolmasters, were effectively deprived of them.

The rulers of these small states began immediately to complain to the Governor General of the heavy burden required to support a schoolmaster. The response of the Governor General in 1755 was to reduce the payment to 3,000 pounds and to permit a partial payment in wax. With this more reasonable quota, all of the recognized states of the island, including Ndao, could support a school; the result was a further increase in green gram production, with the larger states exceeding their quota and receiving, as a reward, return gifts of cloth, muskets, and other valuable objects. A final decade's spurt in production led to a tribute in green grams of over 135,000 pounds in 1769. Thereafter there occurred a decline in this tribute almost as dramatic as the original increase. The reasons for this decline had already begun to appear by 1756, the time of the signing of the Contract of Paravicini.

The remarkable feature of Rotinese schools was the fact that they were foreign language schools. Instruction was in Malay, not Rotinese. Most of the first teachers sent by the Company to Roti came from Ambon. And it seems to have been primarily the prerogative of Rotinese noble children to attend these schools. Both Christianity and education began among the high nobility of the island and gradually, over centuries, filtered down through the society as a whole. Since the Rotinese rulers often came in conflict with Company officers by tending to treat them as near-equals, disputes between these rulers and their pretentious foreign schoolmasters were almost inevitable.

As part of the negotiations preceding the signing of the Contract of Paravicini, the rulers of Roti requested permission to contribute a portion of the support of their own schoolmasters. In typical Company fashion, this request was granted on condition that these rulers attempt the cultivation of pepper, which the Dutch were trying to introduce.[28] (When pepper failed, chiefly because of the state of the pepper plants received from Batavia, an attempt was made to cultivate indigo, but this crop also failed.) In granting the Rotinese rulers' request, the Company set no guidelines on what constituted a schoolmaster's level of support. This forced each schoolmaster to make his own claims, which in turn triggered a spate of charges by the rulers against their schoolmasters. They were accused of attempting to extract excessive payments, of beating their pupils, and of making them work—in Rotinese words—"like slaves."[29] These foreigners had no respect for Rotinese ways.

At this point, the stage was set for a development that was to affect life on Roti for the next two hundred years. The first of a generation of young Rotinese who had been trained in Malay in local schools began, at their rulers' insistence, to replace their own teachers. Malay instruction and religious education passed into the hands of the Rotinese themselves. Christianity and native practice became permanently fused, and no later government interference nor any missionary efforts succeeded in altering these relations.

By 1765, with the beginning of Roti's own school system, half of whose costs were to be supported directly by the Company, there was far less pressure toward green gram cultivation and the crop's importance declined. In the meantime, the Timor area had become more secure and there were other areas of supply. The decline in green grams was as rapid as its brief rise. In 1778, Roti exported only 24,000 pounds; by 1787, this tribute had further declined to 10,500 pounds.

In their short, fitful history, green grams, now an insignificant food crop sparsely planted in a few gardens of Roti, had financed the start of the Rotinese educational system. This rapid rise and fall of green grams demonstrates the responsiveness of Rotinese agricultural production to changing demands. It suggests that in the eighteenth century the Rotinese economy already had some of its diversified base. Furthermore, the educational system that green grams helped to create was used to justify the claim of Rotinese rulers that they were independent, self-educating, and Christian. This made the island almost impenetrable to outside interference and elevated the Rotinese to a unique status among the peoples of eastern Indonesia. When, in the nineteenth century, the Rotinese began to migrate, they had more than a specialized, adaptable economy. They had an absolute lead in education and a traditional school system to maintain this lead.

DUTCH RELATIONS WITH SAVU IN THE SEVENTEENTH AND EIGHTEENTH CENTURIES

Compared to the rich sources of information on Roti during the first hundred years of Dutch contact, those on Savu are meager. This in itself is significant, for it reflects Savu's isolation and its lack of strategic importance in the political struggles of the Timor area. Moreover, it reflects an evident desire on the part of the Savunese to avoid involvement with the Dutch. Mutual disinterest is perhaps the best way to characterize early Dutch-Savunese relations.

The Portuguese who established the earliest contacts with Savu[30] were in no position, in the middle of the seventeenth century, to challenge the Dutch for control of the island. The first recorded visit to Savu by the Dutch occurred in 1648 and is described in an exchange of letters between Opperhoofd Hendrik ter Horst and the Governor General, and in excerpts that have survived from ter Horst's diary.[31] Three rulers on the island consented to trade with the Dutch and swore an ''eternal alliance'' with the Company. Ter Horst reciprocated by temporarily stationing a bookkeeper and a few soldiers on the island for the express purpose of purchasing slaves. He also agreed to send a ship once or twice a year to visit and trade with the island.

His impressions of the Savunese were decidedly unfavorable. In his diary he recounts his visit with the ruler of Menia: "The beach [was] black with men each with . . . swords and spears in their hands . . . a party of barbarous men."[32] And he goes on to compare the Savunese to the Hottentots of the Cape of Good Hope.

These initial impressions, plus his failure to obtain the purchase of a large number of slaves, set a precedent for future relations. Savu could be readily ignored. Relations could be reduced to occasional visits. Only one event appears to have marred these indifferent relations during these first hundred years of contact. In 1674 a Dutch sloop, the *Kerper,* ran aground off the east coast of Savu and for unexplained reasons its entire crew, including its Company officers, were killed by the people of Timu. The following year, after a successful expedition to destroy rebel states on Roti, Opperhoofd van Wijkersloot set out to punish the Company "murders" on Savu. On the island, he was welcomed by the ruler of Seba, who was not implicated in the murder. From Seba, he marched with his army to Timu, where he discovered that about 1,500 persons had withdrawn into a triple-walled redoubt from which they refused even to speak with the Dutch. Since van Wijkersloot estimated this redoubt to be no stronger than the one he had previously stormed on Roti, he attacked; but despite all his firepower, he was unable to force his way into the stronghold. In the end one of his men succeeded in getting close enough to speak to the ruler of Timu, who agreed to pay a reparation of 300 slaves, 150 *teyl* of gold, and 150 teyl of *muti salah* beads on condition that the Dutch were to leave Timu immediately. This they did and eventually on receipt of 240 slaves, 80 teyl of gold, and 70 teyl of beads they withdrew from the island.[33] Although the Dutch could claim satisfaction with this expedition, the fact that they were unable to overwhelm the Savunese, as they had the Rotinese, contributed enormously to the reputation of the Savunese as fierce and indomitable warriors. After this date there appear to have been no other major incidents of conflict between the Dutch and the Savunese. Relations continued to be characterized by mutual indifference.

An indication of Savu's strategic unimportance can be drawn from the fact that whereas the establishment of Dutch relations with Savu dates from the same period as those with Roti, the Company made no effort to sign a formal treaty with the rulers of Savu until 1756. Prior to the signing of this treaty, Savu seems to have served the Company mainly as a recruitment area for soldiers to serve in Kupang. In the decisive 1749 battle with the Black Portuguese for control of Kupang, Savunese soldiers serving under the Dutch outnumbered the combined total of all the other native soldiers.

There were 240 Savunese, compared to only 30 Rotinese—and it was the Savunese who received special commendation for their valor.[34]

With regard to Savu, one of the chief purposes of the Contract of Paravicini was to fix, on a contractual basis, the exact number of soldiers that each of the states would provide when called upon. To this end, the Company recognized five states (see Map 6), whose differing importance can be determined by the men they were required to supply. Seba, Timu, and Mesara had to provide 100 riders and 100 foot soldiers; Liae, 60 riders and 60 foot soldiers; Menia, which at this time was already in the process of being divided between Seba and Timu, only 20 riders and 20 foot soldiers. This secured for the Company a total of 380 horsemen and 380 soldiers from Savu. Roti's assessment under this same contract was almost double that of Savu, amounting to 785 horsemen and 705 foot soldiers.[35] These differences can be somewhat deceiving, however. Savu's assessment was considered a secure number while Roti by this time was already known for its inability to muster a full quota of men.

As one of the stipulations in the negotiations that preceded the signing of the contract with the Savunese, the Dutch had to consent to continue their

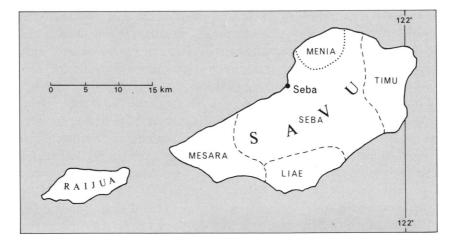

MAP 6 The Savu Islands showing the various states. The map gives the approximate location of the state of Menia, which was recognized by the Dutch in 1756 but had been overwhelmed by Seba by the time of Captain Cook's visit in 1770. Seba continued to expand throughout most of the nineteenth century and this map, based on twentieth-century sources, assigns more territory to Seba than would have been the case in previous centuries.

policy of relative noninterference in Savu's traditional affairs. It was at this time that all of the rulers of Roti were clamoring for their own schoolmasters. For Savu, on the other hand, the Dutch had to agree to recall the one school-teacher whom they had appointed to the island a few years before.[36] Later the Company again sent one or another teacher to Savu, but efforts at school-ing the Savunese in the latter half of the eighteenth century and through the first half of the nineteenth century proved to be remarkably unsuccessful.

If it were not for one event, knowledge of Savu during the entire Com-pany period could consist merely in fragments of information. Fortunately, however, in September 1770, sailing west from New Guinea along the Timor coast and through the straits of Roti, Captain James Cook in the *En-deavour* came upon the Savu islands. Since they were not charted on his maps, he put in at Seba to reconnoiter the island and to purchase supplies. Cook's account of Savu, combined with the notes on Savu in the *Endeavour Journal* of Joseph Banks,[37] present accurate eyewitness descriptions of life on Savu. They provide as well a shrewd and, for the most part, reliable assess-ment of what they were told of the island. Together with the fragments available in Company records and the oral traditions of the Savunese them-selves, it is possible to gain a reasonably ample picture of various aspects of Savunese life in the latter half of the eighteenth century.

Captain Cook was one of the few visitors to Savu to be impressed by its barren beauty. In particular, Cook seems to have been struck by the lontar palms that covered the hills of Savu. He writes:

> The sea-coast, in general, is low; but in the middle of the island there are hills of a considerable height. We were upon the coast at the latter end of the dry season, when there had been no rain for seven months; and we were told that when the dry season continues so long, there is no running stream of fresh water upon the whole island, but only small springs, which are at a considerable distance from the sea-side: yet noth-ing can be imagined so beautiful as the prospect of the country from the ship. The level ground next to the sea-side was covered with cocoa-nut trees, and a kind of palm called *Arecas;* and beyond them the hills, which rose in a gentle and regular ascent, were richly clothed, quite to the summit, with plantations of the fan palm, forming an almost impenetrable grove.[38]

Banks adds in his journal:

> The North side of the Isle appeard scarce at all cultivated, but like that of Rotte coverd with thick brush wood almost or quite destitute of Leaves: among these as we pass'd along we saw numerous flocks of sheep, but no houses or plantations.[39]

Savu at the time of the visit of the *Endeavour*. This drawing, probably by Parkinson, shows a man climbing a lontar in front of a traditional Savunese house. The one inaccuracy is that it is virtually impossible to climb a lontar with leaf-buckets on a carrying-stick over the shoulder. For ascent and descent, the leaf-bucket is hung from a belt around the waist. (Reproduced by permission of the British Library Board, MS. 23920, F.31.)

To their initial surprise, the landing party that Cook put ashore at Seba was greeted by a European and two individuals of mixed descent. The first of these was named Johan Christopher Lange. He was not a Dutchman but a native of Saxony. Cook reports that what was remarkable about Lange was that he had resided on Savu for a full ten years and was to be

> distinguished from the natives only by his colour and his dress, for he sits upon the ground, chews his betele, and in every respect has adopted their character and manners; he has married an Indian woman of the island of Timor, who keeps his house after the fashion of her country; and he gave that as a reason for not inviting us to visit him, saying, that he could entertain us in no other manner than the Indians had done, and he spoke no language readily but that of the country.[40]

Lange was assisted by someone who was described as a native of Timor (the son of a Portuguese) and by a certain Frederick Craig, the son of a native woman and a Dutchman. As political background for relations with the Dutch and the reasons for stationing a European on the island, Cook provides the following outline of the history of Dutch dealings with the Savunese:

> This island was settled by the Portuguese almost as soon as they first
> found their way into this part of the ocean; but they were in a short
> time supplanted by the Dutch. The Dutch however did not take posses-
> sion of it, but only sent sloops to trade with the natives . . . possibly
> their supplies by this occasional traffic were precarious; possibly they
> were jealous of being supplanted in their turn; but however that be,
> their East India Company, about ten years ago, entered into a treaty
> with the Rajas, by which the Company stipulated to furnish each of
> them with a certain quantity of silk, fine linen, cutlery ware, arrack
> [gin] and other articles, every year; and the Rajas engaged that neither
> they nor their subjects should trade with any person except the Com-
> pany, without having first obtained their consent, and that they would
> admit a resident on behalf of the Company, to reside upon the island,
> and see that their part of the treaty was fulfilled: they also engaged to
> supply annually a certain quantity of rice, maize, and calevances [green
> grams]. The maize and calevances are sent to Timor in sloops, which are
> kept there for that purpose, each of which is navigated by ten Indians;
> and the rice is fetched away annually by a ship which brings the Com-
> pany's returns, and anchors alternately in each of the three bays. These
> returns are delivered to the Rajas in the form of a present, and the cask
> of arrack they and their principal people never cease to drink, as long as
> a drop of it remains.[41]

This accurate summary is incorrect in only one particular. Cook alludes to
the Contract of 1756 that established a regular exchange of foodstuffs for
luxury goods. By "calevances" he could only have been referring to green
grams, which Dutch records report that Savu supplied as well as Roti. But it
is unlikely that Savu supplied any maize to Kupang. There is no Dutch men-
tion of maize on Savu at this time, and reports from the middle of the nineteenth century make special note of the fact that only small quantities of
maize were grown on the island. By maize, Cook must have been referring
either to millet or, more likely, to sorghum (*terae hawu*), which has remained Savu's chief cereal crop. Moreover, it would have been impossible
for Cook to have seen any cereals growing on the island because he arrived in
September and, as Banks explains, that year "every crop had failed for want
of Rain."[42]

According to Cook, one of Resident Lange's principal duties was to prod
the rulers of the island into planting crops to be sent to Kupang:

> Lange visits each of the Rajas once in two months, when he makes the
> tour of the island, attended by fifty slaves on horseback. He exhorts

these Chiefs to plant, if it appears that they have been remiss, and observes where the crops are got in, that he may order sloops to fetch it; so that it passes immediately from the ground to the Dutch storehouses at Timor.[43]

Cook mentions "five principalities" with whom the Dutch had formal relations: "Laai [Liae], Seba, Regeeua [Raijua], Timo [Timu], and Massara [Mesara], each of which is governed by its respective Raja or King."[44] It would appear that the final dissolution of Menia had occurred between the signing of the Contract of 1756 and Cook's visit in 1770. Cook goes on to discuss the "martial prowess" for which he reports that the Savunese were famous. Lange, he writes, said that

> the people were of a warlike disposition, and had always courageously defended themselves against foreign invaders. We were told also, that the island was able to raise, upon very short notice, 7300 fighting men, armed with muskets, spears, lances, and targets. Of this force, Laai was said to furnish 2600, Seba 2000, Regeeua 1500, Timo 800, and Massara 400. Besides the arms that have been already mentioned, each man is furnished with a large pole-ax, resembling a wood-bill, except that it has a strait edge, and is much heavier: this, in the hands of people who have courage to come to close quarters with any enemy, must be a dreadful weapon; and we were told that they were so dexterous with their lances, that at the distance of sixty feet they would throw them with such exactness as to pierce a man's heart, and such force as to go quite through his body.[45]

Cook seems not to have questioned the exaggerated and misleading figures that Lange supplied him, for he observed Savu to be a "populous" island. Lange's distortion made Liae, a state on Savu's south coast, about which Cook had obtained no impression, the largest supplier of men on the island. Although Cook had no occasion to witness a demonstration of Savunese martial prowess, he had no lack of evidence of a concern with things military. The moment his lieutenant came ashore at Seba, he was received by "a guard of between twenty and thirty Indians, armed with muskets."[46] And what most impressed the Raja of Seba was to see the precise exercises of Cook's marines, to watch them fire several rounds, and to receive a nine-gun salute as the Raja was returning from the *Endeavour*.

At first, Cook and his men had great difficulties in persuading the Savunese to trade them the animals and other supplies they needed. But after presenting an old man whom Cook regarded as "the Prime Minister" of Seba with an old broadsword, he discovered that the Savunese "were more desirous of goods than money.''[47] And what they most wanted were muskets. In regard to his trading, Cook remarked:

> Most of the buffaloes that we bought, after our friend, the Prime Minister, had procured us a fair market, were sold for a musquet a-piece, and at this price we might have bought as many as would have freighted our ship.[48]

At the assembly house in Seba, Cook saw a great number of weapons: ''hundreds of spears and targets . . . a few swivel guns and pateraros . . . and a great gun before it.'' But he had genuine doubts about the effectiveness of some of this weaponry, which seemed to him ''to be the refuse of old armories.'' No two muskets were of the same make or length, few of them had powder or ball, and many of the guns were consumed with rust.[49]

On the first attempt to put a boat ashore on Savu, Banks reports that the Savunese ''talked much of the Portuguese and of Larntuca on the Island of Ende [Flores].''[50] Later, in dealings with the Raja of Seba, Cook's officers relied on a Portuguese interpreter, while on board the *Endeavour* Cook mentions that ''several of the seamen were able to converse with such of the natives as spoke Portuguese.''[51] It was Cook's surmise

> that the Dutch never teach their own language to the natives of these islands, and have been at the expence of translating the Testament and catechisms into the different languages of each; for in proportion as Dutch had become the language of their religion, it would have become the common language of them all.[52]

In all probability, however, the testament and tracts that Dr. Daniel Solander of the *Endeavour* had the chance to examine were not in Savunese but in Malay. According to Cook, it was the half-caste Frederick Craig's task to use these books ''to instruct the youth of the country in reading and writing and the principles of the Christian religion.''[53] Craig boasted that there were no less than six hundred Christians in Seba; but without a single church or clergyman on the island, Cook doubted Craig's claims about the spread of Christianity.

Some of Cook's speculations on Savunese religion and traditional practices, based on information supplied by Lange, are far from informative. It is clear that Cook visited the hilltop outside of Seba known as *Nada Ae,* whose megaliths he compared to Stonehenge on the Salisbury Plain. He took these megaliths to be monuments erected to mark the reigns of previous rulers, but he wondered about how they had ever been put in place: ''Many of these stones are so large, that it is difficult to conceive by what means they were brought to their present station, especially as it is the summit of a hill."[54] These large hemispherical stones are, in fact, the sacrificial altars of the priests of the different ranked clans of Seba.

On one point of comparison, Cook proved to be entirely correct. He writes: "The chief object of pride among these people, like that of a Welch-man, is a long pedigree of respectable ancestors."[55] This Savunese concern with long oral genealogies has carried to the present day and makes it possible to identify precisely individuals with whom Cook dealt on his visit. Cook gives the name of the Raja of Seba as A Madocho Lomi Djara [Ama Doko Lomi Djara]. Lomi Djara is a name that occurs twice in the royal genealogy of Seba, but this particular Lomi Djara could only have been the son of Djara Wadu, who signed the Contract of 1756. Cook describes Lomi Djara as a personage of

> great authority, without much external parade or show, or much appearance of personal respect. He was about five and thirty years of age, and the fattest man we saw upon the whole island: he appeared to be of a dull phlegmatic disposition, and to be directed almost implicitly by the old man who, upon my presenting him with a sword, had procured us a fair market, in spight of the craft and avarice of the Dutch factors.[56]

It is the position of this second personage, whom Cook referred to as the "Prime Minister" of Seba, that is unclear. Cook records his name as Mannu Djarme, Banks as Mannu Djame. Based on the genealogies of Seba, this could only be Manu Djami.

Whereas Lomi Djara was recognized by the Dutch as the Raja of Seba, he also held the priestly office of Apu Lodo within the ceremonial sphere of Savunese religion. This meant that, for a part of the year, he was the focus of a number of prohibitions that severely limited his activities. As on Roti, the Dutch appointed an executive officer in each state they recognized. This person held the title of Fetor and was often referred to in documents as "the Second" or "Second Regent" in a native state. In most of the states of Roti, the Fetor had little political power compared to the ruler. But on Savu, as long as rulers retained ceremonial functions as Apu Lodo, the Fetors were

---

D. D. Bireludji, hereditary ruler of Seba, with his wife. He is a direct descendant of Ama Doko Lomi Djara, whom Captain Cook met on his visit to Savu in 1770.

allowed considerable political power. In Seba, both Raja and Fetor were members of the same clan, Nataga, but of different lineages. Lomi Djara was a member of Naluluweo; Manu Djami, of Nadjohina.[57]

Undoubtedly the most accurate and, from the point of view of this study, the most interesting portion of Cook's account of Savu is his lengthy description of the Savunese utilization of the lontar palm. The use of this palm was something he had not previously encountered on his voyage and it was sufficiently unusual to merit a careful telling. The *Endeavour* arrived at Savu in September at the high point of the lontar-tapping season in a year when all crops were reported to have failed, so the Savunese must have been involved in extra efforts to secure a food supply for the next six to eight months. Cook and his crew took special interest in the palm, for they too were anxious to obtain supplies. One reason Cook gives for putting in at Savu was that many of his crew were in a state of bad health and still repining at his not having touched at Timor. After the first visit ashore, Banks writes:

> We returnd on board, having only just tasted their Palm wine which had a very sweet taste and suited all our palates very well, giving us at the same time hopes that it might be servicable to our sick, as being the fresh and unfermented juice of the tree it promisd ante-scorbutick virtues.[58]

Besides palm juice, which was offered freely, Cook was able to purchase at a low price "several hundred gallons of palm syrup,"[59] which he found to be "infinitely superior to molasses or treacle."[60]

Both the tapping of palms and the cooking of juice to syrup would naturally have been going on in full view of all of the crew members who came ashore. Cook's account of the lontar, therefore, surpasses even Rumphius' account—which, for the Timor area, was based on information reaching Ambon in the Moluccas. Cook's was based on actual observations and deserves quotation in full as the earliest and most complete account of the lontar and its uses on any of the islands near Timor:

> The fan-palm requires more particular notice for at certain times it is a seccedaneum for all other food both to man and beast. A kind of wine, called toddy, is procured from this tree, by cutting the buds which are

A Savunese tapper ascending a lontar palm. Two leaf-buckets hang from his belt, into which he has inserted his knife and cleaning brush.

to produce flowers, soon after their appearance, and tying under them small baskets, made of the leaves, which are so close as to hold liquids without leaking. The juice which trickles into these vessels, is collected by persons who climb the trees for that purpose, morning and evening, and is the common drink of every individual upon the island; yet a much greater quantity is drawn off than is consumed in this use, and of the surplus they make both a syrup and coarse sugar. The liquor is called *dua,* or *duac,* and both the syrup and sugar, *gula.* The syrup is prepared by boiling the liquor down in pots of earthen ware, till it is sufficiently inspissated; it is not unlike treacle in appearance, but is somewhat thicker, and has a much more agreeable taste: the sugar is of a reddish brown, perhaps the same with the Jugata sugar upon the continent of India, and it was more agreeable to our palates than any cane sugar, unrefined, that we had ever tasted. We were at first afraid that the syrup, of which some of our people ate very great quantities, would have brought on fluxes, but its aperient quality was so very slight, that what effect it produced was rather salutary than hurtful. I have already observed, that it is given with the husks of rice to the hogs, and that they grow enormously fat without taking any other food: we were told also, that this syrup is used to fatten their dogs and their fowls, and that the inhabitants themselves have subsisted upon this alone for several months, when other crops have failed, and animal food has been scarce. The leaves of this tree are also put to various uses, they thatch houses, and make baskets, cups, umbrellas, and tobacco-pipes. The fruit is least esteemed, and as the blossoms are wounded for the tuac or toddy, there is not much of it: it is about as big as a large turnip, and covered, like the cocoa-nut with a fibrous coat, under which are three kernels, that must be eaten before they are ripe, for afterwards they become so hard that they cannot be chewed; in their eatable state they taste not unlike a green cocoa-nut, and, like them, probably they yield a nutriment that is watery and unsubstantial.[61]

Cook's admiration extended not only to the lontar palm and its myriad usages but also to the ingenuity with which the Savunese overcame the major obstacle to the cooking of lontar juice—the scarcity of firewood on the island. Cook's description of the "contrivance" used to save fuel gives an admirably succinct picture of the Savunese cooking oven:[62]

They dig a hollow under ground, in a horizontal direction, like a rabbit burrow, about two yards long, and opening into a hole at each end, one of which is large and the other small: by the large hole the fire is put in, and the small one serves for a draught. The earth over this burrow is perforated by circular holes, which communicate with the cavity below; and in these holes are set earthen pots, generally about three to each fire, which are large in the middle, and taper towards the bottom, so that the fire acts upon a large part of their surface. Each of these pots

A Rotinese woman seated beside a lontar cooking oven of the same sort that impressed Captain Cook on his visit to Savu in the late eighteenth century.

generally contains about eight or ten gallons, and it is surprising to see with how small a quantity of fire they may be kept boiling; a palm leaf, or a dry stalk, thrust in now and then, is sufficient: in this manner they boil all their victuals, and make all their syrup and sugar.[63]

Cook's impression of the Savunese contrasts with that of ter Horst in 1648. The Savunese "appeared to be a healthy and long-lived people." Their morals were "irreproachable, even upon the principles of Christianity." And the "delicacy and cleanliness" of their domestic life were also "very remarkable."[64] It is apparent that Cook was indeed successful in his dealings with the Savunese. When he left the island, he had procured for the *Endeavour* "nine buffaloes, six sheep, three hogs, thirty dozen of fowls, a few limes, and some cocoa-nuts; many dozen of eggs, half of which proved to be rotten; a little garlic and several hundred gallons of palm-syrup."[65] Although many of his conjectures were incorrect, his observations were accurate. Without them, knowledge of Savu would have continued to be meager for almost another century; from them, we can conclude among other things that Savu's palm economy—like that of Roti—was already well developed in the eighteenth century.[66]

It must be admitted, however, that few of the visitors who followed Cook were equally impressed by the island. J. A. B. Dentrecasteaux, who purposely sailed past Savu in October 1792 to see the island that Cook had described, reports with disappointment that Savu's appearance was so inanimate, unpicturesque, and monotonous that Cook's imaginings could only be attributed to his long and perilous voyage.[67] As a later Dutch visitor was to describe it, Savu is "a lump of stone in an immense sea."[68] These appearances were enough to discourage most visitors and to preserve the island's relative isolation.

CHAPTER FIVE

The Rotinese
in the Nineteenth Century

DUTCH EAST INDIA COMPANY involvement in the affairs of the Timor area continued for almost two centuries. It began with Apollonius Scotte's voyage in 1613 and formally ended on 31 December 1799, when the Company's charter expired and was not renewed. A mounting deficit in the previous decade and changing relations among the European powers during the Napoleonic wars put an end to the Company's control of the Indonesian islands. In 1795 Holland was invaded and established as a republic under French protection. The Prince of Orange, who had fled to London, acting as Director of the Company, issued letters to the Governor and officials of the Company and to the commanders of Dutch fortresses to surrender to British authority. In 1797 Kupang briefly surrendered its fortress, only to have it returned and, again in 1811, retaken by the British. For a few years Kupang was joined to the rest of the former Dutch territories under the British governorship of Thomas Raffles. But by the Convention of London in 1814, these territories were returned to the Dutch, with formal reinstatement of control of Kupang occurring in 1816. Despite the confusing succession of official regimes at Kupang, a certain continuity remained.

One man has to be credited for maintaining this continuity. This was Jacobus Arnoldus Hazaart, whose enormous energy and single-minded persistence dominated all aspects of Dutch-native relations for decades. Hazaart was born in Kupang on 8 January 1773 and died on 19 December 1838 on a visit to Savu at the age of 65. Unlike Company officers who held their positions in Kupang for several years at most, Hazaart never left the Timor area, except for brief trips to Batavia, during the entire course of his life. And even more unlike Company officers, who were strictly charged to carry out Company policy in the Timor area, Hazaart seems often to have made his own policies—or at least to have stamped Dutch government policies in his own personal image. No one affected the course and development of native relations in the nineteenth century more profoundly than this Dutchman from Timor.

Hazaart was already the Dutch Resident at Kupang in 1810. In that year he was able to resist a British attack on Kupang, but in the following year was obliged to surrender the town. At first he remained in office as Resident under the British. Later he was replaced but chose to remain in Kupang as a merchant and, after the 1814 Convention of London, was unofficially regarded as the Dutch head of Kupang. Finally in 1816, with the restoration of Dutch rule, he was appointed once more as the Dutch Resident at Kupang. In 1818 he was temporarily dismissed for occupying the town of Atapupu on the north coast of Timor, completely on his own initiative, to prevent the Portuguese from doing so. His decision and actions were subsequently vindicated and he was reinstated a few months later. For the next twenty years, his policies exercised undisputed influence in the Timor area. Even after his death, other Residents seem to have tried to model their own schemes on Hazaart's successful program. The essential components of this program were to end native unrest and rebellion on the islands, to foster the spread of Christianity, and to promote the economic development of Timor. The Rotinese became indispensable to his plans. With Hazaart's impetus, the Christian Rotinese were the population on whom education was to be lavished and to whom the undeveloped areas of Timor were to be given for development.

THE DEVELOPMENT OF CHRISTIANITY AND EDUCATION

Roti's rapid acceptance of Christianity and of education was not initially viewed by the eighteenth-century Dutch as a wholly desirable change for the island. The Company was committed to trade; it recognized a responsibility for conserving Christianity among its personnel, but not the same responsibility for promoting Christianity. The Rotinese conversion was therefore regarded somewhat skeptically. As the Rotinese sensed, there was a definite reluctance on the part of many Dutch officials to encourage this conversion. W. van Hogendorp emphasized this view in his influential summary description of Timor and surrounding islands. He argued that since the Rotinese had "not the least conception of Christian worship . . . it would possibly be better to let them remain in a state of complete ignorance."[1] The contradiction in Dutch policy in regard to Christianity ended with the dissolution of the Company. For Hazaart, the promotion of Christianity was an integral part of his policy and synonymous with economic advancement.

Just before the end of the eighteenth century, an event occurred in Holland that signaled this change in Dutch attitudes toward the East Indies, one that was to have a considerable effect on relations in the Timor area. In 1797, following the inspiration of the London Missionary Society, the Dutch founded the Netherlands Missionary Society (*Nederlandsche Zendeling Genootschap*). This Society was intended to be a nondenominational organization for the teaching of simple evangelical Christianity. Its first representative to reach Kupang was Dr. R. Le Bruijn. He arrived in 1819, just after Hazaart's reinstatement, and almost immediately these two men began work on their common and inseparable plans.

From the time of the first contracts, Rotinese rulers had paid part of their annual tribute to the Company in bees' wax. This tribute was, in effect, continued, but the income from the sale of this bees' wax was granted to the Netherlands Missionary Society to finance education on Roti. Le Bruijn was the first Dutch minister to visit Roti in several decades. Although he found Christianity in a state of decay, he wrote to his Society that Roti offered "an ever open door" to the preaching of the gospel.[2] Within a few years, he had personally baptized two Rotinese rulers and had reestablished much of the old Rotinese school system. By 1825 there were local schools in Landu, Termanu, Talae, Baä, Loleh, Thie, Dengka, and Oenale. Most were staffed by local Rotinese while Le Bruijn remained in Kupang.

Roti, it must be recognized, was never missionized as were some of the other islands of the Timor area. By converting to Christianity in the eighteenth century, the Rotinese tended to regard missionary interference in their religious affairs as misdirected and unnecessary. Most missionary activities were therefore supervised from Kupang and were dependent upon the Rotinese themselves. From time to time, Dutch or German missionaries were sent to reside on the island, but most of them frankly admitted their lack of success in attempts to reform and enhance the conditions of the church on Roti. Despite a host of successive missionaries in the nineteenth and twentieth centuries, none of these—with one or two exceptions—managed to remain two years on the island. The climate of the island, its heat, its dry winds, its malaria, or simply the frustration of dealing with the Rotinese thwarted any continuity in mission efforts.

The glaring exception to this pattern was the German missionary, A. Jackstein, who became blind while on Roti. To this day he is remembered as an almost legendary character who was led on horseback from village to village to preach to the Rotinese. From one or two brief articles that he wrote, he seems to have had a clear perception and appreciation of Rotinese culture.[3] In accordance with Rotinese tradition, a *tutus,* or traditional mortuary monument, was erected in his honor after his death.

More typical of the general pattern was the experience of the first missionary to reside on the island. This was a young Dutchman, J. K. ter Linden, who was appointed by Le Bruijn in 1827. On his arrival he was well received by all the rulers and accompanied by crowds wherever he went. His first letters to the Missionary Society are full of exclamations: "Oh, how charming it is to be among these simple people."[4] Yet within a year of taking up residence in Thie, ter Linden had become so utterly disillusioned with the Rotinese that "on account of the shameful and godless conduct of the instructors" he closed all the schools that Le Bruijn had founded and withdrew to Kupang.

In the following decade, attempts were made again to establish schools under missionary supervision. The missionary who succeeded ter Linden was G. Heijmering. While remaining stationed in Kupang, he reopened the schools on Roti. The first was in Landu; then others followed in Thie, Termanu, Bilba, Ringgou, and Oepao, until by 1842 there were ten schools on the island. In 1839 the missionary F. Hartig arrived on Roti and remained for less than a year before he became ill and had to remove himself to Kupang. During this year the ruler of Termanu was baptized by Heijmering in Kupang, and for the first time a church was allowed to be built in that state. Hartig returned briefly to Roti, where he is reported to have begun the study of Rotinese but to have given this up and to have relied exclusively, as others before and after him, on Malay. Two other missionaries joined Hartig in 1841. One, G. H. Noordhoff, died within a year of his arrival, and the other, F. H. Linemann, only managed to stay until October 1842. In April 1843 a cyclone struck the island and destroyed Hartig's house, school, and church. He moved to Kupang, and missionary work on the island was temporarily suspended. No other European missionary attempted to reside on the island for almost twenty years. Instead, in 1847, the Missionary Society appointed a young Rotinese from Termanu, P. Pello, as a mission assistant and supervisor of schools. A few years later the Netherlands Missionary Society formally withdrew from Roti and Timor.

It is difficult in the missionary literature of this period, or any later period, to find a single, informed, and—at the same time—enthusiastic assessment of the increasing adherence of the Rotinese to Christianity. Roti was, to the missionaries, an area of numerical success and spiritual disappointment. In the harsh judgment of a recent missionary to Timor, "the Rotinese Church is most renowned for its lack of enthusiasm and the low level of its spiritual life. It is a Church that has grown old without ever having been young and vigorous. No doubt its present state is largely due to the sporadic and ineffective way the Christian mission was carried on in Roti from the beginning.''[5]

What was a cause for disappointment to various missionaries was a source of pride to many Rotinese. To them theirs was the only island to accept Christianity from the beginning but to reject outside control of its preaching; the only island in eastern Indonesia to maintain the rudiments of an independent, though interrupted, tradition of local schools, offering instruction in Malay, for a period of over two hundred years; and the only island to resist the wholesale abolition of native practice in the name of religion. In the twentieth century, a number of ordained Rotinese ministers successfully defended bridewealth and mortuary payments by Christians and argued articulately in favor of the fusion of native and Christian practice that had developed on their island.

After the closing of the mission schools on Roti in 1851, there was a period of several years during which these schools were unofficially maintained by the local states. Then in 1855, S. N. Buddingh visited Roti for ten days on a school inspection tour for the government. Wholly unaware of the previous experiences of others on brief first visits to Roti, Buddingh was overwhelmed by his reception and the earnestness with which he was requested to reopen Rotinese schools. He concluded in his report that "the Rotinese are a studious, clever and intelligent people and from an intellectual as well as moral point of view deserve a place of honor among the tropical peoples."[6] His recommendation was accepted. By government decision of 8 May 1857, Roti was awarded an annual budget of 4,380 Dutch florin for the upkeep of 18 schools, one for each state on the island.

With this boost to their education system, there was further development in Rotinese schooling. From the beginning, schoolmasters (*mese* from the Dutch word, *meester*) held special rank and were given considerable prestige. Even today they are accorded the same deference as any clan lord or high noble. After the founding of schools in the main villages of each state, the competition that had persisted among the states extended to the village areas within the states. Still more schools were established. As salaried government employees, schoolteachers were ranked according to training and experience. Official documents for 1862 list three kinds of teacher. On the island, there were 18 Government Instructors (*Gouvernements-onderwijzers*), 11 Local State Instructors (*Negorij-onderwijzers*), and 21 Assistants (*Helpers*).[7] By 1871, in addition to the original 18 government schools, there were 16 village schools. The school population had risen from 2,547 to 3,277. In this same year, a royal decree forbade religious instruction in government schools. Prior to this time, instructors in government schools were also responsible for conducting religious services on Sundays. Although officially severed, the link between religion and education could not in fact be so easily sundered. The link was not merely one of the content of instruction; it existed in the medium of all instruction—the Malay language.

THE ROTINESE USE OF MALAY

Throughout their history, Roti's local schools were structured on the simplest principles and used the simplest materials. Like Rotinese houses, schools and their furnishings were constructed from palms. What could not be obtained from the Dutch was improvised. In place of slates, Rotinese used the soft whitewood boards of *didite* wood; for ink, they used indigo (*tauk*) or fabricated an ink from *dodoa* leaves; rulers were made from bamboo. Malay schoolbooks were used for reading; where these were lacking, reading was taught from the Malay Bible.[8] There were six grades to the school, with boys and girls attending school together. Instruction was regimented: class was held for approximately four hours each weekday, and there was no automatic advance to the next grade at the end of each year, so the age of the students in the same school ranged from 6 to 18. Most rulers enforced attendance and required the payment of a water buffalo or horse before a child would be allowed to conclude his education. Rulers apparently competed with each other to sustain high attendance at their schools.[9] N. Graafland, a school inspector for the Netherlands Indies, provides this description of a nineteenth-century village school in Baä, which might hold for many of the schools on Roti today:

> The building is a spacious, oblong, four-sided, open shed, not recently erected, with some masonry—a surrounding, upright course of brickwork and on this a partition four feet high. The beams, on which the roof rests, stand in the ground, are well cut, but not planed and are only six to seven feet high. Notches are cut through the middle of the upper ends so that the cross-beams on which the roof will rest can be fastened on them with cord from the lontar or gewang palm. No nail is used in the entire building: everything is tightly bound with cord made from twisted tree bark or the leaf-ribs of the palms. The roof beams are also gewang slats and the leaves that serve as thatch also come from the palm while they are tightly bound with tiny cords of twisted leaf-ribs . . . There is no loft and thus one notices the entire roof-work above with drooping leaves and cords in all their rustic simplicity. After a long

A classroom in a Rotinese school. The schools are much the same as they have been for centuries: a building of lontar beams, a lontar-thatched roof (here visible outside), a dirt floor, crude benches, and a simple blackboard for each classroom.

time, one ceases to notice that but what is really bothersome is that in these sheds there is no sound, no form of good acoustics. The furniture is to a certain extent sufficient to the appropriate demands: there are school tables with fixed benches, but the proportions are not judicious. The benches are mostly too low for the table and too far removed from it . . . There are a couple of blackboards but no proper easels. They are apparently not much used . . .

The reading went tolerably well but dryly and without the least emphasis from which to determine a good understanding of what was read. It appeared after further conversation that the pupils did understand but not enough together. They are well versed in Malay schoolbooks in which the reading materials give a good opportunity for useful and stimulating conversation.

I spoke there of Malay schoolbooks and thus involuntarily named one of the obstacles to comprehensible instruction for these youth: for Malay is for them a totally foreign language, just as Spanish is for our Dutch youth. There are no books in their local or mother tongue and they must thus begin to learn in a foreign language and in this way learn to think and speak.[10]

What missionaries and educators alike decried was precisely this use of

Malay in all Rotinese schools and churches. Yet from the time of the first contact with the Dutch, Malay was the exclusive means of access to the outside world. To the Company, in dealing with the Rotinese there was no question but that the language of communication had to be Malay. Early on, they transported Rotinese to Kupang to learn Malay. In 1679, when the Company had firmly decided on Termanu as its base of operations, the young ruler of Termanu was brought to Kupang for the express purpose of learning Malay.[11] Later, Company "interpreters" on Roti worked through Malay, and the annual letters sent to the Governor General were written for the Rotinese rulers in Malay by the Company's scribes in Kupang. Having one's own schoolmaster was thus, in effect, like having one's own state scribe. This tradition persisted through the nineteenth century. Although Le Bruijn, in accordance with the principles of his Missionary Society, urged that preaching be in the native language, he produced the first Malay hymnal. It seems that at no time were church services ever conducted entirely in Rotinese. The same has always been true of instruction in Rotinese schools. The full title for schoolmasters in the nineteenth century, as recorded by Jonker,[12] was *mese malai;* "Malay masters."

There was only one missionary in Roti's history to remain for a long period on the island—a full ten years—and to learn some form of Rotinese. This was G. J. H. Le Grand, who was on Roti from 1890 to 1900. He admitted that during his ten year stay he managed to baptize only about 350 persons. He did master Rotinese ritual language, and his only published letter to his Missionary Society is filled with Rotinese chants and proverbs by which he hoped to illustrate to his directors aspects of Rotinese spiritual life. While Le Grand saw his task as promoting Rotinese schoolteachers and preachers, he fully recognized that Malay had become the "vehicle of Christian thought" on the island. At the beginning of his stay, however, to counteract this use of Malay, he encouraged a Rotinese Government Instructor from Baä, J. Fanggidaej, to translate the Gospel of Luke into Rotinese. This was published by the Netherlands Missionary Society in 1895. As Le Grand quickly discovered, "the reception [of this translation] was not as cordial as I had expected."[13] In fact, the translation was rarely used and gradually forgotten.

There are various reasons why it was probably impossible by this time to impose a Rotinese translation of the scriptures on the Rotinese. One reason has to do with the general linguistic situation on the island and the political structures that fostered it. All evidence suggests that the Dutch encountered a good deal of diversity on the island at the time of their arrival and that they exploited this diversity to create, by the end of the eighteenth century, a political division of the island into 18 petty states. To preserve the distinctiveness of these various states the Rotinese, for their part, seized upon their minor differences and intentionally exaggerated them as marks of identity. Each state came to be distinguished not only by dress, styles of presentation, and court traditions but also by its own separate "language" (*dedea nusak*). The assorted minor linguistic shifts that characterize the chain of mutually intelligible dialects ranging across the island were given a political reality and a conscious native justification. A translation of the scriptures into Rotinese would have to be in some dialect of Rotinese; while this might conceivably be acceptable in that particular state or dialect area, it would almost certainly be rejected in others. In the case of the Fanggidaej translation, the dialect used was approximately that of central Roti. Neither in the east nor in the south or the west of Roti would the use of this dialect be appropriate, and even in central Roti, certain words and phrases would betray the text as a product of someone from Baä rather than from Termanu, Talae, or Keka.[14]

Moreover, for rituals the Rotinese have a special poetic form of speaking that exploits dialect differences. It happens that the parallelism that distinguishes this ritual language is, formally and stylistically, similar to the parallelism that dominates the verse structure of the Old Testament. The Rotinese have intuitively recognized this. The Old Testament of the Malay Bible was and remains even now the linguistic as well as the religious model for Christianity among the Rotinese. High Biblical Malay was, for Rotinese Christians, a complement as well as an equivalent to their own ritual language. In a culture like that of the Rotinese, which is so emphatically verbal, the distinctions between levels of language are as important as the distinctions between dialects. Translation of the scriptures into any form of ordinary Rotinese would tend to debase them as religious texts whose significance ought to be preserved at an elevated level of speech. For the Rotinese in the nineteenth century, Malay had already become an integral, though compartmentalized, "literary language" associated with Christianity and the outside government. Education meant learning to deal with these forces in their own proper language.[15]

By the twentieth century, Christianity and Malay were inseparably equated, a fact that served as a check on conversion. The rulers and high Rotinese nobles were the first to become Christians and to enjoy the full benefits of an education in Malay. Only gradually did these benefits encompass the entire populace. In 1900 Le Grand reported that less than a sixth of the population was formally Christian. Conversions proceeded slowly. In a collection of early twentieth-century church records in the town of Baä is recorded a portentous interview with a pagan Rotinese who stoutly opposed his son's conversion to Christianity. Only after the child had learned Malay in school did the father agree that it was appropriate for his son to become a Christian. The same thing happened throughout the island. On conclusion of Indonesian President Sukarno's national literacy campaign in the 1950s, when the island was certified as literate in Indonesian (the modernized Malay of the nation), mass conversion to Christianity occurred. By this time Roti was incorporated in a new nation-state whose adopted medium of communication was, fortunately for the Rotinese, a long-standing element of their own indigenous traditions. To appreciate the consequences of Rotinese involvement in extraisland affairs, we must first consider the Rotinese migrations that began in the early decades of the nineteenth century.

THE MOVEMENT OF ROTINESE TO TIMOR

The Dutch East India Company's policy toward native states was, in certain respects, as contradictory as its policy toward native Christianity. The Rotinese seem to have exploited these contradictions. Initially, Company officers tried to do no more than openly recognize what they took to be the de facto rulers on Roti. In doing this, they divided the island into a number of small states whose rivalries could be turned to the Company's advantage. This, in effect, froze what had undoubtedly been a more fluid situation. By involving themselves with specific ruling clans in the various states, however, the Company officers were continually called upon to determine the legitimate lines of rule, to quell internal dissension within these states, and to arbitrate disputes among all the states. Thus the Company created on Roti a situation from which it could not extricate itself. With a dozen or more states the situation was unstable.

To stabilize the island, the Company seems tacitly to have developed a special relation with Termanu, which still today has the largest area of any state on the island. In the seventeenth and eighteenth centuries it was considerably larger, and in all probability relatively more populous. Based on native evidence, Termanu seems to have been in the process of political expansion at the time the Dutch arrived. Prior to this, Termanu may have dominated much of the area between Bilba and Dengka. In addition to the Company's official enclosure (*pagar*) located at Kota Leleuk near Namo Dale on Termanu's north coast, there was for a time a small Chinese settlement in the state.[16] And from the beginning, the Dutch seemed to have treated the rulers of Termanu as the foremost political figures on the island. This was already evident in 1679, when the Dutch chose Termanu's young ruler, the Lord Pelo Kila, as the person to be taken to Kupang to learn Malay. Thereafter he became the Company's intermediary and spokesman and retained this position even after 1700, when he relinquished his title to his brother, Sinlae Kila. Certainly from the standpoint of the Dutch, Termanu (whose territory embraced all of the east central region) was the key to controlling the island. Yet precisely because of its large size and population, Termanu included the largest number of dissident territories clamoring for separate recognition from the Company. In the course of the eighteenth century, while still relying on Termanu, the Company was drawn into the politics of dismembering the state.

The first check on Termanu's domination came early in the eighteenth century when the Company recognized the autonomy of some of the smaller states on Termanu's western border, such as Baä, Lelain, Loleh, and Thie, and thereby freed them from the tribute that they were apparently obliged to pay Termanu.[17] The next areas of dispute were Diu and Bokai. By the contract of 1700, Diu was divided between Korbaffo and Termanu, although both states continued to war with Bilba over parts of the territories of Diu and Bokai. To end this, the contract of 1756 granted recognition to Diu as an independent state and gave Bokai to the Rotinese commander of the Company's native mercenaries.

Most of the formal dismemberment of Termanu came, however, after the fourth and last Company contract with the rulers of Roti in 1756. Within a few years of this contract, Lelenuk—between Diu and Bokai—was recognized as an independent state with its own ruler. Arguing explicitly in terms of the precedent set by Lelenuk and Bokai, the populations of Talae and Keka gained separation from Termanu in 1772. Immediately afterward, a village area on Termanu's southern border with Keka and Talae, Ingu Fao, began agitating for separation as well. Ingu Fao's case was advanced by a branch (and eventually a lineage) of the royal clan descended from Termanu's former ruler, Ndaomanu. Ingu Fao was soon joined by Hoi Ledo, another village area near Termanu's border with Baä, that also began to demand autonomy.

At this point resistance to further dismemberment hardened. Ingu Fao, like Talae and Keka, was at some distance from the royal center of Termanu at Fea Popi, but Hoi Ledo was much nearer; its former rulers were once ancient rivals of the rulers of Termanu, and they claimed irrigation rights to some of the finest wet-rice fields in the state. Dutch recognition of Hoi Ledo, or even Ingu Fao, was a major threat to the rulers of Termanu. For the Dutch, too, the point had been reached where they realized that the recognition of additional states on the island had to be stopped. There seemed to be no end to the number of areas that might wish to become autonomous. Yet there seemed to be no way to prevent the agitation for autonomy within the traditional pattern established by the Company. It continued into the nineteenth century without a solution.

When Hazaart assumed control in Kupang in 1816, he was neither committed to perpetuating Company policy nor was he strictly constrained by directives from the Dutch colonial government in Batavia. He was confronted not only with claims for autonomy by village areas within Termanu, but also by a long-standing dispute between Delha and Oenale over local autonomy. His solution was direct and unequivocal, and it formed part of his larger design for pacification of the interior of Timor and for economic development of that island.

In the coastal areas around the Bay of Kupang were extensive savannahs of lontar and gewang palms. If the sketchy references in the early Dutch literature can be taken as an indication, the area around the bay and along the north coast was more populous at the time of the arrival of the Dutch than it was in Hazaart's time. For more than a century it had been a battleground between those Timorese who had early allied themselves with the Dutch and the majority of the Timorese who were allied with the Black Portuguese. Between 1652 and 1749, the Dutch-allied Timorese frequently suffered severe reprisal raids and often had to retreat to the protection of the fort at Kupang. After the defeat of the Portuguese and Timorese at Penfui, there seems to have been a partial retreat of the Timorese to avoid reprisals from the Dutch and their allies. Much of the territory around Kupang became a no-man's-land. Furthermore, the palm savannahs of Hazaart's time suggest that the process of swidden exhaustion in this dry region also contributed to the withdrawal of the previous populations toward the interior. Although no longer suitable for swidden agriculturalists, it was an ideal area for a palm-tapping people.

Thus, to end internal strife on Roti, to gain a ready supply of potential native soldiers for the pacification of Timor, and to form a buffer zone around the town of Kupang, Hazaart—immediately on taking office—began to transport the population of Ingu Fao (about three to four hundred persons) to the area around the village of Babau outside of Kupang. Two or three years later, in 1818 or 1819, Hazaart transferred the dissidents of Hoi Ledo to Pariti, another area near Kupang. Both of these groups, under pressure from the ruler of Termanu, apparently agreed to their transportation to Timor. But the people of Delha, whom Hazaart also wished to transport at this same time, resisted and Hazaart resolved to move them by force. A note in the *Register* of the Governor General in Council, for 16 December 1819, cautions the Resident to use less brutal methods:

> As regards the criminal and restless inhabitants of Dela on the island of Rotti who are to be uprooted by vigorous means from there and established in a suitable part of Timor, the Resident should, however, prior to proceeding further, have recourse once more to gentler measures.[18]

Nonetheless a portion of the population of Delha was transported to join the other Rotinese on Timor. With this new source of manpower and the regular required levy of armed men from each of the rulers of Roti—in all, a force of 400 Rotinese men—Hazaart in 1822 led a major expedition into the interior of Timor to crush the rebellious state of Amanuban.

Within six years of the restoration of Dutch authority, Hazaart was proceeding successfully on all fronts. There was said to be "good harmony" among all the native rulers loyal to the Dutch; Christianity was being taught; and the last openly rebellious Timorese state was under attack. At this point, the Governor General in Batavia sent the first of several Commission officers to report on the situation on Timor and the surrounding islands. J. D. Kruseman visited Timor in 1825 and was very favorably impressed with Hazaart and his efforts. In its enthusiasm for developments on Timor, his Commission Report could have been written by Hazaart himself.

Kupang at this time comprised a handful of Europeans and their descendants, an estimated 200 Chinese in the town itself and some outlying villages, and 800 mardijkers and Papangers. The mardijkers were an Indonesian native free soldiery. The Papangers were originally Philippine soldiers who had fought on behalf of the Spanish in the Moluccas and were eventually incorporated into the Dutch forces. They served in various regions of Indonesia, and a contingent of these soldiers was permanently settled on Timor. Both the mardijkers and Papangers were mainly Moslems. In addition to these 1,000 persons, there were 2,600 Rotinese, Savunese, and Solorese and 1,200 slaves. Rotinese already made up the majority of outside islanders on Timor —approximately 2,000 according to Kruseman.

The principal foods for Kupang were rice, maize, and vegetables. To judge from Kruseman, food and social class were closely associated. The Chinese were heavily involved in trade and could afford to have their rice imported from Java. Most mardijkers ate local rice, while a few like the Papangers and the slave class, had to subsist on maize. Chinese, mardijkers, and Papangers relied on slaves to do agricultural labor outside the town of Kupang. The alluvial plain surrounding the town had already been settled by these slaves, who had planted some wet rice and maize. Kruseman was convinced, as was Hazaart, that proper wet-rice cultivation on this plain held the key to the development of Timor. This great plain, centered initially

on the settlement at Babau (then known as Bau-Bau), was to be opened to
Rotinese colonization. Kruseman, in his recommendation to the Governor
General, was explicit:

> Of all the colonies, Bau-Bau is the most important and has therefore
> the most inhabitants, its rice fields are the most fertile and hence it is
> the key to the whole land, for, with the exception of Amarassij to the
> south and west of Koepang, access from all the parts of Timor is
> through the place.
>
> Bau-Bau is an immense plain . . . comprising a surface area of 60
> square miles . . . and the hundreds of buffalo that graze on this plain
> find the finest pasture . . . [so] nature, as it were, appears to have
> formed this region for a colony; the ground is fertile, water in abun-
> dance, *bebak* to build houses [here Kruseman appears to be referring to
> the palms rather than to just their leaf stalks] grows most beautifully,
> the climate is very pleasant and the sea well situated for ships . . . [and]
> with the exception of a part at the foot of the mountains, this whole
> plain is inhabited by no other Timorese than a few people from Amabiij
> who have mixed with the colonists.

Kruseman then goes on to explain the circumstances for the Rotinese colonization of Babau:

> The disturbances in Amanoebang provided the occasion for the pro-
> motion of the colonization of Bau-Bau, to which the banishment there
> of a Radja of Rotti with 600 of his subjects who had, a few years before,
> set themselves against the Government on that island has greatly con-
> tributed; all these Rottinese feel so happy to be in Bau-Bau that one
> could not force them to return to their island.[19]

Among the children of these new Rotinese colonists, Kruseman notes, the
missionary Le Bruijn had opened a small school for Christians to teach
"reading, writing and the basic principles of the reformed worship."

On the basis of present sources, it is difficult to determine the exact number of Rotinese who were transported to Timor. Hazaart was not under the
obligation Company officers were to provide a careful accounting of all his
actions. The "Radja of Rotti" who was banished to Babau may have been
the ruler of Delha, the claimant to the lordship of Termanu from Ingu Fao,
or the actual ruler of Termanu. In a later letter to the Governor General, entered in the *Register/In Council* on 24 December 1827, Hazaart explains his
newly adopted "gentle measures" for ending native unrest on Roti. He
states that under pretext of an expedition against Amanuban, he "enticed"
the ruler of Termanu, Mauk Amalo, to Kupang and there, before an assembly of the other Rotinese rulers, deposed him and appointed his successor. In

what year this occurred is unstated, and whether Mauk Amalo was the Raja banished to Babau with 600 of his followers is uncertain. The oral traditions of Termanu that tell of Mauk Amalo's banishment describe him as a clever political opponent of the Dutch, one who resisted interference in what he defined as his own affairs. He was also the last pagan ruler of Termanu. His successor was baptized by the missionary Heijmering and let the first church be built in Termanu. So even though Hazaart gave no reasons for deposing Mauk Amalo, one can see that there were various possible sources of the conflict between the two men.

Several facts are clear. The first "migrations" from Roti were not spontaneous nor were they motivated by scarcity or overpopulation. They were politically inspired as part of an explicit colonial design. Furthermore, it is clear that Termanu was the primary state on Roti from which the early immigrants came. Perhaps as many as 1,200 persons from Termanu were transported in less than a decade. This had implications for the direction given to later migrations. Whether by accident or design, in terms of Roti's own local economic orientations, it happened that first immigrants to Babau came from one of the most intensive wet-rice-growing states on the island.

What is most strikingly apparent, in Hazaart's grand design for Timor, is the underlying set of ethnic stereotypes based on economic pursuits that was used by the Dutch in dealing with the various peoples of the Timor area. The Chinese, though industrious and indirectly involved in agriculture, were viewed as traders. The mardijkers and Papangers were town dwellers and apparently lazy. Savunese were best fit to be soldiers. The Timorese were unreliable, and not even the long loyal allies could be safely counted on to colonize the plains of their former territories. They were, according to Hazaart, too easily tempted to join other rebellious Timorese in the interior. In addition, they were maize cultivators and, in general, not disposed to Christianity or education.

The Rotinese were the only people who had the qualities Hazaart seems to have regarded as necessary. They were inclined to be Christians and knew something of wet-rice agriculture. Although they were always difficult to deal with, once forced into something, they recognized what was to their advantage. Yet even after the success of the first several Rotinese settlements, Hazaart seems to have had lingering doubts about the suitability of the Rotinese as wet-rice cultivators. In the same letter in which he announced the dismissal of the ruler of Termanu, he requested of the Governor General "a hundred Javanese and their wives and children" who, he argued, would extend rice cultivation on the fertile plains of Timor. When, in response to this request, he was offered a hundred Javanese convicts instead, he quickly withdrew his request and abandoned his scheme. He was left with no choice but to leave the development of this plain to the Rotinese. Once initiated, the colonization program committed the Dutch and Rotinese to one another and it gradually became impossible to regulate the Rotinese advancement into Timor.

THE ROTINESE PENETRATION OF TIMOR

Officially, the Rotinese were settled in what was known as government territory (*governements grondgebeid*). By contract and long-standing agreement, this was a band of land extending 6 *paalen*, or approximately 9 kilometers,[20] inland in a semicircle around the Bay of Kupang. It was this territory of Kupang that the Dutch had, in the previous century, repeatedly defended against the allied incursions of Black Portuguese and Timorese. The rulers of the original loyal allies of the Dutch frequently needed to seek protection near Kupang and eventually they established permanent residences within this government territory. Their states and, in particular, that of the so-called Emperor Sonba'i underwent attrition and division, contributing to the creation of the virtual no-man's-land into which the Rotinese were moved. By 1831 the ruler of Kupang who first ceded to the Dutch their land had moved his residence to Semau, whereas the rulers of Amabi, of Taebenu, and of Lesser Sonba'i maintained residences near Kupang and held diminished authority in what remained of their former states.

The Emperor Sonba'i, whose residence was in the interior of Timor, had sent his brother to live near Kupang and to serve as his spokesman. This brother subsequently declared his separation from Sonba'i and created the state of Lesser Sonba'i. Soon other territories claimed separation from the kingdom of Sonba'i. Amfoan, on the north coast of Timor, was the first state to separate itself and to obtain recognition by the Dutch. Between Amfoan and the government territory of Kupang were two disputed areas, Pitai and Takaip, that both asserted their independence from Sonba'i. But their autonomy was recognized neither by the Dutch nor by Sonba'i. In the euphemism of a Dutch commission report for 1831, these areas were in "a relationship of neutrality."[21] Pitai was a small area with a population of approximately 3,000, on the northern hook of land overlooking the Bay of Kupang, not too far from Pariti. Takaip, with an estimated population of 11,000, comprised all the territory along the northern coast and a considerable distance inland between Pitai and Amfoan. Another state to declare its independence from Sonba'i was Manobait, a small area with a population of about 3,000, to the north of Babau, in the mountains above the plain. Although given tacit recognition by the Dutch, this state was not similarly recognized by Sonba'i. Almost inevitably the Rotinese, once established on Timor, came in conflict with Pitai, Takaip, and Manobait. The local rulers of these areas, former subject lords or Fetors of Sonba'i, were, almost as inevitably, branded as rebels and subjected to attack by both the Dutch and the Timorese. Although they were, in fact, popularly accepted rulers in the lands that were to be most affected by the new Rotinese settlements, they were in a limbo-like position that undermined their own defense.

Within a decade or two of the initial settlement, the plains area around Kupang became dotted with Rotinese settlements: Tarus, Oesapa, Babau, Oesau, Nunkurus, Pariti. (Map 7 indicates the location of some of these settlements.) One reason for this is that the Dutch were not transporting a homogeneous population. It was a population that had for centuries maintained distinct and separate states. Whatever Hazaart had intended, the Rotinese recreated on Timor, in villages and subvillages, the divisions that existed on Roti. This gave the Rotinese migration a centrifugal tendency. Rather than concentrating in a few strategic areas, Rotinese settlements from the different states scattered over the entire government territory. Rotinese from Termanu had been settled in Babau and Pariti and spilled over into Oesau. In 1839, or shortly thereafter, the Dutch settled families from Dengka at Tarus and some of these families later founded the village of Nunkurus. A significant number of persons from Thie, for example, settled in Oesapa and, at a later period, people from Bilba settled at Sulamu and began to move onto the island of Semau.[22]

Timorese attacks on these settlements came early and continued sporadically through the nineteenth century. P. J. Veth mentions an attack from Pitai on Pariti almost immediately after it was settled, and a devastating dawn raid on Nunkurus by Manobait in 1847.[23] Rotinese settlements became armed camps of agricultural pioneers. More than one visitor to Timor remarked on how well armed the Rotinese were. For every raid, the Dutch organized retaliation. Responsibility for the success of these retaliatory responses lay with the Dutch, not the Rotinese. Their own traditional factiousness prevented them from maintaining even the semblance of a united opposition to the Timorese. The Dutch were therefore forced to muster the Rotinese to defend themselves on the basis of a solidarity that the Rotinese themselves hardly recognized.

In the previous century, it had taken months—sometimes even a year or more—to assemble a force for an attack on the interior of Timor. In the nineteenth century, this could be done in a few days or weeks. The main contingent for these forces came not from the Rotinese settlers on Timor but from the island of Roti itself. It became relatively easy to gather rapidly an armed body of Rotinese men to defend their fellow islanders on Timor. Thus, with Dutch organization and transportation, the tiny individual settlements could be defended by the armed force of the entire island of Roti. This force was never directed against all Timorese, but against specific, threatening factions of Timorese who did not even have the support of the main Timorese rulers.

Buddingh, the government school inspector who was so passionately taken by his Rotinese reception, recounts with evident dispassion what was occurring on Timor at the very same time in 1855 that he was enthusiastically touring Roti. Apparently a Rotinese from Pariti had stolen a water buffalo from some Timorese of Takaip. He was caught and ordered to return two buffalo for the one that was stolen. The Fetor, Bakekooi, of Takaip was said to be dissatisfied with this and to have "declared war" by staking the head of a water buffalo on a pole near Pariti. This, according to Buddingh, was interpreted as a declaration by Bakekooi that "this land belongs to me." The Fetor then began, at night, to steal all the livestock he could round up in the government territory around Pariti. The Resident therefore decided to launch an expedition against him and sent two ships, the *Celebes* and the *Lansier,* to bring 1,300 "auxiliaries" from Roti to Timor. These auxiliaries were landed near Pariti and from September 9th to 13th, they engaged the Timorese of Takaip, attacking with cannon and burning the village of Batu Iki. On September 15th, in less than a week from their day of initial engagement, these same Rotinese were back on their island.[24] The Timorese had no defense against these brief, lightning attacks that propelled the Rotinese penetration of Timor.

Restraining the Rotinese proved to be, for the Dutch, a worrisome impossibility. Van Rhijn's 1847 sketch map of Timor, for example, locates the limits of Rotinese settlement at Sulamu on the other side of what had once been the Timorese village of Pitai. By the 1870s, however, Rotinese settlement had moved along the north coast of Timor well into the territory of Amfoan. By then the village of Naikliu was described as a flourishing Rotinese settlement, harbor, and trading post. Ormeling has noted what he has called a "twin village" phenomenon around Kupang: Tabung Rote adjoins Tabung Timur; Koinino Rote adjoins Koinino Timur; Oematanunu Rote adjoins Oematanunu Helong.[25] In the early twentieth century, the Dutch government began a full-scale "pacification" of Timor and by 1923 had opened a trunk road into the interior. Some Rotinese settlement and a great number of Rotinese traders followed this road into the mountains. As peddlers, as middlemen in the roundup of cattle for the export trade, and as

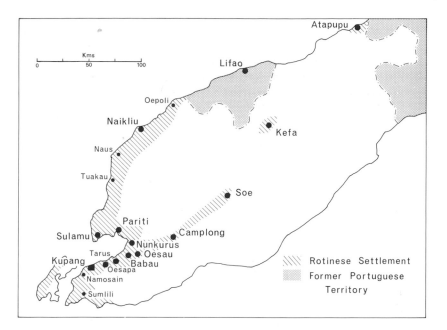

MAP 7 Rotinese settlements on the island of Timor. The map gives an approximate indication of the main areas of Rotinese settlement as of 1970. In towns such as Kupang, Soe, Kefa, and Atapupu, Rotinese are mainly civil servants or laborers; elsewhere they have permanently settled on the land.

retailers of lontar gin, the Rotinese traveled throughout Timor in the dry season.

The Rotinese migration was not simply a gradual movement along the north coast and the interior trunk road. As lontar-tappers, Rotinese vaulted themselves into the midst of the Timorese areas. At some time in this century the Rotinese established a settlement at Tuasene on an extensive lontar savannah in the valley of Noil Leke in south central Timor. From this colony has come another settlement, Tepas. (Near Tepas there is also a small Savunese village.) Ormeling has described this new enclave in the middle of Timor:

> In the valley, Rotinese and Savunese live amid thousands of lontar palms. They have little economic and social contact with the original inhabitants whose kampungs [villages] are on the hills bordering the Noil Leke valley and whose farming consists of shifting cultivation. Administratively, Tuasene as a *kampung ketjil* [small village] belongs to the Timorese ketemukungan [a multivillage administrative unit] of

Tepas Molo. Within this greater unit the Rotinese, however, have their own temukung and village organization and generally show little inclination to follow Timorese regulations. The Timorese in the hills have a closed village with beehive-shaped huts, quite different from the Rotinese rectangular bebak houses scattered among the valley's lontar palms. Only near the kampung chief's dwelling are the Rotinese houses somewhat closer together.[26]

This modern description of a Rotinese settlement is not unlike the nineteenth-century descriptions of Rotinese settlements near Kupang.[27]

The Rotinese migration to Timor (see Map 7) was more than a movement of a palm-tapping people to new lands on another island. The immigrants did, of course, reestablish on Timor the whole range of their traditional economic activities. In 1874, the Dutch botanist Teysmann, for example, described most of these activities, including lontar-tapping, in the area surrounding Kupang. With the aid of the Dutch, the Rotinese also reestablished their traditional school system on Timor. Within a year of the first settlement at Babau, the missionary Le Bruijn was able to open the first school among the Rotinese. New schools were begun as new settlements were founded: at Oesapa, Oelio, Oesau, Nunkurus (until it was overrun by Timorese), and Pariti.

The Rotinese situation on Timor was not the same as on Roti. For one thing, Rotinese education was subject to greater scrutiny and direction than on Roti. Le Bruijn and his successor, G. Heijmering, generally relied on the Rotinese to staff their own schools. But one of the next missionaries to arrive on Timor, W. M. Donselaar, took a dimmer view of Rotinese education; whenever possible, he attempted to raise standards by appointing to Rotinese schools Ambonese teachers from the Institute Roskott on Amboina, which specialized in teacher training for native instructors. The issue became one of control over education. In the administrative reshuffle of school personnel in 1847, Le Bruijn's and Heijmering's principal Rotinese assistant, P. Pello, was appointed supervisor of the schools on Roti; but Donselaar was stationed at Babau to oversee the schools outside of Kupang. When the Netherlands Missionary Society withdrew from Timor and the Dutch government assumed responsibility for native instruction, Donselaar remained at Kupang.

Reporting on the schools in 1862, Donselaar had this to say:

> The reestablishment of a number of new schools on the island of Rotti presented an enormous difficulty in obtaining proper or near proper instructors. The eighteen schools on Rotti are now provided with instructors, although most of them are unsuited and incompetent in

their profession. Some of these masters were formerly employed by the Netherlands Missionary Society but were dismissed for immoral conduct. A couple of masters were again recently dismissed for having illicit relations with schoolgirls. The schools on Timor are provided with proper instructors. Three teacher-students from the Roskott Institute at Amboina were this year assigned to Babauw, Olio, and Oissauw.[28]

Donselaar's views on the value of Ambonese teachers were disputed in less than ten years by another in the series of school inspectors who were periodically sent to tour the area—in this case, J. A. van der Chijs. Roti had had only a few Ambonese teachers. In his view, they had proved unsatisfactory and their replacement on Roti was advantageous. In his report for 1871, van der Chijs wrote:

> The instructors on Rotti are presently all natives. There are no more Ambonese there, as were formerly found in that profession; and this lack is, by no means, a misfortune for Rotti. For in addition to the fact that the Ambonese instructors on Rotti had to work among a strange people whose language they did not understand, they appear, in general, to have done more harm than good.[29]

Although van der Chijs never gave all his reasons for rejecting Ambonese instructors, he seems to have been impressed by the Rotinese desire to retain control over their own educational system. Such control at the higher level of education that was demanded meant that the Rotinese would have to obtain further training. Van der Chijs therefore recommended that a teacher training school be established at Kupang, but this goal was not achieved until much later;[30] in the meantime, Rotinese were sent to Amboina for further training. The first Rotinese graduated in 1877 and was soon followed by a stream of other Rotinese who returned to Timor to assume positions in the schools there. A new pattern began to emerge. By the end of the century, Rotinese schoolteachers were an educated elite on Timor. In 1884, for example, the schoolteacher D. P. Manafe wrote an introduction to Rotinese grammar that was eventually published in Holland by the Dutch linguist Kern; J. Fanggidaej, the Bible translator, while stationed as an instructor at Babau, wrote two articles on Rotinese, in Malay, that were similarly published in the *Bijdragen tot de Taal-, Land- en Volkenkunde*.[31] More importantly, these teachers created the second stage of the Rotinese educational system. The pattern that developed, and one that has continued to this day, was for students—in particular, the eldest sons of the nobility—who finished their elementary education on Roti to move to Timor and to live with relatives while they continued their education in Rotinese-controlled schools in and around Kupang. This education equipped many Rotinese to serve in the ever-burgeoning bureaucracy of the district capital in the twentieth century.

Rotinese migration involved a movement to Timor at two levels: an educated elite, developed through Rotinese schools, which competed for niches in an administrative bureaucracy centered in the district capital of Kupang; and a large population of industrious palm-tappers and rice-growers who moved into the plains around Kupang and from there spread further into Timor. These Rotinese, despite their endless factions, assisted one another in their mutual advancement. For a time, the humorous remark circulated among the Rotinese in Kupang that TIMOR was an acronym which stood for the Indonesian saying: *Timor ini milik orang Roti,* "This Timor is the property of the Rotinese."

Before we look at the events of the nineteenth century that led to the movement of the Savunese to Sumba, it is instructive to consider the demographic background and basis of the Rotinese migration to Timor.

DEMOGRAPHIC ASPECTS OF THE ROTINESE MIGRATION

There are always two aspects to any migration: its effects on the areas of immigration and its effects on the areas of emigration. The early migration to Timor scattered Rotinese in settlements throughout the government territory in a pattern largely determined by area of origin on the island of Roti. The differences among these areas of origin make an examination of their demographic history a potentially revealing undertaking.

Population figures for Roti in the nineteenth and twentieth centuries provide an embarrassment of seeming riches—a wealth of dissimilar data that requires cautious and circumspect analysis. The figures begin in 1824 and continue, at frequent intervals, through 1971. They were gathered at different times for different purposes by Commission officers, missionaries, school inspectors, *Controleurs,* and—more recently for the Indonesian government —by schoolteachers and village headmen. One of the most ambitious censuses ever undertaken on Roti was the initial one carried out in 1831. Conducted on an island-wide basis, it included population figures for all of Roti's 18 states. The further breakdown of these figures is, however, given in terms of Roti's hundred-odd clans, a feature that no later census ever attempted to duplicate. Of the twelve subsequent censuses, seven provide a record of the population for each state. Yet the most recent of these, that of 1971, unfortunately no longer reports population according to state; instead enumeration is based on the *kecamatan* into which these states have been grouped.

The difficulties in using these figures with any precision are considerable. There is first the fact that the Dutch did not succeed in imposing fixed boundaries on the states of the island until 1887. Until this date, there was a fluctuation—in some instances considerable—of the populations between border states. After this date, some minor shifts of population continued in border areas. In addition to major emigration from the island in these two centuries, internal migration occurred among the states. Therefore a decline in the population of one state cannot be immediately interpreted as evidence of emigration of that state's population to Timor. Moreover, during the second half of the nineteenth century, Roti suffered several devastating smallpox epidemics, whose effects in the various states can only be guessed. What is more, none of this information, with the exception of the last census, gives any estimate of the age composition of the population from which one might conceivably construct, however crudely, an interpretable demographic pyramid. Given that migration and epidemic factors cannot be accurately determined, it would be rash to calculate a hypothetical growth rate for the island's population. Finally, in the majority of the records, published and unpublished, that give any population figures, there is no hint of how these data were assembled. The combination of all these difficulties constitutes a formidable obstacle to analysis; yet the information does bear scrutiny and can, with reservations, be considered revealing.

We may begin this analysis by examining the general contour of population increase and decline. The 12 enumerations of Roti's population in the nineteenth and twentieth centuries are as follows:[32]

Year	Population
1824	36,000
1831	40,771
1863	64,132
1879	52,090
1885	52,819
1890	56,600
1921	44,341
1930	58,515
1954	67,186
1957	71,591
1961	70,568
1971	74,133

It is immediately evident from these figures that Roti's population reached a high point in the 1860's, declined in the 1870's, and only after 1921 began slowly to increase. Between 1890 and 1930, this increase, in absolute terms, was about 2,000 persons, less than 5 percent in 40 years. It was evidently not until the late 1940's that Roti's population surpassed that of the previous century. Despite some fluctuation, this population has continued to rise since independence. Even this increase has been slight—only 7,000 persons between 1954 and 1971. Overall, it has taken approximately 150 years for Roti's population to double.

The 1860's provide the most useful baseline for considering the Rotinese migration to Timor. The fact that Roti had a high population at this time was not overlooked by the Dutch. In a letter of report dated 25 April 1866, the Resident of Timor, W. G. Coorengel, wrote: "The islands of Rottie and Savoe are heavily populated, indeed, overpopulated."[33] The decline in Roti's population dates from this period. One immediate cause was a fearsome smallpox epidemic that occurred in 1869 and recurred, with less intensity, in 1874. Donselaar, who witnessed the spread of this epidemic through the Timor area, estimated a loss of 5,000 persons on Roti.[34] If one takes into account the fact that the population figure for 1879 is inflated by the inclusion of at least 2,000 inhabitants of the island Ndao,[35] then the population loss from the two epidemics is hardly sufficient to account for a decline of 14,000 over 15 years. It is apparent therefore that the migration from Roti to Timor, initiated in 1815, increased considerably from 1870 with the approval of the local colonial administration.

To get a better understanding of this migration, we can consider those census figures in Table 3 that provide the eight enumerations based on the states (or kecamatan) of the island.

The census figures for 1831, when they are broken down according to the states, appear to be estimates rather than exact enumerations. This census was originally included as an appendix to Francis' Commission Report on the Timor area.[36] One of the main reasons for wanting to know the population of Roti's states was to determine the quota of armed men that could be required of each state. But just as the Resident at Kupang could demand a varying levy of men from each state, so too the ruler in each state, to fill his quota, had to assess the clans of his court in terms of their size. This is probably the reason that the census of 1831 also recorded clan populations.

In this census Termanu's population stands at a low, while Dengka's population, relative to the other states at this time, appears remarkably high. Termanu's low population reflects both the dismemberment to which it had been subjected and the fact that Termanu was the principal area from which in the preceeding 15 years several successive settlements of early emigrants had come. Dengka, on the other hand, was probably at the height of its

TABLE 3   The population of Roti by state (in 1971, by kecamatan).

State	1831	1863	1885	1921	1954	1957	1961	1971
Landu	1,500	1,670	1,478	1,481	2,476	2,550	2,745	} 11,303
Ringgou	3,000	5,771	4,136		3,511	3,736	3,761	
				3,171				
Oepao	500	2,431	791		498	510	561	
Bilba	4,750	7,121	5,585	2,942	3,396	3,650	3,613	
Diu	650	895	802	1,356	2,028	2,052	2,260	} 8,279
Korbaffo	1,500	3,500	3,383	2,466	3,429	3,524	3,358	
Lelenuk	165	185	313		748	763	806	
				598				
Bokai	300	340	395		1,045	1,356	1,131	
Termanu	1,900	7,523	7,429	4,586	5,606	5,668	5,759	} 10,112
Keka	500	960	1,453	1,148	1,855	1,883	1,972	
Talae	500	1,931	834	974	1,461	1,472	1,462	
Baä	1,450	2,162	2,075	2,663	5,310	5,805	6,134	} 13,062
Loleh	2,550	4,724	3,013	3,928	5,080	5,374	5,609	
Lelain	475	337	247			766	650	
				7,390	13,997			
Dengka	12,931	8,761	11,473			13,216	13,678	} 16,973
Oenale	3,650	6,315	4,124	2,394	3,288	3,500	3,002	
Delha	1,050	1,370	1,604	1,333	1,827	1,943	1,951	} 14,404
Thie	3,400	8,136	3,684	7,911	11,631	13,823	12,116	
Total	40,771	64,132	52,819	44,341	67,186	71,591	70,568	74,133

territorial expansion. Soon after this census was taken, Dengka was invaded by the combined forces of the other states of Roti under Dutch direction and made to relinquish some of its lands to the states on its borders, principally Baä, Thie, and Oenale. Some prisoners from Dengka were settled on Timor; others, according to native sources, were settled in Termanu. Thus most of Dengka's population decline (4,170 persons), as indicated in the 1863 census, is probably a result of redefinition of its borders and the partial redistribution of its population.

A comparison of the population figures for the states between 1863 and 1885 is further revealing. With the exception of four smaller states on the south coast of the island (Lelenuk, Bokai, Keka, and Delha), along with Dengka on the north coast, all of the states of Roti show some decline in population. Dengka and Thie during this period were still disputing their common border, and it must be assumed that Dengka's population increase (+ 2,712) is related to Thie's population decline (– 4,452). Taken together, these two states evidence an overall decrease. Significantly, the states of both Termanu and Korbaffo show only slight population declines. The states showing large population declines are the three neighboring states of Ringgou, Oepao, and Bilba in the east and that of Oenale at the northwestern end of Roti. (Bordered on two sides by states showing an increase, Oenale, as an area of major emigration from Roti, must be considered with some reservation.)

The decline in population of Ringgou, Oepao, and Bilba accounts for 42 percent of Roti's total population decline for this period. Since there is no mention of Dutch assistance in the transportation of Rotinese to Timor, migration could only have been accomplished by native perahu. It is significant therefore that these three states have by far the best sailing access to the Kupang area. Sea currents make it extremely difficult to sail from the south coast of Roti to Timor. From any of the inlets and harbors that dot Roti's north coast, it is—at very best—two days' sailing by native boat. But from the small port of Pepela in Ringgou, directly across the straits of Puku Afu from Timor, it is only a day's voyage to Kupang. With this ease of access from the port of Pepela and from a few ports on the north coast, and with already well-established populations on Timor, the Rotinese in the second half of the nineteenth century seem to have developed a continuing two-way traffic between Roti and Timor—one that has been maintained to the present. The *Algemeen Verslag* (or General Report) for Timor notes a substantial increase in the number of Rotinese settling there around 1888;[37] and in 1890, it was reckoned that there were 6,000 Rotinese traveling annually between the two islands.

A comparison of the population figures for the states in 1863 and in 1961 provides a clear picture of how a century of emigration has affected the relative distribution of the population on the island. Table 4 gives the figures for these two dates as well as the comparative densities of the populations in the various states.

The most significant changes in population density have occurred in the three states of Ringgou, Oepao, and Bilba. In 1863, these three states taken as a whole had the highest population density ever reached by any area in Roti's history. Prior to 1863, the Ringgou-Oepao-Bilba area was a region of recurrent (and in the Dutch records always unexplained) endemic local

TABLE 4   Comparison of the population of the 18 states of Roti in 1863 and 1961.

State	Area (sq km)	Population 1863	Population 1961	Population density 1863	Population density 1961
Landu	169	1,670	2,745	9.9	16.2
Ringgou	⎞	5,771	3,761		
	57			143.9	75.8
Oepao	⎠	2,431	561		
Bilba	59	7,121	3,613	120.7	61.2
Diu	61	895	2,260	14.7	37.1
Korbaffo	60	3,500	3,358	58.3	55.9
Lelenuk	⎞	185	806		
	52			10.1	37.3
Bokai	⎠	340	1,131		
Termanu	177	7,523	5,759	42.5	32.5
Keka	42	960	1,972	22.9	46.9
Talae	33	1,931	1,462	58.5	44.3
Baä	48	2,162	6,134	45.0	127.8
Loleh	77	4,724	5,609	61.4	72.8
Lelain	⎞	337	650		
	178			51.1	80.5
Dengka	⎠	8,761	13,678		
Oenale	64	6,315	3,002	98.7	46.9
Thie	93	8,136	12,116	87.5	130.3
Delha	44	1,370	1,951	31.1	44.3

instability—a region with frequent native uprisings, feuds, and unruliness. One suspects that the area was reaching a point at which the local economy may not have been able to support the population. Still, the importance of an identity with a particular state—an allegiance to a particular form of local adat—would seem to be evident from the fact that this high-density region was surrounded on both sides by states of relatively low density (Diu and Landu). In the end, it proved easier for the separate populations of Ringgou, Oepao, and Bilba to migrate to Timor and pioneer new settlements in which they were able to maintain their own distinctive traditions than to move to neighboring states where they would be under a different ruler. The people from this area seem to have settled on Semau, at Sulamu north of Pariti, and then apparently moved along the north coast of Timor. By 1885, migration had significantly reduced population density to about 91 persons per square kilometer while by 1961, further migration had reduced this population to about half that of the previous century. The pattern suggests that, unlike the first Dutch-instigated transportation of Rotinese from Termanu, from Delha, and then from Dengka, this later emigration was spurred by definite population pressure, and that ready sailing access to Timor was undoubtedly an important factor in maintaining it as a spontaneous movement.

Map 8 is a graphic illustration of the changes in population densities on Roti, some of which can best be discussed individually. The increase in the populations of Landu, Diu, Lelenuk, Bokai, and Keka suggests a certain natural increase in areas with relatively low population densities. Landu is a special case in that it once had a much higher population. However, in 1750, as a result of Dutch involvement in an extremely bitter dispute over rule in that state, more than a thousand persons were rounded up, transported to Batavia, and sold into slavery. Many of Landu's surviving inhabitants went into hiding to avoid capture or fled to other states. For some time the state was virtually closed to immigrants from other states or to the return of those who had fled. Within several years of their transport to Batavia, all of the enslaved people from Landu were summarily freed, but they were never allowed to return to Roti. Instead they were settled permanently just outside Batavia. As a consequence of this incident, Landu never regained the position it once held on the island. Much of its land reverted to secondary forest. By contrast, Diu, Lelenuk, Bokai, and Keka are all states that were once claimed by Termanu. In the eighteenth century, disputes and open raiding probably limited the population in these areas. More importantly, all of these small states, with the exception of Keka, lack natural sources of water —not just water for irrigation, but water for drinking as well. The lack of water, a general feature throughout Roti, is particularly exaggerated in these areas and must be considered one of the major constraints on the density of population that these states can support.

Korbaffo, Termanu, and Talae all show a decline in population density between 1863 and 1961. These three states are recognized areas of emigration. Of these, Korbaffo shows the least decline and has the fewest known villages of immigration on Timor. On the other hand, a portion of Korbaffo's population has moved across its formerly disputed western border with Termanu to occupy sparsely settled land in eastern Termanu. This has been possible because of almost a century of close marriage alliances between the rulers of Termanu and Korbaffo. Talae's population decrease is somewhat greater than Termanu's although it follows a pattern much like that of Termanu, from which it separated in the latter part of the eighteenth century. According to local tradition on Timor, the major movement of people

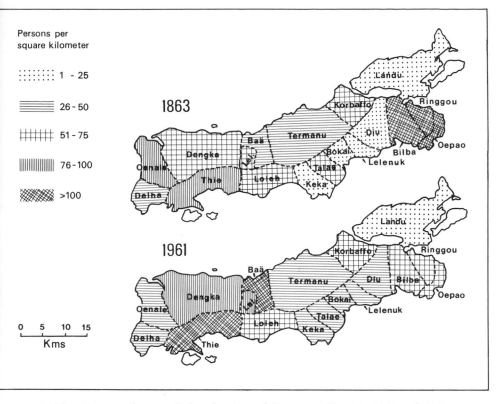

1863

1961

0 5 10 15
Kms

MAP 8 Comparative population densities of the states of Roti in 1863 and 1961.

from Talae occurred in 1904 with the settlement of the village of Sumlili at the westernmost tip of Timor.[38] Earlier migrants may have settled with the people from Termanu whose dialect they speak.

With the exception of Oenale, which shows a marked decrease in population, all of the states of west Roti show a population increase from a relatively high population density base. Baä shows the greatest increase, but this is artificially inflated. In the nineteenth century the Dutch transferred their post from the harbor Namo Dale in Termanu to the harbor Namo Dale in Baä and this became the one town, known as Baä, on the island. The state of Baä therefore includes the town of Baä which has, in addition to a small population of Chinese and Moslem shopkeepers and traders, a large and growing number of administrative personnel. Besides subsidies from outside, the whole of the island contributes directly and indirectly to the support of the population of the town of Baä.

In the past century, the contrast between east and west Roti has increased. If one divides the island, as the Rotinese themselves do, into two named divisions, the eastern division, *Lamak-anan*, comprises a territory of 710 square kilometers compared to 504 square kilometers for the western division, *Henak-anan*. Traditionally, the dividing line for these divisions is said to run through Termanu; there is disagreement, therefore, among Rotinese on whether Termanu, and with it Keka and Talae, belong to the east or the west. For our purposes we shall follow the majority opinion and locate Termanu, Keka, and Talae in the eastern division, thereby dividing the island along the borders of Baä and Loleh. The western division, although smaller in size, is the more heavily populated region of the island and includes the more lontar-intensive states. Table 5 summarizes the changes that have occurred in these two divisions over the century.

As a first approximation of the processes that have occurred, Table 5 is instructive. A century ago, west Roti was already the more densely populated region. Migration from the pocket of highest density in east Roti and a later migration, probably in the early twentieth century, from the states of Termanu and Korbaffo, both of which have good sailing access to Timor, have reduced the overall population of east Roti and only heightened the contrast between these two divisions. Even while west Roti's population was declining, its lowest density remained above east Roti's highest density level. Now west Roti's population density considerably exceeds its density of a century before, while east Roti's population density is below that of last century. East Roti, with its lower population density but better access to Timor, clearly seems to have contributed the higher proportion of immigrants to Timor.

These figures may also be interpreted as a reflection of the relative economic orientations in the two divisions. East Roti's economy, with its less intensive pattern of palm utilization and special emphasis on wet-rice culti-

TABLE 5   Population differences between east Roti (Lamak-anan) and west Roti (Henak-anan).

Year	East Roti		West Roti	
	Population	Population density (per sq km)	Population	Population density (per sq km)
1863	32,327	45.53	31,805	63.10
1885	26,599	37.46	26,220	52.02
1921	18,722	26.36	25,619	50.83
1954	26,053	36.69	41,133	81.61
1957	26,164	38.25	44,427	88.14
1961	27,428	38.63	43,140	85.59

vation, has a lower carrying capacity than west Roti, with its heavier emphasis on palm utilization and semi-intensive pig-rearing. On the assumption that their total territory has not changed radically, Thie and Dengka's population density, for example, has gone from 64 persons per square kilometer in 1863 to 98 in 1961. A more adequate interpretation of these same facts would argue that it is not simply that west Roti's economy has a higher carrying capacity, but rather that the intensive palm utilization methods of this economy place a heavier demand on individual labor. West Roti's economy has been better able to absorb its population increase. It is the combination of these two factors that has probably retarded emigration from west Roti.

By way of summary, it is possible to present the results of a computer analysis of the six censuses for the states of Roti between 1863 and 1961. Although not unlike some of the analyses in the first part of this study, this analysis is somewhat more complex. It is therefore discussed and assessed separately in Appendix C. The results of the final scaling of the states can be represented in a simple 2 x 2 matrix (Figure 3) whose dimensions can be interpreted in terms of relative migration versus population density. This diagram provides a well-segregated and well-clustered grouping that tends to confirm the previous discussion. It must be remembered, however, that the diagram is a scale and that each state's location represents its position relative to the other states on the island.

In quadrant I, Talae and Termanu give evidence of a high migration but a relatively low population density. In quadrant III are Landu and the small states of the southeastern coast that also have a low population density but show, in contrast, a low emigration. Ringgou, Oepao, Bilba, and Korbaffo in quadrant II show a high population density and a high migration in comparison with Thie, Baä, Dengka, and Lelain in quandrant IV, which have just as high a population density but a far lower emigration. Delha and Loleh have a nearly identical migration scale but differ in their population densities.

Only Oenale presents a pattern that is strikingly different from that of most of the rest of west Roti. (This has already been indicated by the findings of a previous analysis in the first part of this study, which demonstrated that Oenale's ratio of pigs to population grouped this state with Korbaffo and implied less reliance on the lontar than elsewhere in west Roti.) Oenale has obviously had a high emigration, and there are villages on Timor that attest to this well-known fact. In the early nineteenth century, at the time of the first movement to Timor, Delha was still in the process of separation from Oenale, one of the earliest states to be recognized on Roti. Given the clear discrepancy in emigration from Oenale and from Delha, it is possible

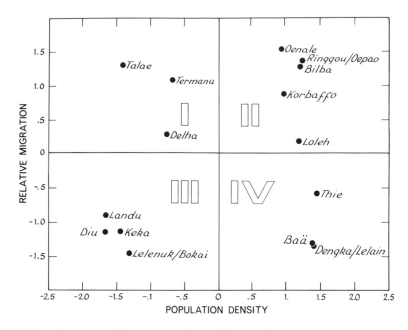

FIGURE 3 The states of Roti clustered according to relative migration and population density over a period from 1863 to 1961. Quadrant I contains states with high
migration and low population density; II, states with high migration and high population density; III, states with low migration and low population density; and IV,
states with low migration and high population density. For a full explanation of the
derivation of this figure, consult Appendix C.

that in the initial transportation of Rotinese to Timor, those individuals
whom the Dutch labeled as "people from Delha" were, in fact, from
Oenale. This early settlement may have laid the foundation for a migration
that seems to have occurred in a way comparable to that of Ringgou, Oepao,
and Bilba.

Just as the Rotinese were provided niches on Timor, so too the Savunese—
potentially their competitors in palm-tapping—were provided similar niches
on Sumba. The historical events that led to the Savunese migration had,
however, quite a different cast from those that prompted the Rotinese migration. And it should be pointed out that this seemingly fortunate separation of potential competitors was not based on ecological constraints, but on
complex political and social factors. Events in the eighteenth century were
such that this separation very nearly did not occur. Between 1759 and 1769,
Dutch Company officers considered a plan to settle Rotinese from Dengka

on the northeastern coast of Sumba to form a beachhead on this uncontrolled island. This plan had the active cooperation of the ruler of Dengka and not until initial preparations had begun was the plan abandoned. One can only imagine how emigration from Dengka to Sumba in the eighteenth century might have transformed the demographic history and structure of Roti and created new patterns for Sumba. Since this scheme was never carried out, it was left to the Savunese at a later period to settle on Sumba.

CHAPTER SIX

The Savunese
in the Nineteenth Century

AS STIPULATED IN the contract of 1756, Savu was obliged to supply a levy of armed men to assist the Dutch in their campaigns on Timor. Even before this formal agreement was reached, Savunese served in the Company's forces in the defense of Kupang and gained the reputation of being outstanding soldiers. This stereotype, by no means unfounded, of Savunese as superb soldiers was a major factor in determining Savunese relations with the Dutch. It gained them a distinction among the peoples of the Timor area, and it afforded them certain tacit rights to manage their own affairs without undue interference from the Dutch. This view of the Savunese was repeated dozens of times in the course of the records on the island. Interestingly, it was not just the Dutch who subscribed to it; the British too repeated it. J. H. Moor, summarizing materials on the Timor area from the short period of British role, remarks of Savu that "obtaining men for soldiers . . . is the only advantage derived by the government from this island."[1]

The Dutch attitude toward the Savunese was, however, tempered and in a sense further enhanced by their recognition of the Savunese quality of uncompromising firmness. Whereas the Rotinese tended in unexpected ways to copy the Dutch and to encompass them as counterparts in their local intrigues, Savunese for centuries treated the Dutch with formal disregard. Until late in the nineteenth century, they expressed virtually no interest in Christianity nor in Islam and responded not at all to Dutch proposals of education. Since their island held little of value, the Savunese were permitted their isolation and the only problem that presented itself to the Dutch was that of finding someone both willing and hardy enough to suffer a post on the island. For long periods there was no one to be found, and when someone was located, that person usually was of mixed descent or of some unlikely origin. Men like Lange who were willing to go native and adopt Savunese ways, or like the poor shipwrecked Dane who was stranded in Kupang in 1860 and pressed into service on Savu—these were the only persons whom the Dutch could post on the island. Yet despite Savu's stony barrenness and scorching heat, the Savunese themselves showed little willingness to settle elsewhere.

Hazaart, in particular, was convinced of the Savunese abilities as soldiers and so after his expedition against Amanuban in 1822, he settled a contingent of 300 Savunese near Kupang, almost in the town itself. But it is apparent that Hazaart was neither able nor willing to recruit a large number of Savunese, who might prove to be more difficult to handle than the Rotinese. J. D. Kruseman, in his unpublished report on Timor in 1824, was undoubtedly reflecting Hazaart's view of the Savunese when he wrote:

> The Savunese are an able people, but to control them one must know their ways well; a few of these people are useful in Koepang but too many would perhaps cause unpleasant incidents; they should make good soldiers but the Resident Hazaart has not been able to persuade them to take employment in the native military service.[2]

Later, in his published description of Timor, Kruseman modified and slightly edited his comments on the Savunese:

> The Savunese are a good and industrious people, but to control them one must know them well. They should be very suited for native military service, but to this, they are utterly indisposed.[3]

Those Savunese who did serve as soldiers for the Dutch maintained the reputation of their people. S. Müller reports that on expeditions into the interior of Timor the Savunese, who comprised a small fraction of the total native force, "were charged with the direct supervision of the diverse bands and especially with the maintenance of order and the deportment of proper vigilance."[4] Savunese discipline was what the Dutch respected, and there is a certain irony in the fact that the Dutch, who frankly admitted their inability to control the Savunese, should put these uncontrollable Savunese in charge of supervising other native groups.

THE FIRST MOVEMENT OF SAVUNESE TO SUMBA

In the eighteenth century and throughout most of the nineteenth, Sumba, to the west of Savu, was even less well known than Savu itself. In the seventeenth century, the Sultan of Bima claimed Sumba as a tributary island; the Dutch tacitly disregarded these claims and eventually, in 1756, signed contracts with eight rulers on the island, most of whom held territories in eastern or central Sumba. For the remaining years of the Company's presence, the ruler of Mangili attempted repeatedly to embroil the Company in his feud with the ruler of Melolo, but the Governor General stoutly resisted involvement in Sumba's local wars.[5] It seems that only one Company officer visited the island for any length of time. This was an officer named Tekenborgh; his report was not considered sufficiently informative for the Company to take action on the island. Later, for the early part of the nineteenth century, the Dutch had to rely for information on a report written by the survivor of a shipwreck, J. A. Batiest, who was taken captive and lived for a time in the interior of Sumba.[6]

In the seventeenth century, eastern Indonesia was pocketed by mixed groups of opposing forces. The Dutch held Kupang. The Black Portuguese were first vested on Solor, but later transferred to Larantuka on the northeast coast of Flores and to Oekussi on the north coast of Timor. The Makassarese were another contending group in the area. Although they were unable to drive the Portuguese from their strongholds on Flores and Timor, they did manage to rout the Portuguese from the bay of Endeh on Flores' south central coast, directly north of Sumba. At Endeh a new native force developed: Islamic seafarers who, still identified with the Makassarese, joined other Islamic sailing groups in raids throughout the area. The main force of Endehnese directed their efforts toward Sumba. Their principal source of wealth was a trade in slaves. The Company concluded a contract with the Endehnese in 1793 but later, in 1838, the Dutch had to lead an expedition (made up largely of Savunese) to Endeh in an attempt to force them to abandon their slave raiding on Sumba.[7] Thereafter, although restricted in the export of slaves, the Endehnese who had settled on Sumba continued their plunder by siding with various native Sumbanese rulers who warred among themselves and were eager to purchase their share of local slaves.

In the early nineteenth century, besides the Endehnese on Sumba, there were also some Savunese. In his Commission Report for 1831, Francis notes that "the people of the island Savoe have, through marriages contracted on Sumba, established a village there."[8] Evidence suggests that this first village of Savunese was established through a royal marriage alliance between the ruler of Melolo on Sumba and the ruler of Seba on Savu. Francis expressed his hope that through the "encouragement" of the Savunese, the Dutch government would be able to form closer relations with Sumbanese. Ironically, as it turned out, nothing alienated relations with the Sumbanese more than this Dutch encouragement of the Savunese.

The rulers of Savu, and in particular the ruler of Seba, appeared quite willing to provide men wherever they could be employed. While they supplied the Dutch with an elite native soldiery, they also began to supply armed men to serve the local rulers of Sumba in their constant warfare. On Timor and Flores, they were used to put down "native unrest"; on Sumba, they were used to foment it. A good number of Savunese soldiers settled on Sumba and, like the Endehnese, formed an independent force on the island. These armed settlers created the basis for later migrations of Savunese to Sumba and, despite several reports directly questioning the procedure, it became official Dutch policy to rely upon the Savunese in later attempts to pacify the island.

The person whose schemes most affected the development of Sumba was one of Hazaart's successors at Kupang, the Resident D. J. van den Dungen Gronovius. In 1838, he directed the sea expedition to Endeh to put a stop to the slave trade on Sumba and in the following year, as his personal representative among the Endehnese, Gronovius appointed a remarkable individual, the Sjarief Abdulrachman bin Abubakar Alqadrie, who belonged to the Sultan's family of Pontianak. The Sjarief married the daughter of one of the leading nobles at Endeh and, using his influence among the Endehnese, explored Sumba for the possibilities of establishing trade on the island. With 14,000 Dutch florin personally advanced him by Gronovius, the Sjarief established himself at Waingapu on Sumba's north coast and in 1841 began the export of horses, a trade that expanded so rapidly and extensively that it radically affected the political economy of the island. Horses were to the rulers of Sumba what cattle, at a later date, were to the rulers of Timor, a means of amassing enormous wealth and power. Horses were also a stimulus to further warfare on the island.

Like Hazaart, who had a vision of Timor's future, Gronovius had a vision full of economic possibilities for Sumba. He visited Sumba in 1846 to inspect the island and to assess for himself the expanding export trade he had financed. Within five years of the first shipload of 98 horses to be exported, more than 4,000 of these animals were shipped from the island. Gronovius' scheme called for the expansion of this trade and for the settlement of Sumba by Dutch planters who were to be given land, on credit, for the cultivation of coffee, sugar, cotton, pepper, tobacco, and other products. To

Gronovius, the population of Sumba was "a dumb, superstitious, and idle but yet hospitable and good-natured race of men, far surpassing the Timorese in attractiveness."[9] In this vision, there was a special place for the Savunese. Gronovius wrote:

> The great number of lontar trees, that are found on Soemba, but from which the population derives not the slightest use, will serve, in no minor way, to stimulate emigration from some of the neighbouring islands to Soemba . . . From year to year, these migrations will increase, and there is no doubt that in a very short time, by means of these Savunese, the lontar tree of Soemba will supply an important export article for trade.[10]

No Dutch planters were sent to Sumba and, to the Netherlands government, Sumba was judged to be of little value—"a scantly regarded and neglected island." Sumba's horse trade passed into the hands of Sjarief Abdulrachman's family. Yet Gronovius, until shortly before his death, continued to urge the colonization of Sumba:

> To the idea of colonizing the Sandalwood Island, I still remain devoted. My stay there and my travels through the island convince me that such an undertaking would be crowned with success. There would be great blessings in this for the development, civilizing and protecting of a dumb but good-natured population, who are now the prey of usurious traders, pirates and insignificant but vexatious radjas. I would hope that if the Government agreed to such an undertaking, a colony of Rottinese and Savoenese would be transferred to Sumba.[11]

Few Rotinese came to Sumba. Although they brought no "blessings" for the Sumbanese, Savunese did come but in limited numbers. The first group to bring with them their wives and children settled at Kadumbu on Sumba's northeast coast in 1848. Later commentators took a very dim view of these Savunese.

Thus the first Savunese movement to Sumba was unlike the first movement of Rotinese to Timor. The Dutch were motivated to transfer Rotinese to Timor as much to settle internal disputes on Roti as to form a buffer zone around Kupang from which to begin the economic development of the island. A small number of Savunese were also settled in Kupang but strictly as native soldiers. In contrast, the Dutch had little to do directly with the earliest Savunese settlement on Sumba. Initiated through a royal marriage alliance between specific rulers on the two islands, it developed surreptitiously by the sending of Savunese mercenaries to Sumba; only toward the middle of the nineteenth century did the Dutch become involved in the attempt to transfer Savunese to Sumba. The fact that this migration of the Savunese took a very different form from that of the Rotinese had a great deal to do with conditions on the island of Savu in the second half of the nineteenth century. To understand Savunese emigration, we must first understand the situation on Savu itself.

SAVU IN THE SECOND HALF OF THE NINETEENTH CENTURY

Before 1850, Savu was one of the most isolated islands in the Timor area. There were five states that had originally signed contracts with the Company: Seba, Menia, Timu, Mesara, and Liae. When the Company's officers ceased their annual visits to Savu, these states were left to settle their own internal affairs. In the ensuing warfare, Seba—the largest state and the one on which the Dutch relied most heavily—managed to expand its territory on all sides and eventually, with Timu, overwhelmed the state of Menia. The tiny island of Raijua, with its separate population and isolated from even the main island by a dangerous strait, never signed a contract with the Company.[12] For almost a century (1775-1862) no Dutch officer was posted in Seba. There were no schools and no Christian mission, and the Dutch at Kupang frequently quoted Captain Cook as their authority on Savu. But in the decade after 1860, Savu had contact thrust upon it. Suddenly, within the span of a few short years, the Savunese opened their island to education, to Christianity, and then to demographic decimation from smallpox and cholera.

In 1862 the Resident at Kupang, a man named Esser, sent an Ambonese by the name of Manuhutu to found a school at Seba that was to be paid for by the population itself. How long Manuhutu stayed is unclear but another instructor of "Timorese descent," S. Mae, was sent to Savu in 1866. He soon quarreled with the ruler of Seba and left the island in the following year. Another Ambonese, W. Pati, was sent in 1869 and he was still in charge of the Seba school when the school inspector, van der Chijs, visited the island in May 1871. Van der Chijs found that, of the 47 pupils in this school, 3 understood a form of "Ambonese Malay," and that it was usually the 12-year-old daughter of the ruler of Seba who assisted with instruction or took over the class entirely whenever Pati was sick with malaria. Mesara, however, had built its own school structure and had appointed to the school a Savunese named Djadjar.

Developments similar to those on Roti in the eighteenth century do not seem to have occurred, or at least not so rapidly, on Savu. In 1889, there were reported to be only seven schoolteachers on Savu and all of them were from Ambon. By 1903, however, there were eight schools on Savu (though none on Raijua) with a total of 3,332 pupils. Still, all but one of the schoolteachers were from Ambon and all instruction was in Ambonese Malay. Even as late as 1920, there was no radical change in this situation, only a gradual increase in the number of pupils in schools on Savu. But by this time there was also a school on Raijua.[13]

Prior to 1860, there were few Christians on Savu and it was rumored that the ruler of Seba, interested in Islam, had gone so far as to give up eating pork. The missionary Donselaar made no secret of his reasons for directing a mission to Savu. In a letter to his Missionary Society, he wrote:

> If the access to Christianity had not opened, the Savunese would have thrown themselves into the arms of Islam . . . By the conversion to Christianity of the first and foremost Savunese families, the way for Mohammedanism is now cut off.[14]

Yet the Savunese do not seem to have been eager to accept either Islam or Christianity. The first missionary, M. Teffer, arrived on Savu in 1872 and remained stationed there, with four or five years' intermission, until 1883 when he left to become a tobacco planter in Portuguese Timor. To the dismay of his Missionary Society and his successor, after he had gone there was little evidence to be found of the transformation that he exuberantly claimed to have effected. The next missionary, P. Bieger, arrived in 1888, contracted malaria, and left in the following year. The same year another missionary, J. K. Wijngaarden, arrived and, with periods of sick leave, managed to stay until 1892. The last missionary to reside on Savu in the nineteenth century, J. H. Letterboer, came in 1896 and remained until 1903. To his Missionary Society he admitted at the end of his stay that he had made little progress in the preaching of Christianity. Less frank than the Dutch officer Heiligers, who claimed that "without exception the Christian Savunese is, in his heart, still pagan,"[15] Letterboer expressed his hope that not all of the Missionary Society's work had been in vain.

Savu's isolation in the middle of the nineteenth century can also be judged by the sudden, shattering effect of disease on the island. In 1869 both Savu and Roti suffered smallpox epidemics. Roti may, according to estimates, have lost perhaps one-twelfth of its population; Savu, by these same estimates, lost almost half of its population in a few months. The missionary Donselaar, who visited Savu in the year after the epidemic, describes the disastrous spectacle:

Everywhere there are still now traces to be seen of the sorry devastation caused by the frightful disease, especially in the numerous empty and abandoned houses whose inhabitants have died. From many houses there remain but a few children who have now been placed in the care of village heads. The reports told to me by eye witnesses at the time of the rampant height of the disease were pathetic. In some houses, where not a single person was left unscathed, the corpses of those who had died were pushed and shoved out of the house with great difficulty by sufferers still alive, where these corpses then became the prey of dogs and pigs. Apparently there were cases where someone needed help and no one could offer help and these died from lack of water. Some took flight to remote spots and hoped there in caves and grottos to avoid the menacing danger. I was told of groups of four and five persons who were later found alone, in their refuges, dead of the pox.

The deaths of Randjoewa were dreadful. What follows I have as the word of mouth of the radja of Seba who visited that island just after the epidemic. The pox broke out on Savoe at a time when the radja of Randjoewa was here. Randjoewa still at the time remained free. The radja returned bringing with him money from the sale of a horse to the Resident and a few household furnishings that he had received from the *Posthouder*. After his return, the disease also broke out on Randjoewa and when its cause was attributed to the money and goods he had brought there, the radja decided to throw both into the sea on the strong insistence of the population. When the disease did not in the least abate its fury, such that in one village of about 300 inhabitants, only one child remained, it was decided to offer a human sacrifice in expiation. But when everything for this was made ready, the headman who was charged with the performance was himself struck by the pox and died shortly afterwards. So the proposed sacrifice did not occur.[16]

Donselaar estimated that Savu lost over 12,300 persons during this epidemic. It is possible that Donselaar's estimate is too high. But even if Savu did not lose half its population, it almost certainly lost one-third. Unquestionably, the epidemic of 1869 was a catastrophe for the Savunese people. This was only the first of three epidemics that took a high toll on the island. Around 1874 the Savunese were struck by a cholera epidemic, and then in 1888 again by a smallpox epidemic.[17] Compared to Roti, where the loss in human life was far less severe during these various epidemics, Savu paid heavily for its isolation.

A comparison of the population figures from Roti with those from Savu in the nineteenth and twentieth centuries illustrates the differing demographic histories of these islands. The figures for Savu are as follows:[18]

Year	Population
1824	25,000
1831	28,660
1869	30,000
1871	16,000
1880	23,026
1890	19,026
1920	27,153
1930	33,573
1961	44,956
1971	51,002

On first examination, there appears to be some superficial resemblance. The populations on both islands reached a high point for the nineteenth century in the 1860's. Then both populations declined, and neither regained its previous population level until some time in the 1930's. Since that period both islands have shown a general population increase.

Close examination reveals various differences between the figures for Savu and Roti. There is first the precipitous drop in Savu's population between 1869 and 1871. It is clear that 1869 marks a sharp break in the growth of Savu's population. Roughly speaking, in the 1860's Savu's population was half of Roti's. By 1890, after the three major epidemics, Savu's population had decreased by over a third, while Roti's population over the same period had decreased by about an eighth. There is then a gap of 30 years between population enumerations. During this period Savu's population recovered while Roti's continued to decrease. For Savu, this trend continued. The turnabout in Savu's population began earlier than in Roti's and in absolute terms has shown a greater increase. Whereas in the 1860's Savu's population was half of Roti's, it now totals five-sevenths of Roti's population. Table 6 highlights these differences between the two islands.

The historical evidence is sufficient to warrant an interpretation of these differences. The decrease in Savu's population between 1869 and 1890 was primarily the result of losses from epidemics. Emigration from Savu was far less a factor. The reverse is true for Roti. Emigration was the primary factor in Roti's population decrease, whereas epidemics were secondary. In 1890 Roti still had a relatively high population density, while Savu's had been decreased considerably. It was precisely at this time that the Dutch government attempted to encourage the migration of these two populations, the one to Timor and the other to Sumba. In the case of Roti, the government

TABLE 6   Comparison of population figures for Roti and Savu.

| Years | Population | |
	Roti	Savu
1863-1869	64,133	30,000
1890	56,600	19,026
1920-1921	44,345	27,153
1930	58,515	33,573
1961	70,568	44,956
1971	74,133	51,002

had no difficulties at all. The Rotinese migration was by this time in full swing and needed no additional stimulation. Dutch-sponsored emigration of Savunese to Sumba, however, met with resistance from all the rulers of Savu. They refused to allow a massive exodus from the island. Although this was attributed by the Dutch to the fear that thereby these rulers would suffer a loss of their power, it is apparent that a further underlying reason was the need to recoup the loss in manpower that the island had suffered over the two previous decades. Even the Dutch offer of payment failed to stimulate migration. The Dutch campaign to settle Savunese on Sumba came at a point in time when the island was relatively depopulated. Instead of a mass colonization of Sumba, there was only a slow, steady seepage of Savunese to the island.

One of the arguments of this study has been that despite the cultural, social, and religious differences that have played an important part in the history of these two island peoples, there has been and continues to be a fundamental similarity in their lontar-centered economies that has consistently distinguished the Rotinese and Savunese from other peoples in the Timor area. This is particularly true of the intensive lontar economies of Savu and west Roti. As yet another point of comparison between these two islands, we can contrast the population figures of Savu with those of both east and west Roti (Table 7).

West Roti, including Oenale (which has a demographic and economic pattern unlike the rest of the region), comprises roughly the same area as Savu. In the 1860's, west Roti and Savu had comparable population levels. And, interestingly, if one discounts Savu's epidemic losses, the populations of the two areas have remained comparable until this past decade. This confirms, in other terms, the previous conclusion that the major emigration

TABLE 7   Comparison of population figures for east Roti, west Roti, and Savu.

| Years | Population | | |
	East Roti	West Roti	Savu
1863-1869	32,327	31,806	30,000
1885-1890	26,599	26,220	19,026
1920-1921	18,726	25,619	27,153
1961	27,428	43,140	44,956
1971	29,694	44,439	51,002

from Roti came from the island's eastern region. It does not in any way discount the fact that there has been emigration from both Savu and west Roti. It only emphasizes the point that the lontar economies of these two areas have been better able than that of east Roti to absorb a certain increase in population.

If, therefore, the emigration from Savu was not on the same scale as that from Roti, the nature of the emigration to Sumba that definitely did occur remains to be determined.

LATER SAVUNESE MIGRATION TO SUMBA AND TO TIMOR

Toward the end of the nineteenth century, the Savunese were still a little-known and little-understood population in the Timor area. Compared to the Rotinese who had already begun to publish articles about themselves and their island in Dutch journals, the Savunese remained a mystery. What knowledge there was came from Captain Cook, some fragmentary government documents, a few missionary reports, and dealings with those Savunese who had left the island to settle either in Kupang or on Sumba. Unlike the Rotinese, few Savunese had a good command of Malay; but they were willing to do hard labor or serve as policemen and as sailors, still keeping their special reputation in the Timor area for bravery and daring based, in particular, on their exploits on Sumba. A brief note by the Dutch Resident at Kupang, H. C. Humme, summarizes Dutch impressions of the Savunese. Humme's statement deserves full quotation, for it emphasizes those characteristics on which the Savunese renown was founded:

The Savoenese learn other languages with great difficulty. The omission of the final consonant is so marked that they do it in each syllable of a word. So they say, for example, for *meester: me-te;* for *opziener:*

o-si-ne; for *oewang: hoewa;* for *kantor-post: kata-po,* and so forth; so that for the uninitiated, it is often difficult to understand them when they speak Malay.

Notwithstanding the easy, idle life that the Savunese lead in their land, one cannot say that their nature and character is in keeping with this.

Many Savoenese leave their island to seek a more active life and thereby to earn money, an opportunity that is not offered them at home.

Those doing coolie labor in the capital Koepang are almost exclusively Savunese; the corps of armed police assistants here consists of two-thirds Savoenese who apply themselves with particular delight to the exercise in the use of arms; also most of the attendants and the crewmen of the cruise-boats are Savoenese.

Through lack of training and contact with more developed groups, their comprehension is very limited; though they may not have learned to respect the property of others in their own land, here they are rarely guilty of theft.

They are generally small in stature, lightly built, but hardened against fatigue.

In this archipelago, the Savunese generally have the reputation of being brave in the face of the enemy, though I am inclined to take this as an usurped reputation.

It appears that their conquests on Soemba have given rise to their reputation. Under the leadership of a former Radja of Seba (the largest province on the island Savoe) who truly showed signs of personal courage and of an enterprising spirit, a handful of Savoenese crossed over to the large but sparsely populated island Soemba and there established a colony after having driven away the inhabitants of those parts.

If, however, one realizes the timid and cowardly nature of a Soembanese who, never having left his island, considers any foreigner a dangerous wild animal from which he quickly takes flight; and that the Soembanese did not then know anything of the effect of firearms with which the Savoenese were provided, then that heroic deed, such as it was, loses much of its value.

The Savoenese have at present three settlements on the island Soemba, of which one is near our establishment at Kabaniroe. In this way they also serve as protection to the European officials against the perfidiousness of the Soembanese.[19]

Although the Dutch did indeed rely on the Savunese in dealing with the Sumbanese, not all Dutch officials were convinced that the Savunese were an asset to the island. When the Dutch established their first resident officials on Sumba in 1866, van Menckelum, one of these *Controleurs,* described the Savunese "colony": "The Savunese in Melolo are the riff-raff of the nation; they resemble more a bandit troop than a peaceful colony."[20] An even clearer assessment of the situation can be found in an official statement for 1876:

> The course of affairs on Soemba demanded, on repeated occasions, the Resident's presence. The many foreigners, above all people from Endeh and Savoe who were originally employed as auxiliary troops by the radjas of Soemba in their wars with one another and who later settled for good on the island, have acquired such an influence for themselves there that they have gradually—the Endehnese over the western and the Savoenese over the eastern parts—begun to exercise a kind of supremacy. These people live mainly from warfare which they conduct in an inhuman fashion and in which they consider only the creation of slaves who are exported in large numbers by them to Endeh.[21]

The Sjarief Abdulrachman's family was implicated in continuing the slave trade via Endeh. Despite their accurate realization of this situation, the Dutch were forced to ally themselves with the Savunese, since to the Sumbanese the Dutch and Savunese were inextricably associated. In 1875 there was an attempt by the ruler of Batakapedu to drive both the Dutch and the Savunese from his territory. The ruler of the state of Seba on Savu was called upon to negotiate a settlement with the ruler of Batakapedu; when this failed, the Dutch furnished the ruler of Seba with a gunboat to enable him to bring more armed men from Savu. These men were then supplied with additional weapons and employed to crush the rebels, who had retreated to a stronghold at Kiritana.

The conflicting elements of Dutch policy were difficult to resolve. Local Dutch policy favored the "Christian" Savunese—who, it was thought, could be partially controlled—over the "Moslem" Endehnese—who could not be. The Endehnese were regarded as the more fearsome slavers and plunderers,[22] but they were the ones who, in the late nineteenth century, were making the greater inroads on Sumba. Unlike the Savunese, who maintained themselves as a separate group, the Endehnese married Sumbanese women and adopted Sumbanese dress and language.[23] It was this fear of Endehnese encroachments and the spread of Islam on Sumba that prompted the renewed Dutch campaign, beginning in 1890, to encourage Savunese to settle on Sumba. Although their efforts to lure a large number of Savunese failed, they did obtain what they were most interested in gaining for Sumba, namely, Christian Savunese.

There is firm evidence to suggest that a high percentage of the emigrants from Savu were persons who had converted to Christianity and were pressured into leaving their island. The missionary Letterboer, for example, had to report to his Missionary Society a steady fall in the Christian community during his residence on Savu. The number of Christians there declined from 4,008 in 1898, to 3,969 in 1899, to 3,388 in 1902, to 3,332 in 1903. In his report Letterboer expressly attributes this decrease not to a lack of effort on his part but to the emigration of Christian Savunese to Sumba and Timor. He writes:

> When one compares the total of souls from 1902 (3,388) with the total from 1903 (3,332), we have declined about 50 souls. What is the reason for this? It is possible that this is partially due to the large number of families that have left Savoe to seek needed livelihood either on Soemba or Koepang. It is well known that the [Christian] congregations on Soemba consist entirely of Savoenese. Also at Koepang there is a village with many Christian Savunese.[24]

This accords well with what is known of traditional Savunese religious practice and evidences a marked contrast to the religious practices of the Rotinese. The Rotinese readily assimilated Christianity. Their social organization could accommodate new converts, since it was based on nonlocalized, often highly segmented, clans. The converted and unconverted never needed to reside together, nor did they threaten each other's well-being. Rotinese clansmen shared obligations to members of their clan or to members of other clans in terms of the rituals of the individual life cycle—mainly at birth, marriage, and death. Only certain clans in each state had the right to carry out a self-contained sequence of rituals in a short, annual postharvest celebration, and these public ceremonies were the only rituals that succumbed to Christianity throughout most of Roti. Individual rituals became a permissible amalgam of Christian and traditional practice, with different emphases and different forms of language depending on the person for whom they were performed. Personal religious obligations to deceased ancestral spirits were maintained. Offerings were private affairs and could continue to be performed within the house. In explaining the general attitude toward offerings made to these ancestral spirits, one Rotinese Christian made the simple comment: "One never asks what a man does in his house when the doors are closed." Given these circumstances, and the time the Rotinese have had to adapt and develop their religious practices, Christianity did not become a divisive force on the island. On Savu, however, the descent group was a residential unit and the main rituals were required public ceremonies, performed strictly and unerringly, in each state, according to a fixed lunar calendar. A hierarchy of priests performed these rituals on behalf of the entire community.[25] Conversion in these circumstances compromised the entire cosmic cycle. It created a group of nonparticipants in a situation where participation was required. A decreasing number of participants diminished the dramatic effect and comprehensiveness of the ceremonies. For this reason, it seems, Savu resisted conversion to Christianity and apparently expelled many of its early converts. As late as 1955, according to the official figures of the Evangelical Church of Timor (*Gereja Masehi Injili di Timor:* GMIT), only about one-third of the island's population were Christians.[26]

A further aspect of this contrast is important. For the Rotinese, syncretism was possible; and today few Rotinese see any conflict between their present practices and the demands of Christianity. With the insistent verbalism by which they preserve the essential features of their culture, they were able to transport much of this culture to Timor and continue the connections that united them with their homeland. For the Savunese, the conflict with Christianity was real and apparent. After their movement to Sumba there was no way to recreate the local priesthoods or maintain the complex lunar cycle of ceremonies. Many Savunese had, in fact, been expelled for nonparticipation in these ceremonies. The variant of Savunese culture that developed on Sumba lacked the essential ceremonial basis of the home island. Emigrant Savunese tended to be staunch Christians who regarded themselves as having made a break with their homeland. Only as Christianity made headway on Savu itself were there reasons for renewing associations with the island.

Other features distinguish the Rotinese and Savunese migrations. Historical records indicate that the Rotinese migration was very largely a transfer of households from one island to another, whereas the initial Savunese migration both to Sumba and to Timor consisted predominantly in small settlements of soldier bands. Records indicate that this pattern persisted and that the Savunese emigration involved a higher proportion of lone males intent on seeking their fortune than did the emigration from Roti. It happens that three census enumerations for Savu record the total number of males and females in the population. Using the reverse of the representation method employed by the Dutch in their 1930 census, we can see that the ratio of males to females left on Savu declined after 1880 and had risen only slightly by 1930. Table 8 gives the number of males relative to 1,000 females, together with the percentage of males in the total population on the island, compared to similar figures for Roti in 1930.

The 1930 Dutch census was the last one to distinguish the populations of the outer arc in terms of their ethnic origin. This census must therefore be the basis for comparing the Rotinese and Savunese migrations and is summarized in Table 9. What these figures make clear is that the Rotinese migration was larger, not only in absolute numbers but proportionally as well. Of the total Rotinese population, only 77 percent were located on Roti. Of the total Savunese population, 83 percent were on Savu itself.

TABLE 8   Male-female ratios for Roti and Savu.

	Year	Males relative to 1,000 females	Percentage of total population
Roti:	1930	970	49.2
Savu:	1880	982	49.5
	1890	926	48.1
	1930	937	48.3

Another difference between these migrations was that the Rotinese emi-gration was almost exclusively to one island, Timor, whereas the Savunese migration divided in two directions, the larger to Sumba, the lesser to Timor. Of the total Rotinese population, 22 percent were on Timor. Of the total Savunese population, 9 percent were on Sumba; 7 percent on Timor. On Sumba, most Savunese were concentrated in the east, primarily in the state of Melolo; on Timor, they were to be found mainly in Kupang. The figures in Table 10 show, as has already been indicated, that the ratio of emigrant males to females was higher among the Savunese than among the Rotinese: 1,093 males per 1,000 females for the Savunese as compared to 1,057 males per 1,000 females for the Rotinese. A breakdown of individual

TABLE 9   Population distribution of Rotinese and Savunese according to the 1930 census.

	Rotinese		Savunese	
Location		Percentage of total	Number	Percentage of total
Savu	—	—	33,573	83
Roti	58,515	77	—	—
Sumba	—	—	3,718	9
Timor	17,146	22	2,734	7
Other islands	706	1	663	1
Total population	76,367	100	40,688	100

TABLE 10   Proportions of males and females: Rotinese on Timor, and Savunese on Timor and Sumba.

Population	Location	Males	Females	Total	Sex ratio (males per 1,000 females)
Rotinese	Timor	8,811	8,335	17,146	1,057
Savunese	Timor	1,466	1,268	2,734	1,156
Savunese	Sumba	1,904	1,814	3,718	1,050
Total Savunese		3,370	3,082	6,452	1,093

figures for Savunese emigrants to Sumba and to Timor reveals a disproportionate number of males to females among the Savunese on Timor. On Sumba the ratio was 1,050 males per 1,000 females, while on Timor it was 1,156 males per 1,000 females. By 1930 Kupang, not Sumba, was the magnet that attracted Savunese men.

Historically, there have been two discernible and unequal streams of migration from both Roti and Savu. The major migrations from both islands were of populations who continued their traditional economic pursuits. For historical and ecological reasons, these migrations were to separate islands: Rotinese tappers and cultivators migrated to Timor; Savunese tappers and cultivators migrated to east Sumba. There was also a secondary migration, directly from these two islands and indirectly from the emigrant settlements on the coastal plains of Timor and Sumba, brought about by the desire for advanced education. There was only one direction this migration could take —to the district capital of Kupang on Timor, where there was opportunity for further schooling and for employment after this schooling. As we have seen, the Rotinese had the initial lead in this advancement and for a time held higher positions in the bureaucracy; eventually a balance of numbers and positions between the two groups seems to have emerged. This pattern is already suggested by population figures in the 1930 census. Of the 17,146 Rotinese reported on Timor, 1,721 were in the town of Kupang itself; of the 2,734 Savunese on Timor, the majority—1,704—were in Kupang. The town was a common niche in which both populations were, at the time, in balance.

CHAPTER SEVEN

Ethnic Relations
in the Twentieth Century

IN THE EARLY decades of the twentieth century, the Dutch colonial administration made a series of attempts to deal with the bequest of centuries. For social improvement, the Dutch fostered increased education. To rationalize an administrative structure that consisted in dozens of small self-governing states, they embarked on a program of successive compromises that attempted to incorporate traditional political positions into a bureaucratic order. To modernize the economy, they introduced Bali cattle. And to counter the spread of the lantana shrub on Timor, they introduced lamtoro.

The results of these efforts never turned out quite as they were intended. Increased education benefited primarily the Rotinese and Savunese, produced a group of individuals who felt capable of handling their own affairs, and exposed these individuals to revolutionary ideas. The right solution was never found for the rationalization of administration. Some states were subject to far greater tinkering than others. There was a persistent confusion between political and ritual offices within the various states. Problems of succession increased, along with a growing uncertainty about the political order. And in a matter of a few decades, the combination of lantana, lamtoro, and cattle radically altered the pattern of agriculture on Timor. The situation was primed for change.

POLITICS AND NATIONALISM IN THE TIMOR AREA

One effect of the lead in education gained first by the Rotinese and then by the Savunese was to give these two populations a predominant position in the nationalist movement in the Timor area in the 1920's and 1930's. As new political organizations were formed to represent the stirrings of national consciousness in the Dutch East Indies, the Rotinese and Savunese collaborated to create equivalent political groups to represent their region. Arising in response to developments in Java, Sumatra, and Celebes, these groups were initially viewed with suspicion by the local populations of the Timor area. The Dutch attempted to isolate and outmaneuver these organizations by pointing to their preponderant Rotinese and Savunese membership—which, it was claimed, made them exclusive and nonrepresentative of the region. To counter them more effectively, however, the Dutch had to sponsor similar organizations and, inevitably, they had to depend upon other Rotinese and Savunese for the creation of these rival groups. As a result, throughout the period prior to independence, nearly all the political and educational organizations of the Timor area were dominated by these two peoples.

The first organization to be formed, *Het Timorsch Verbond* (The Timor Alliance), was founded by Rotinese who were studying in Makassar: a schoolteacher, D. S. Pella, and a member of the royal family of Termanu, J. W. Amalo. Although the Verbond began innocently enough with government permission in 1922, as a group dedicated to the "promotion of the intellectual development and material prosperity of the Timorese people" (the Rotinese, by this time, identifying themselves with the Timor residency rather than with their island alone), the Dutch soon began to view this organization as revolutionary. The Verbond produced a Malay monthly, *Soeloeh Timor* (Timor Torch), and with Savunese assistance began to agitate against certain Dutch colonial officers (one of whom was stationed on Savu, the other on Sumba). Encouraged by its success when both officers were found guilty of misconduct, the Verbond began a campaign to reorder the informal structure of education. At one important meeting, J. W. Amalo managed to get a motion passed calling for the separation of church and school. Ministers and their assistants were not to be allowed a hand in the direction of the state schools of the Timor area. After this meeting the Dutch attitude turned to hostility. Active participation in the Verbond became highly suspect and members of the organization who held government positions were threatened with dismissal.[1]

Rotinese factionalism, however, could be counted on to produce a full spectrum of organizations and opinions. Within a few years of the formation of the Timorsch Verbond, two Rotinese, J. W. Toepoe and Christian Pandie (who had become a member of the Communist party while on Java), formed another political organization, *Kerapatan Timor Evolutie* (Gathering of Timor's Evolution), which in turn split when Pandie attempted to form his own organization, *Sarekat Timor* (Timor League) on the "fundamental socialist principle that all men are brothers." This organization soon changed its name to *Sarekat Rajat* (People's League) and in its revolutionary newspaper, *Api* (Fire), waged a campaign against the powerful Timorese ruler of Amarasi. Pandie was jailed in 1926 as a result of specific objections to his activities and out of a general fear of Communist-inspired insurrections in Indonesia. Toepoe, on the other hand, went on to establish another short-lived party, *Pelita-Neratja* (Lamp and Scales). At the opposite end of the spectrum two other Rotinese, C. Frans and J. Kedoh, formed a pro-government and pro-church organization, *Perserikatan Timor* (Timor Union) that quickly obtained the financial support of the colonial government in its publication, also called *Perserikatan Timor*. This party with its official periodical became the main vehicle by which the government opposed what it considered to be the radical opinions of the period.

In 1930, J. W. Amalo revived the Timorsch Verbond in Surabaya, after government pressure had forced it into virtual dissolution. The rallying point was again a campaign to obtain an investigation of the conduct of a Dutch officer in the handling of a local matter. The case centered on the actions of the *Controleur* on Roti and his dealings with a complicated case in Delha. The leading Savunese political figure of the time, E. R. Here Wila of Seba, who headed a branch of the Verbond in Makassar (where the Ministry of Justice carried out its deliberations), coordinated this new campaign. Its success led the leaders of the Verbond to hold a "congress" of the party in Kupang in June 1932. There it was decided that the Timorsch Verbond would join Sukarno's national organization, *Permufakatan Perhimpunan Politik Kebangsaan Indonesia*.

Renewed government pressure and fierce internal squabbling among the scattered branches of the Timorsch Verbond led to another decline in the party's influence. The Verbond was able to instigate only one more investigation into a case of local injustice—this one on the island of Adonare in 1937. Thus although it was unsuccessful in strictly political affairs, the Verbond achieved a remarkable record in forcing the colonial government to correct its own mishandling of native affairs. One of the reasons for this success was the fact that the Colonial Service had itself come to rely upon numerous Rotinese and at least some Savunese. The Verbond could count on many of these Rotinese and Savunese to provide the necessary information to prosecute an investigation. Not only on Savu, Sumba, Roti, and Timor, but throughout the Timor residency, there were Rotinese and Savunese in government service. The case on Adonare, for example, was uncovered in part with the aid of another member of the royal family of Termanu, J. S. Amalo, who was a *Bestuurs-Assistant* for Solor.

By 1933 a new generation of political activists had begun to emerge. Several Rotinese and Savunese students in Bandung on Java formed an educational organization, *De Timorsche Jongeren* (Timorese Youth), which was intended to unite all of the students from the Timor residency who were pursuing studies throughout Indonesia. The founder of the Jongeren was a Rotinese, H. Johannes; he was joined by two other Rotinese, Ch. F. Ndaomanu and J. H. Toelle, and by two Savunese, S. K. Tibuludji and I. H. Doko. On their return to Kupang in 1937 and with the active encouragement of Here Wila of the Timorsch Verbond, Doko and Ndaomanu transformed the Timorsche Jongeren into a new party, the *Perserikatan Kebangsaan Timor* (Timor National Union).

This organization had only been active for a short time when war broke out in Europe. Holland was invaded, and the Dutch colonial government in Indonesia forbade native political activities that might threaten its position. Suddenly, on the night of 19 February 1942, the Japanese landed on Timor and overwhelmed both the Dutch and the contingent of the Australian army that had been sent to defend the island.

During the Japanese occupation a number of local leaders served in various governmental capacities. Prominent were the Raja of Amarasi (H. A. Koroh), C. Frans of the pro-Dutch Perserikatan Timor, and I. H. Doko of the Perserikatan Kebangsaan Timor. A Savunese, D. Adoe, was put in charge of the police in Kupang, while a Rotinese, T. Pello, served in a number of positions of prominence during the period. (Frans was always considered suspect because of his prior Dutch allegiance, and he was kidnapped and secretly executed by the Japanese in September 1943.) As the war progressed, plans were made to entrust local government to several of these leaders. At the final moment, on 11 September 1945, as Australian troops began to enter the town, the Japanese command hastily surrendered Kupang to a committee of three men: Dr. A. Gabelar, an Indo-European who had not been interned but had served as a doctor during the occupation; T. Pello, a Rotinese; and I. H. Doko, a Savunese.

Accused by the Dutch of collaboration, various local leaders (Doko, Pello, Ndaomanu, and Koroh) resurrected the Perserikatan Kebangsaan Timor and in March 1946 changed its name to the *Partai Demokrasi Indonesia* (PDI), whose express aim was independence within a united Indonesia. They were joined by other important local figures: the Raja of Kupang (A. Nisnoni), the Savunese Titus Uly, and the Rotinese J. S. Amalo (who had been interned by the Dutch on Sumba on charges of collaboration). A Savunese, M.

Rihi, who had already taken part in the first revolutionary encounters on Java, returned to Timor to organize the party's youth, which comprised largely Rotinese and Savunese from Kupang. In previous decades most political parties had suffered because their membership was too exclusively Rotinese and Savunese. This was also true of the Partai Demokrasi Indonesia; to counter this inescapable fact, the PDI's leaders attempted to create a balanced representation of the major ethnic groups of Timor in its official delegations.

When the Dutch extended an invitation to the PDI to attend the Malino conference in Makassar to discuss the postwar status of the territories of eastern Indonesia, opinion within the group was sharply divided. A Rotinese faction led by Pello and Ndaomanu was opposed to attendance, whereas Doko and Koroh argued for attendance as the only means to express their demands for immediate independence. In the end Doko and Koroh prevailed, and they were delegated to represent Timor on behalf of the PDI. Their political opponents, a coalition of five pro-Dutch parties,[2] tried to unseat them at the conference; since none of these parties, despite their various claims, had an indigenous base on Timor, the move was unsuccessful. By astute maneuvering, the PDI assumed almost complete representation for Timor and the surrounding islands.

Locally, two councils were formed to represent Timor. The first was a Council of Rajas (*Dewan Radja-Radja Timor*), which the Dutch expected to rely upon by appealing to the oath of the allegiance to the Dutch crown that each of the Rajas of Timor had sworn. Instead, as a result of the efforts of Rajas Koroh and Nisnoni, the majority of the Council sided with the PDI and elected Koroh its chairman and Nisnoni its vice-chairman. At this time, as a result of earlier Dutch efforts to reduce the number of Rajas on Roti and to establish a single "Raja" as ruler over the island, Roti was in the peculiar situation of being ruled by a governing committee composed of members drawn from the different royal houses of the states. Since the Rotinese were not properly represented at the Council of Rajas, many were able to gravitate to what was purportedly the more democratic of the two governing councils, the People's Representative Council (*Dewan Perwakilan Rakjat*). The chairman of this Council was Th. Messakh, a member of the royal family of Thie, and the roster of prominent members of the Council was, in fact, a mustering of representation from the leading noble lineages of Roti.

Through the control exercised by the PDI in both councils of local government, the Timor area was one of the few regions of eastern Indonesia that did not waver in its support for national unification and independence. When, in December 1946, the *Negara Indonesia Timur* (State of Eastern Indonesia) was created in an effort to thwart national unification, Timor joined this state as one of its 13 autonomous regions, under the condition set down by the PDI that this move was not an end in itself but a means to an end: that of full unification within the Republic of Indonesia.

In its efforts at full unification, the PDI was supported by the Movement of the Indonesian Peoples of the Lesser Sundas or GRISK (*Gerakan Rakjat Indonesia Sunda Ketjil*), which had been founded in Yogyakarta. GRISK was headed by the Rotinese H. Johannes, the previous founder of De Timorsche Jongeren and member with Doko and others of the Perserikatan Kebangsaan Timor. GRISK's active opposition to the Dutch on Java was extended on a military level by a group formed within the Indonesian army and known as the *Laskar Sunda Ketjil*. From this group emerged a number of young Rotinese and Savunese, such as Ch. Mooy and El. Tari, who were to play a prominent role in the politics of Timor. Having fought for independence on Java, their commitment to the republic was unchallengeable.

Beginning with the formation of the Perserikatan Kebangsaan Timor in 1937, the Savunese leader Doko embarked on a career that made him one of the most consistent and steadfast of the political organizers on Timor. Much of his training during the Japanese occupation had been in the Office of Propaganda, and it became his goal, as well as that of his party, to maintain some control of the offices of information both locally and in the newly formed Negara Indonesia Timur. In successive cabinets of Anak Agung Gde Agung, Doko was appointed first Assistant Minister, then Minister, of Information for the state. He also managed to get Here Wila of the old Timorsch Verbond appointed head of the Office of Information in Kupang, an office that was already heavily staffed with nationalist Rotinese. In the end, it was Doko who was deputized on 1 October 1949 to oversee the transfer of civil authority from the Dutch to local officials of the Negara Indonesia Timur in Kupang. This was a prelude to the transfer of Timor from the Negara Indonesia Timur to the Republic of Indonesia, which occurred within a year. The First of October 1949 thus became the locally recognized date for independence from Dutch rule—an era that had had its formal beginnings in Kupang in 1613.

ROTINESE AND SAVUNESE ON TIMOR AFTER INDEPENDENCE

There is no study of Sumba from which to assess the impact of the Savunese there. However, an excellent study of Timor exists that documents the effect of the Rotinese and, to a lesser extent, the Savunese on that island. In the early 1950's, F. J. Ormeling, Director of the Geographical Institute of Jakarta, carried out an extended and coordinated governmental study of the overall problems facing the island of Timor. His report, published in 1956 as a book, *The Timor Problem: A Geographical Interpretation of an Underdeveloped Island,* is an exceptionally detailed examination of both physical and social conditions on the island. Ormeling's remarks about the Rotinese and Savunese are scattered throughout his book. By piecing together these observations, one obtains a clear, though somewhat patchy, picture of the immigrants in the early independence period. These observations are particularly important because they bring the historical narrative nearly up to date, and they represent the impressions of an astute and careful observer who had only the barest understanding of the centuries of historical developments that had given rise to the contemporary situation.

To begin with, Ormeling has only a brief explanation of the presence of Rotinese and Savunese on Timor. He writes that

> the Company attracted inhabitants from the surrounding islands, chiefly Roti but also from Savu and Solor, as protection against possible attacks by Sonbai and the Black Portuguese. They were assigned dwelling places in the immediate neighbourhood of the Dutch fort . . . Thus Kupang and environs became an immigration area through Dutch influence . . . In 1950 roughly sixty percent of Kupang's swapradja's circa sixty thousand inhabitants were not of Timorese origin. Rotinese are far in the majority among these non-Timorese elements.[3]

Although he was unaware of the fact that Malay schools on Roti dated from the 1730's, Ormeling certainly recognized the importance of the Rotinese school system in the nineteenth century:

> At the close of the previous century, Roti was the teacher's Arcadia in the Timor Residency. Several generations of schooling have made the Rotinese suitable for public administration in an environment whose development is fairly low. For some decades Rotinese government officials, teachers, and preachers have been familiar in the Timor archipelago.[4]

What seems to have impressed Ormeling most was the overwhelming penetration of the Rotinese into all levels of administration and government service:

> Due to their higher level of educational development the Rotinese have played a large part in local government administration in the Timor archipelago. They filled minor posts in numerous government services during the Dutch administration. Before the war practically all local

government offices in the Timor Residency employed one or more Rotinese as writers, clerks, etc. They acted, moreover, as teachers and over-
seers in agricultural, forestry and veterinary services. *Bestuurs-assis-
tenten*, minor civil servants who assisted the European official in the
practical execution of his work, were largely drawn from the Rotinese in
this Residency, and several of them gained valuable experience in these
jobs. The Japanese, too, relied on Rotinese civil servants, and some of
them held responsible posts during the occupation . . . The young Indonesian Government, finding itself short of trained civil servants in
1949, readily availed itself of Rotinese experience and appointed several
of them in positions vacated when the Dutch left. There was no other
choice in view of the illiteracy of the Timorese proper. In 1953 it looked
as though Timor were governed by a Rotinese minority.[5]

In attributing the Rotinese position in the government administration to
their previous schooling, Ormeling recognized too that the Savunese were
the other group on Timor who were heavily represented in the schools, especially in the secondary schools at Kupang. Of the students attending govern-
ment-operated secondary schools in 1950, 54 percent were either Rotinese or
Savunese; only 10 percent were Timorese.[6]

Ormeling's scheme divided the Rotinese population on Timor into three
occupational groups: civil servants, farmers, and retailers. The Rotinese, he
observes, were the only group of "foreign islanders" to settle on Timor as
farmers. "As such," in Ormeling's words, "they form the only serious competition for the Timorese in their constant and intense struggle for existence."[7] The Rotinese, he maintains, "settled in the most favorable places,
in the plains, along the coast, and pushed inland along river valleys and recently along roads."[8] Originally, however,

they were assigned settlement areas in the Oesau-Pariti plain . . . The
immigrant found a broad, almost unpopulated, virginal plain inter-
sected by numerous small rivers and surrounded by lontar and gebang
savannahs. There were possibilities for collecting *tuak* [lontar juice] and
cultivating rice. Kupang Bay nearby enabled him to fish and obtain salt.
Apparently the Rotinese colony immediately utilized these resources.
Within a short time the Oesau-Pariti plain became Kupang's rice gran-
ary. Further groups of Rotinese settled in this period as farmers along
the road from Kupang to the Oesau-Pariti plain and as craftsmen in
Kupang itself.[9]

Although unfamiliar with the economy of the Rotinese on their home island, Ormeling in his various descriptions of Rotinese activities on Timor
presents a succinct description of the lontar-centered economy that the Rotinese had been able to transfer to Timor. By collating Ormeling's various ob-

servations, it is possible to review all the significant features of this unusual economy, chief among them the utilization of palms: "The most characteristic Rotinese industry is lontar-tapping."[10] As on Roti itself, these immigrants, "surrounded by a superabundance of lontar palms, do not bother with replanting."[11] Ormeling goes on to explain:

> Firstly the tree provides the familiar series of food and drinks: *tuak* [lontar juice], *gula air* [lontar syrup], *gula lempeng* [crystallized lontar sugar], *laru* [lontar beer] and *sopi* [lontar gin]. Ladang cultivation and lontar-tapping combined afford the Rotinese a guarantee against famine. In times of harvest failure he falls back entirely to the level of food gatherer and keeps alive with lontar products. In normal times he welcomes them as a source of additional food . . . The average adult Rotinese consumes fairly large quantities of lontar syrup and laru. A daily eight to ten bottles of tuak or laru is not exceptional. Even urban Rotinese continue this habit. Besides food and drink, *Borassus flabellifer* provides raw material for numerous consumer goods. Practically all articles used in the Rotinese and Savunese household are made from lontar material . . . Finally, the lontar palm serves as a commercial crop. The sale of lontar products provides a welcome addition to the Rotinese budget. For years lontar products, mainly syrup and sugar, have been exported to the surrounding islands. Deep in the interior of Timor, as far as Insana, Amanuban, and South Belu, Rotinese gula air is found today in Chinese distilleries as raw material for *sopi* preparation. Furthermore, Roti exports some of its own sopi production. Sopi Roti is renowned in Kupang.[12]

In addition, Ormeling notes that all of the so-called "modern" houses in the Kupang and Amarasi area are made from *bebak* (gewang leaf stalks).

> In the widespread gebang savannahs round Kupang Bay, bebak gathering is an industry in itself providing incomes for many people—mainly Rotinese. Kupang is largely built of bebak, undoubtedly Timor's most important construction material.[13]

Ormeling observed another attendant palm industry:

> The pig rearing and fattening industry in Europe used to depend on oak forests: here it depends on gebang and lontar areas . . . in gebang and lontar areas on the dry north coast Rotinese spend extra care on the animals by giving them *putak* [gewang pulp] and lontar syrup, in their fodder.[14]

Besides water buffalo and pigs, livestock included goats and sheep. Goats were found throughout the island. The possession of sheep was distinctively Rotinese:

> Domestic sheep play a very insignificant role on Timor . . . Only in the environs of Kupang Bay are small flocks of sheep kept by Rotinese, and then only for local meat consumption.[15]

The opportunities for rice cultivation were, however, greater on Timor than on Roti:

> The largest sawah area (1,200 hectares) anywhere on Timor lies on the higher situated southern part of the plain, which is irrigated from the Oesau river by means of a primitive flooding system.[16]

The whole of this wet-rice area was worked by driving herds of water buffalo through the fields until they became, as Ormeling describes it, "a smooth sea of mud." Unlike other regions of Timor, cattle had not replaced water buffalo in any areas of Rotinese settlement:

> The preponderance of water buffalo in certain districts of Kupang swapradja—in Amabi for instance—is evident. Undoubtedly the influence of sawah cultivation on the heavy clay soils in the adjacent plain of Oesau-Pariti is making itself felt. As in many other sawah areas of Indonesia water buffalo are preferred here as working animals.[17]

This becomes of greater social significance when coupled with the evidence of Ormeling's surveys, which indicate that the distribution of water buffalo was strikingly more equitable than that of cattle[18] and that despite a greater number of cattle on the island, registers showed a significantly larger number of water buffalo slaughtered for local consumption.[19] One of Ormeling's major conclusions is that the bulk of the Timorese population gained little from the cattle-raising industry on their island. The figures he uses to demonstrate this conclusion suggest that, in contrast to the Timorese, the Rotinese benefited by the retention of their water buffalo. In fact, they have benefited doubly as a result of the situation on Timor, since it is the Rotinese who have usually acted as the chief middlemen and cattle buyers in this Chinese-financed export trade.

Many Rotinese economic activities on Timor, however, involve more than palm utilization and rice cultivation. The Rotinese, Ormeling observed,

> make more use of the long dry season when agriculture is forced to a standstill . . . Besides lontar-tapping they engage in fishing, salt-making, collecting bebak, and lime and charcoal-burning. With the Savunese they are active in the commercial field, although far behind the Chinese in this respect. Their main interest is the small retail trade known as *papalele*. As early as the previous century, mention was made of

Rotinese visiting the interior for trading purposes. Their settlement at Naikliu, on the coast of Amfoan, where Buginese and Alorese perahus meet, has long been a commercial center of local importance. Today Rotinese retailers sell lontar products, milk, vegetables, lime and *bebak* in Kupang. Like the Savunese they regularly visit pasars [markets] in Amarasi, Fatuleu and recently even Molo, where fruit, potatoes and vegetables are purchased from the local Atoni. Thus, practically the whole djeruk [citrus] harvest from Central Timor's highlands finds its way to the consumer in the kotas [towns] via Rotinese and Savunese intermediaries.[20]

By 1950 it was misleading to describe what was occurring as simply "migration" to Timor. Connections between the islands involved a two-way traffic, and the Rotinese considered that western Timor had become a part of his social world. Ormeling noted:

The Rotinese immigrant still keeps firm contact with his home island and traffic between Timor and Roti is quite impressive in the dry season. The immigrants go to Roti by hundreds and by hundreds their relatives visit Timor.[21]

This travel was done almost exclusively by native perahu. Winds from May through August favor access to Roti; September through December is the better sailing period for Timor. Although concentrated in the dry season, two-way traffic between the islands is maintained throughout the year, even against contrary winds. In 1953 the number of registered perahus sailing to Roti from Kupang—one of a number of departure points—averaged roughly one per day. In 1965-1966, adult Rotinese who had never been to Timor were a decided minority; those on Timor who had never been on Roti were even fewer.

From all of this, Ormeling's conclusion is simple:

The immigrants utilize the environment's possibilities more fully and have a greater variety of economic activities than their hosts. Due to this Rotinese immigrants are generally economically stronger than the Timorese. Actually in the coastal area around Kupang Bay they are clearly winning the day.[22]

REFLECTIONS ON THE HISTORY OF THE CLASH OF ECONOMIES

Ormeling's conclusion returns us to the argument with which Part One of this study was concerned. The evidence of the ethnographic present makes it abundantly clear that the Rotinese and Savunese migrated from their small islands to the coastal regions of the larger islands of Timor and Sumba and that with their efficient palm-centered economies, they are continuing to advance themselves noticeably on these two islands. This study initially concentrated on assessing the importance of the economic and ecological factors that favor the palm-tappers as opposed to the swidden cultivators. In returning to these earlier assessments by way of a lengthy consideration of the developments of the past three hundred years, we have added a perspective with which to comprehend more adequately the complex combination of factors that have contributed to these immigrants' success in "winning the day" on Timor and Sumba. This historical perspective in no way refutes the earlier conclusions of this study. But the added amplification that it provides allows us to alter our perception of the relative significance of the various factors that led to the migrations of the Rotinese and Savunese.

The thrust of the accumulated ethnographic literature on the eastern islands of the Lesser Sundas has tended to portray these islands as a kind of forgotten region of the former Dutch East Indies. Compared with what occurred on the large islands of Sumatra, Java, or Celebes or on the islands of the Moluccas, Dutch involvement in the Lesser Sundas was indeed relatively slight. The political incorporation of many of these islands as self-governing territories with their own rulers and their own adat law preserved at least the impression of noninterference in local affairs. Yet it is one thing to recognize the relative lack of Dutch involvement and another to ignore it entirely.

The fact is that the effects, direct and indirect, of the Dutch presence have been profound. They cannot be discounted or ignored in any ethnographic account of these islands. What is locally conceived of as traditional can, in many instances, be shown to be the result of particular responses to Dutch intervention.

This Dutch influence was not confined to a few limited aspects of native life. It had unintended and incalculable effects, at many levels, on the various islands. Both those societies that appear to have resisted this influence and those that appear to have responded were affected by it. It could be argued, for example, that the introduction of maize and the later indirect, Dutch-financed support given to the export trade in horses from Sumba and in cattle from Timor did more to affect the lives of ordinary cultivators and to shore up the aristocracies above them than all the Dutch involvement with the Rotinese and Savunese, whose principal mode of production remained unaltered and whose palm products offered little of commercial value.

Given the widespread effects of European influence, it is equally misleading to view the traditional societies of these islands as the manifestation of internal developments within separate, self-contained social systems. A simple modular view that considers each of these societies as an entity cannot distinguish their varying social structures from their common history. On the other hand, the diversity of cultures, peoples, and environments in the eastern islands of the Lesser Sundas makes it apparent that the influence of even so monolithic an organization as the Dutch East India Company or that of the later colonial administration could not have been everywhere the same. To interpret the differing impact of these organizations requires the recognition of a variety of local situations and indigenous conceptions.

The fortunate fact of the availability of historical records on some of these societies thus provides a perspective for evaluating what has become established as "tradition." It also provides a perspective from which to avoid oversimplified generalizations. An anthropology concerned with the representation of society by structural models must face the challenge posed by an open historical perspective. If as a result, one's conclusions are theoretically less neat and tidy, if they admit the possibilities of what might have been and are less assertive in the determination of what actually occurred, such are the consequences of recognizing a rich array of historical evidence. In the light of such evidence, we can briefly review and perhaps better comprehend the clash of economies that has developed and continues to dominate ethnic relations in the outer arc of the Lesser Sundas.

To BEGIN WITH, the adverse environmental conditions on the small islands of Roti and Savu in a sense may have been their initial blessing. Their lack of sufficient water, the unreliability of the rains, the desiccating effect of the long, dry monsoon on these low-lying islands seem to have prompted an earlier development toward palm economies than was necessitated on Timor or Sumba. The smaller islands had the luxury of developing their economies in relative isolation and without the intrusion of outside forces. It is apparent from the early records that their palm economies were already well developed by the time of the European arrival.

From what can be determined of these economies, they were potentially diversifiable. They were capable of rapid, minor subsystem adaptations, provided their pivotal palm base was not affected. Thus the islands were in a better position to respond to the Portuguese and Dutch. Indications are that these palm subsistence economies supported higher densities of population at the time of the European arrival than did the swidden-based economies of Timor or Sumba. This meant that the "well-peopled" islands had a more ready supply of manpower. As small islands, Roti and Savu had seafaring populations and no interior into which to retreat. Both islands were basically indefensible to the power of the Dutch. They had no choice but compliance. The early decades of contact convincingly demonstrated to the Rotinese the consequences of resistance. Unlike Timor, neither Roti nor Savu ever became the battleground for outside contending forces. And when the Dutch had firmly established their control in the area, both islands became relatively closed and protected sanctuaries. From these backwaters, Savunese and Rotinese could be used in the pacification of Timor and Sumba. Once transported to these islands, they had the advantages of Dutch protection and of economies better adapted to local conditions.

Timor was divided between the Dutch and various factions of Portuguesespeaking forces. Part of the Timorese response to these opposing forces was a retreat into the interior of their island, leaving many coastal areas depopulated. Even in the interior, the native economies were affected first by the search for sandalwood, then by the rapid spread of maize, which became the major subsistence crop through most of the island, and finally and decisively by the introduction of cattle and the creation of an export trade that tended to undermine the basis of the subsistence sector of the Timorese economy. Maize reached Sumba later than Timor, but its spread plus the creation of a royal export trade in horses had similar though less pronounced effects than on Timor.

Maize did not spread at all on Savu. As a consequence, with its hardy, drought-resistant sorghum and high-protein green grams, Savu suffered fewer disastrous famines than Sumba or Timor, where reliance on a single potentially precarious crop became so marked. The spread of maize on Roti has been largely confined to eastern and central Roti; this may partially explain some of the dislocations that have occurred in these areas. Even where maize has spread, it has never become an exclusive crop. The Rotinese system of fertilized house gardens for maize, the intercropping of other foods in separate gardens, and the use of all sources of water for irrigation divide potential risks. The historical evidence of the ability of the Rotinese economy to increase green-gram production for a special purpose and to reduce this production after that purpose had been met tends to confirm the adaptability and versatility of this economy. The equally evident and consistent ability of the Rotinese to sell a certain quantity of their harvest points to a fact that is true for both the Rotinese and the Savunese, namely that these populations have their palms to provide for their needs. The preservation of a secure and highly productive subsistence base is one feature that distinguishes these peoples from their neighbors on Timor and Sumba. The unusual nature of this base, made up as it is of palm syrup, seaweed, seaworms, and pork—together with a material culture based on a hundred and one easily replaceable palm products—gave them what they needed and what few others wanted.

These palm economies provided more than mere subsistence, however. They affected the concentration, distribution, and accessibility of the populations they supported. The formal settlement pattern of the Savunese, for example, resembles that of the Sumbanese, to whom they are culturally related, in that both have nuclear villages composed of genealogically defined residential groups. By contrast, the scattered settlement pattern of the Rotinese is formally like that of the Timorese. Circumscribed residential villages of the kind found on Savu and Sumba do not occur among either the Rotinese or the Timorese. But the effects of differing population densities and subsistence patterns go a long way toward attenuating these formal cultural resemblances. Although the Sumbanese have nuclear villages, the necessities of planting, guarding, and harvesting distant swidden fields keep a considerable segment of the population scattered for a good part of the year. While the Sumbanese may congregate for ceremonies within their villages, their seasonal dispersion is, in fact, more like that of the Timorese than the Savunese, whose nuclear villages form permanent year-round residences. On Roti, despite the Dutch imposition of fictional village structures, the density of population in most areas and the peculiar drift to scattered settlement among palm trees creates the effect of a loose but near-continuous residential arrangement. Since houses and gardens are fixed and there is no seasonal shift between them, this continuous sort of settlement, though unlike the discrete village settlement of the Savunese, is similarly permanent and relatively concentrated.

The economic dependence upon trees as opposed to shifting fields required of the Rotinese and Savunese a concentration of persons quite unlike that found on the larger islands. Since their palm-centered economies were able to meet subsistence needs in most years and to produce a surplus in good years, the concentration and settlement of the Savunese and Rotinese had probably, at the time of the Dutch arrival, already led to a greater degree of formal organization than on Sumba or Timor. Moreover, since these palm economies directed necessary labor into several peak periods—planting, harvesting, and tapping—and allowed the intervals to be filled with optional subsistence activities, Rotinese and Savunese men were left with a greater amount of free time per year than either the Timorese or Sumbanese. The political history of Timor attests to the fact that certain Timorese rulers could call upon a larger number of men to oppose the Dutch than any or all of the Rotinese or Savunese rulers. Yet these men were available for only a limited portion of the year. The whole "empire" of Sonba'i, for example, reverted to the level of scattered kin groups as the time for burning swidden fields drew near.

Nowhere is this difference between the two types of economies more apparent than in the field of education. Palm-tapping is an activity that requires skill and coordination. Boys begin to learn these skills at about the age of 14 or 15. Before this, although there is always some kind of work that can be found for them to do, their labor is not absolutely required by the economy. Even after a boy has begun to tap trees, he can do his work early in the morning and late in the afternoon and still have much of the day for other activities. By contrast, in a swidden economy child labor can be important, if for no other purpose than to guard the fields against birds, pigs, and rats. Since settlement is at least seasonally scattered, convenient location of schools, which is a minor problem on Roti and Savu, is a major one among the Timorese and Sumbanese. Even today the imposition of compulsory education on swidden agriculturalists poses a threat to their increasingly precarious economy. For the Rotinese and Savunese, on the other hand, it presents few problems and has become established as a traditional occupation for the young.

It therefore seems reasonable to conclude, if only on the basis of present-day evidence, that the productive base of the Rotinese and Savunese economy gave them certain clear advantages in responding to the opportunities provided by the presence of the Dutch. Highlighting the characteristics of a swidden as opposed to a palm economy makes clear their different potentials for reacting to outside influences. Examining the historical distinctions between two societies with similar palm economies makes it equally clear that a palm economy in itself does not determine, in any very specific sense, the actual responses that these two societies make to outside influences. An economy may set certain limits, or establish certain potentials, but it is the interplay of a host of complex social and cultural factors that create the historical developments that characterize the societies. Insofar as a pattern can be said to emerge, this has less to do with specific historical events and more to do with constraints and potentials.

Certainly the initial tendency of the Savunese to ignore the Dutch or to accept only a limited involvement with them as members of their armed soldiery was unlike the response of the Rotinese. The Rotinese were initially drawn into an involvement with the Dutch for strategic reasons, but seem to have relished their entanglements and embraced what they could of Dutch cultural forms. By the nineteenth century, Christianity and education in Malay were part of an aristocratic tradition among the Rotinese, while they were foreign to the Savunese. The Rotinese could thus use these new cultural forms to proclaim their autonomy, exaggerate the differences among themselves, and prevent further outside interference in their local affairs; whereas the Savunese in the nineteenth century appeared, especially to missionaries, to be dangerous, unrepentant heathens. When, however, the Savunese began to turn to education—some hundred and fifty years after the Rotinese did—they seem to have pursued it with the determination characteristic of their other endeavors. Even though fewer in number, they rapidly attained as many positions of prominence in the Timor area as the Rotinese. The Savunese qualities of discipline and organization are as apparent in the historical record as are the Rotinese qualities of fractiousness and factionalism.

One can hardly avoid the impression evident right from the first records of contact that the Rotinese and Savunese have acted in ways remarkably similar to those in which they presently act. Nonetheless, it would be unwise to attribute these consistent patterns of social action to distinct cultural qualities without recognizing the remarkable continuity of the institutions that have maintained them. The Savunese ceremonial system with its strict lunar calendar, its priestly organization, its required communal participation, and its ritual glorification of physical confrontation has nurtured Savunese virtues, just as the local court system on Roti with its insistent verbalism and its emphasis on cunning and cleverness has nurtured Rotinese virtues. Given a secure economy and the relative lack of forceful interference in their affairs, these and other institutions have persisted since the seventeenth century. The Dutch stereotypes of the Rotinese and Savunese, which developed in response to their distinct cultural traits, fed upon them and fostered them, effectively channelling these peoples toward separate occupations. Even today, it is an established tradition in Kupang that Savunese make the best policemen, Rotinese make the best lawyers, and—depending on one's philosophy of education—either one group or the other make the best schoolteachers.

There has been another level of discernible continuity. Although very different in structure, the system of clans on both Roti and Savu has remained remarkably unchanged. The early nineteenth-century lists of clans on both islands are still reasonably accurate guides to the clans of the present. Of these clans, certain ones stand out as historically more important than others. The Rotinese royal clans of Termanu, Thie, and Loleh, for example, whose dynasties have retained unbroken lines of succession since the seventeenth century, have contributed a large number of important historical figures. The same is true of the powerful royal clan of Nataga of Seba. From Lomi Djara and Manu Djami, whom Cook met in the eighteenth century, through a succession of forceful rulers in the nineteenth century, and a variety of revolutionary politicians like Here Wila and Doko in the twentieth century, to the present Governor of the province, El. Tari, this one clan through its various lineages has produced an impressive array of political figures.

When we turn from a recognition of these continuities to an examination of the factors involved in the movement of the two populations to the larger islands, the historical record indicates that both peoples have managed to achieve roughly the same end—but not for the same reasons and not exactly by the same means. It would be an inadequate assumption to attribute the seemingly fortunate migration of the Savunese to Sumba and Rotinese to Timor to some simple principle by which conflict was averted through the separation of potential competitors into different ecological niches. The involvement of the Dutch in the history of these two peoples is enough to cast doubt on any such assumption. Had the Company persisted in its plan to move Rotinese to Sumba in 1759, the early Savunese incursions into east Sumba might have been frustrated or, as is also possible, these incursions might have brought Savunese into conflict with the Rotinese established on Sumba. Only in a general and perhaps unintentional fashion, however, can the Dutch be credited with directing these populations to separate islands.

The first movement of Rotinese was not a spontaneous migration but the result of a Dutch solution to political problems on Roti itself. The cause of the first Savunese movement to Sumba is less easy to determine. It appears to have been spontaneous in the sense that the Dutch had no part in it. It came about because of royal marriage relations between the two islands and was probably motivated by the gains that could be made through military action on Sumba, using the weapons supplied to the Savunese by the Dutch in their pacification campaigns on Timor. When, later in the nineteenth century, the Dutch attempted to stimulate large-scale migration, the situation on the two islands had changed radically. The opening of Savu to wider contact with the outside world around 1860, after a period of relative isolation, was probably responsible for the very high loss of life in the epidemics that struck the island. Since Roti suffered the same series of epidemics but without the same proportional loss of life, it is likely that the Rotinese had built up greater immunities through long and established contact with the outside. The epidemic of 1869 alone precluded any possibility of a large-scale, Dutch-assisted migration of Savunese to Sumba. On Roti, very little stimulation was needed to effect the movement of considerable numbers to Timor, especially from the more densely populated states of east Roti. There was still good land, especially palm savannah, available on Timor, land that an earlier generation of Rotinese had already partially secured. When, on the other hand, the movement of Savunese to Sumba began again, this migration appears to have consisted, in large part, in Christian converts who were expelled from their island.

The acceptance of education by both Rotinese and Savunese made their migrations more than the movement of palm-tappers to new lands. The requirements of further education, especially for the upper classes of both islands, and the possibilities for employment thereafter, directed Rotinese and Savunese (both from their home islands and from their new territories) toward the town of Kupang and, eventually for an educated elite, from Kupang to other areas of Indonesia.

This is another remarkable achievement, if one considers that the total combined population of Rotinese and Savunese comprises only about one-tenth of one percent of Indonesia's vast population. Yet Rotinese and Savunese occupy positions of importance in the nation out of all proportion to their actual numbers. Many Rotinese and Savunese have gone abroad, earned advanced degrees—in fields such as economics, linguistics, anthropology, and medicine—and have returned to serve their country. Already Indonesia's two leading universities have had Rotinese as rectors: Professor Dr. W. Z. Johannes at the University of Indonesia in Jakarta from 1950 to 1952, and Professor Ir. H. Johannes at Gadjah Mada in Yogyakarta from 1961 to 1966. Rotinese and Savunese can also be found to represent the full range of national opinion. Francesca Fanggidaej, granddaughter of the Bible translator from Baä, was for many years an active organizer of the women's movement of the Communist Party of Indonesia and, having once nearly lost her life in the uprising at Madiun, happened to be in Peking on an official visit at the time of the political upheaval in Indonesia in 1965.

During the same upheaval El. Tari, a Savunese with military rank and administrative experience, acted firmly in the defense of Kupang, as Savunese have done for centuries, and was eventually promoted and elected to the governorship of the province. A Rotinese, K. Amalo of Termanu, was elected Assistant Governor of Nusa Tenggara Timur. The election of these two men, one Savunese and one Rotinese, may be seen as the symbolic culmination of several hundred years of historical development in the Timor area.

PART THREE

Some Comparisons
of Palm Economies

CHAPTER EIGHT

Introduction to the *Borassus* Palm

THE THIRD PART of this study consists in the comparison of three palm economies, a comparison intimately related to the two previous parts. Part One established the special features of the Rotinese and Savunese economies based upon exploitation of the *Borassus* palm. It focused on the utilization of this palm as an adaptive mode of production in an area otherwise dominated by swidden cultivation. Part Two considered the historical consequences of the existence of these societies with their special economies and the complex course of Dutch involvement with both palm-tappers and swidden-cultivators in the Lesser Sundas.

Part Three introduces another kind of comparison. Instead of distinguishing the Rotinese and Savunese use of the lontar as an isolated and peculiar mode of production, it analyzes the general and widespread use of *Borassus* palms throughout the drier regions of south and southeast Asia. The first issue is to establish the distribution of species of *Borassus* throughout this area and to consider their taxonomic status. It is necessary, however, to distinguish the casual employment of these palms from the comprehensive exploitation of their full possibilities. This is itself a complex issue that cannot be considered in the abstract but only in relation to specific instances of specialized exploitation. The "full possibilities" of the use of these palms are difficult to determine, and the question of whether certain uses limit or preclude others immediately arises. Given the common botanical features of the *Borassus*, it is apparent that these palms can be effectively exploited in a variety of ways. This in turn raises the third and most significant issue in this comparison. The specialized use of *Borassus* palms by different peoples has

199

to do both with the nature of the palm and with the social and economic situations in which these various peoples are to be found. To obtain some general idea of the variations, this part of the study will examine three ethnographically distinct cases of intensive palm utilization: (*a*) the Rotinese in eastern Indonesia, (*b*) the Madurese in western Indonesia, and (*c*) certain caste groups of south India.

A comparison of such culturally varied populations cannot be expected to provide any simple answers to the questions it poses. Despite the common features of these palm economies, it must be recognized from the outset that these case comparisons do not reveal unambiguously the inherent properties, potentialities, and limitations of this mode of production. They set out only to explore and reflect upon the variety of uses to which the *Borassus* palm has been adapted. Since the information presently available on these palms and the populations that depend upon them is sufficient only to begin such explorations, it is hoped that this comparison may prompt others to extend it.

THE *BORASSUS* AND ITS SPECIES

In *The Natural History of Palms,* Professor E. J. H. Corner writes:

> Of all land plants, the palm is the most distinguished. A columnar stem crowned with giant leaves is the perfect idea, popular or philosophic, of what a plant should be. It suffers no attrition through ramification. In all the warmer parts of the earth this form stamps itself in grand simplicity on the landscape. It manifests itself in more than two thousand species and several hundred genera, every one restricted more or less by climate, terrain, and geographical history.[1]

Certain palms are inextricably involved in human history. For centuries they have offered various peoples of the world a means of sustenance and, at times, of near-total subsistence. Whole cultures can legitimately be described as adaptations to certain species of palms, a list of which evokes an impressive history. There is the doom palm (*Hyphaene thebaica*) of ancient Egypt and the date palm (*Phoenix dactylifera*) of the Middle East; the coconut palm (*Cocos nucifera*) and the oil palm (*Elaeis guineensis*)—commercially, the world's most exploited. Among sap-producing palms, there is the wild date palm (*Phoenix sylvestris*) of India, the sugar palm (*Arenga pinnata*) and the Nipa palm (*Nypa fructicans*) of Indonesia and the Philippines, and the African wine palm (*Raphia vinifera*). In a class by itself is the sago palm (*Metroxylon sagu*) and its related segregates. A single felled trunk of this species can actually yield up to 1,200 pounds of edible crude starch. In addition, there is the Areca palm (*Areca catechu*), whose nuts are chewed with betel throughout India, southeast Asia, and the Pacific; there are also the pandanus palms, the rattan palms, and the royal palms of the Caribbean. Those who have studied these trees—among them A. von Humboldt, Wallace, Fischer, and Corner—have repeatedly pointed to the remarkable facets of human dependence upon palms.

Among the palms on which human populations rely, *Borassus* are outstanding. It is estimated that there are more of them in the world than any other kind of palm with the exception of the coconut. But the undeniable fact is that palms of the genus *Borassus* are among the least studied of all the world's palms. Their numbers, wide distribution, immense size, and the fact that they grow wild in some regions and are cultivated in others has made the determination of species of this genus exceptionally difficult. There seems little doubt that man has helped to shape and distribute this palm and thereby has contributed to the taxonomic problems that these palms present.

The literature on *Borassus* palms, both popular and botanical, is beset with contrary statements and confusing nomenclature. It was customary, in the early literature, to refer to all forms of *Borassus* as *Borassus flabellifer* (or *Borassus flabelliformis*) Linn., thereby subsuming under a single rubric all occurrences of this palm from west Africa to New Guinea. In 1836 Martius made the first break with this tradition by suggesting the distinction between an African variety of *Borassus,* which he termed *Borassus aethiopum,* and the Asian variety, for which he retained the name *Borassus flabellifer.* This dichotomy marked the extent of the botanical classification of *Borassus* palms until 1914, when the distinguished Italian botanist Beccari devoted a monograph to establishing a fuller species classification and ventured an outline of species distribution.[2] In this study Beccari recognized seven species of *Borassus: aethiopum, deleb, sambiranensis, madagariensis, flabellifer, sundaicus,* and *heineanus.*

Beccari subdivided B. *aethiopum,* the African *Borassus,* according to three varieties. The first is located in the Ivory Coast, the Congo, and Nigeria; the second, in Senegal and Chad; the third, in east Africa. He located a separate species, B. *deleb,* in the Sudan and two species, B. *sambiranensis* and B. *madagariensis,* in Madagascar. The remarkable feature of most of these African species and varieties, something of which Beccari was only partially aware, is that they are put to the same human uses in Africa as in Asia. The African literature is scattered but is, on this point, consistent and emphatic.[3] Species difference within the genus *Borassus* seems not to have an appreciable effect on utilization. With this in view, it is possible also to appreciate Beccari's classification of the Asian *Borassus* palms.

Beccari located the *B. flabellifer* L. in a wide area of India, Ceylon, and Indochina. For the Indonesian archipelago, he distinguished a separate species, *B. sundaicus,* and in New Guinea, another species, *B. heineanus.* Beccari had traveled in the Indonesian archipelago and even recounts seeing lontar palms in east Timor. To all outward appearances, even to the trained specialist, they seemed the same. He assumed that the tree had been transported from India and had spread through Indonesia. He reports, however, that later a microscopic examination of a single specimen of *Borassus* sent him from the botanical gardens at Bogor on Java revealed appreciable differences between the palms, particularly in the outer covering of the leaf. Beccari argued that the leaf covering of the *B. flabellifer* might be an adaptation, in the transpiration system of this palm, to a prolonged dry season. The leaf surface of the *B. sundaicus,* he suggested, might reflect an adaptation to a humid region. Yet the fact is that except for a few areas of Java, lontar flourish almost exclusively in the driest regions of Indonesia.

Beccari was thus considered unconvincing in regard to the species identification of most of Indonesia's lontars. Dutch botanists writing on Indonesia tended to discount his conclusions and continued to refer to the lontar as *Borassus flabellifer* L. Heyne's comments on the lontar in his monumental study, *De nuttige Planten van Nederlandsch-Indie* are typical of this attitude:

> In Beccari's posthumous work *Palme della tribù Borasseae,* on the evidence of a single Javanese specimen grown in the State's Botanical Garden, there is established a new species for the Malay Archipelago, *Borassus sundaica* Becc. which, in general occurrence, is not distinguishable from *B. flabellifer.* Until the time when more materials are examined or until consistent botanical differences of satisfactory value warrant the separation of these species, I will keep firmly to the old name, being under the firm impression that our lontar is a cultivated palm in regions with a sharply pronounced dry monsoon, long ago introduced from India as indicated by its popular names here.[4]

This general view of the classification of the lontar has persisted in the recent literature on the area. In the edition of Burkill's *Dictionary of the Economic Products of the Malay Peninsula* published in 1966, this single-species view of the Asian *Borassus* is maintained, but with a recognition of Beccari's alternative classification:

> Around the coast of most of India there is no tree more conspicuous than this palm. It makes great groves, chiefly in the Bombay and Ma-

dras Presidencies in hot places. Then again inland it is, in parts, very plentiful. To the westward it is abundant on the shores of the Persian Gulf. To the eastward it is conspicuous in the relatively dry parts of Burma, and it is very abundant in the parts of Siam near and behind the head of the Gulf of Siam. Down the peninsular part of Siam it extends rather freely, reaching Kedah. Farther south the climate becomes too wet for it, and such palms as exist in Penang, Malacca, and Singapore are few and are clearly maintained by cultivation. In Java the same state is met with, but gradually eastward the palm becomes more and more abundant, until, in places, it is again very abundant in a natural state. It occurs throughout the eastern islands of Malaysia, and in Timor wide groves of it are found.

Beccari regarded it as probable that all these are his *B. sundaica;* but he only established the occurrence of *B. sundaica* as in cultivation in western Java. It is of no use to treat the Malaysian tree, therefore, as distinct from *B. flabellifera,* until it is proved to be so; but the recognition by Beccari of differences vastly alters the views, which must be held, on the history of the palm in the East.[5]

Since Beccari's determination of *B. sundaicus* hinged on such slender evidence, I arranged to supply Professor Harold E. Moore, Jr., of the Bailey Hortorium at Cornell University, with specimens and photographs of the palms of the Timor area. On the basis of these materials (sent to him in 1973), Professor Moore confirmed Beccari's original judgment. In terms of their shape and overlapping form, the petals of the lontar are those of *B. sundaicus.*[6]

In light of this new evidence, we can refer to the Rotinese palm as *Borassus sundaicus* Becc. and can reasonably assume that the palms found on Madura are of the same species. These palms are now to be distinguished from those of India and Ceylon, which continue to bear the original name, *Borassus flabellifer* Linn. For the purposes of discussion, it is still possible to follow the established convention and refer to the Indonesian palm as the ''lontar'' and the Indian palm as the ''palmyra.'' The geographical dividing line between these two species has yet to be determined. The specific differences that exist between these palms are mainly evident at the microscopic level; they certainly do not seem to have affected popular views of the palm, nor do they appear to be a critical factor in its utilization. From India to Roti the techniques for tapping this palm are barely distinguishable. Cognate forms of its accepted Sanskrit name, *tala,* can be traced as far east as Sumbawa and Makassar. While these do not prove an Indian origin of the lontar, they do point to a borrowing of techniques and of terminology. The natural history of this palm must await further study based on thorough botanical research.[7] The field is open and in the interim, with the materials at hand, this study will be concerned with the Asian *Borassus* in both its forms.[8]

THE SOCIAL USE OF THE ASIAN *BORASSUS*

Although the distribution of this Asian *Borassus* extends, as Burkill has indicated, from the Persian Gulf through India to both mainland and island
southeast Asia, the concentration of the palm in certain areas, as opposed to
its sporadic occurrence, determines its significance for human utilization.
Such concentrations are found in a wide belt north of Bombay down the
entire Malabar coast, in the northern areas of Ceylon (particularly the Jaffna
region), then upward along the Coromandel coast with immense numbers in
Madras and still appreciable numbers well into Bihar. In Burma it is said
that the *Borassus* abounds along the Irrawady near Ava. In Thailand it is
found along the Gulf Coast, and in Cambodia its largest numbers occur in
the southern regions of the delta from Kompong-chnang through Phnom
Penh to Takeo and Kampot, and from there into the lower Mekong of south
Vietnam. In Indonesia the largest concentrations of lontar are found in east
Java, on the island of Madura, on the islands of the Lesser Sundas, and in
southern Celebes.

Given its importance and its wide distribution, this tree has been accorded
literally hundreds of names. "Lontar," the term used in this study, is its
Malay name—the name established in the Dutch literature on Indonesia.
Originally, however, the Dutch referred to it as the *jagerboom*. The Portuguese saw this tree as the palm par excellence and named it *palmeira*, which
eventually was adopted in English as "palmyra." But the British in India
also called it the "brab tree." In Indochina the French referred to it as the
rondier, although in Africa they used this same term for the African *Borassus*
and a number of other tappable palms.

In Sanskrit the lontar is called *tala*, and it is known by cognates of this
word in related Indian languages—*tal* in Bengali, and *tal gaha* in Singhal-
ese. In south India the tree has been subject to finer discriminations. There
are separate terms for a young tree, a male tree, and a female tree. A general
term in Tamil, according to Ferguson, is *panay-maram* and in Telegu, *tate-
chuttu*. In Cambodian it is called *dom thuot;* in Vietnamese *cay thot lot;* in
Thai, *tanta note*. In Java the palm is generally known as *siwalan,* but also as
ental or *tal*. On Madura, as in south India, male and female palms are distinguished by different names. The male palm is called *manjangan* or *tagha-
jan;* the female, by the Sanskrit-derived term *ta'al* or *ta'alan*. Cognates of
this Sanskrit word can be traced further eastward through the islands: on
Lombok, *tal;* in Bima on Sumbawa, *ta'a;* and in Makassar and Salayar, *tola*.
To the south of these islands, in parts of Flores, the tree is *kori* or *koli,* and
this term's cognates can be traced northward to Ceram (*kolir watan*) and

eastward to Kei (*koil*). On Roti and Timor, it is *tua;* on Savu, *duwe;* on Solor, *tuak pokang*. Of all these terms tuak causes the most confusion since, in popular Malay, the term is used to refer to any local palm (which can also be an arenga or coconut) that is tapped to obtain juice to be made into liquor. Thus tuak may refer to a variety of trees, their juice, and their fermented by-products. In the ethnographic literature the frequent references to tuak-drinking provide little information.

The spread of the Sanskrit or south Indian terminology for the tree and its parts raises the obvious question of the origin of the techniques for utilizing the palm. In large areas of south India, for example, the word *ola* (*olla*) refers to the lengths of dried lontar leaf which were used, traditionally, as writing strips and were then bound together in manuscript volumes. On Java, Madura, and Bali, ola was used to refer to similar strips of lontar leaf. On Roti, however, where the word ola can also be found, it refers to the dried strips of lontar leaf that are folded in certain forms to represent the ancestors. These clearly traceable appearances of a diffused Indian influence have led most commentators to assume an Indian origin for Indonesian forms of tapping. Most authors have gone further and assumed the diffusion from India of the palm itself. While the botanical evidence for the spread of the lontar is now disputed, it still could be that the traditional techniques were applied to an almost indistinguishable palm species without any appreciable change in results. The basic techniques of palm-tapping are virtually the same on Roti and in south India. This may, however, have a great deal to do with the fact that there seems to be only one way of extracting a continuous flow of juice from the palm. Certain peripheral techniques of tapping, particularly the use on both Roti and Madura of a lontar-leaf bucket for collecting juice, appear to represent an advance over Indian techniques, while the astonishing diversity of commercial products into which extracts of the palm are transformed by Indian tapping castes represent a clear advance over Indonesian uses. The spread of Sanskrit terms, which continues even today in Indonesia, cannot be taken as definitive; nearly everywhere, these terms occur as a "higher" form of speech (as do Sanskrit terms in Dravidian-speaking areas of India) in coincidence with local terms. Tapping in India has a long traceable history, yet folk traditions claim that tapping castes came to their present areas from the south, primarily from Ceylon, another area of intensive palm-tapping. On balance, there is no conclusive evidence of origin, but present appearances point clearly to India and Ceylon.[8]

From even the most cursory survey of the *Borassus* emerge a number of characteristic associations linked with the palm and with the social groups who obtain their living from it. The *Borassus* is the poor man's palm. In

India those who tap these trees are members of the lowest castes, and elsewhere it is normally the poor, the landless, and—by definition—the nonagriculturalist who must rely most heavily on the palm. Ferguson, in 1850, was one of the first to note this fact:

> It is not the wholesomeness or nourishing qualities of the edible products of the Palmyra tree that make it so important to the inhabitants of India; but simply the fact, that thousands, perhaps millions of the people can procure these from their Palmyra groves, or purchase them for a low rate from their neighbours; whilst Rice and other articles of food, are frequently so expensive as to be placed beyond their means. The Palmyra tree is, in this respect, what the Potato has so long been to the poor Irish and Scotch.[9]

Borassus sugar is "native" sugar. Compared to sugarcane, the *Borassus* palm is more efficient as a sucrose-producing plant. Commercially, however, the various difficulties of extracting juice, maintaining yield, and slowing inversion have prevented the palm from becoming the focus of systematic cultivation. In areas of colonial control, the lontar was never successfully commercialized. This does not mean that its products never entered the market, but rather that the market was an internal one and that, during the colonial period, it was not monitored as the export market was. For a few years the French in Cambodia attempted to arrive at some idea of the production of *Borassus* sugar. In 1897, for example, the agricultural service estimated the output at just under 2.5 million kilograms, all but a fraction of which was for "consumption and utilization within Cambodia."[10] For many a Javanese peasant, it seems to have been the case that he produced cane sugar for export under the colonial regime while he himself consumed lontar sugar.

Besides associations with the poor, the literature on the *Borassus* gives the impression that those who live from these trees are generally unreliable, unaccountable, and, worst of all, untaxable. Half-settled, usually in areas with an overabundance of palms, practicing a profession whose techniques are only partially understood by their neighbors, selecting their palms from a myriad of seemingly similar trees, and extracting undetermined quantities of a somewhat suspect juice, palm-tappers have usually been considered by those who have had to deal with them as the wastrels of society. Since everywhere the lontar is associated with the production of liquor, the poor toddy-tappers were often, as a class, branded as shiftless drunkards whose lowly condition was itself the result of constant inebriation. Not just colonial government officials but upholders of orthodoxy in Hinduism, Buddhism, and

Islam have seen in the tapping profession a degrading and corrupting way of life. In India, for example, with independence and the establishment of prohibition, the tapping industry suffered considerably. Producers of *Borassus* sugar were suspected of illegal traffic in alcohol. Bootlegging was added to their crimes.[11]

To a few, however (mainly missionaries and occasional foreigners), lontar-tappers have appeared not as persons justifiably condemned to the lowest rungs of society but as children of nature who, though superficially corrupted, were blessed in abundance for their simple life. Yet it remains a curious fact that both their detractors and their advocates have agreed that the only means to social improvement for palm-tappers was an alteration in their way of life. In all the cases we are to consider, status improvement for these palm-tappers has meant the abandonment of palm-tapping. In approaching the subject of comparative palm-tapping, one has to deal with a mode of food production that has indeed supported millions of people, but one that has been generally ignored, only rarely described, and when recognized at all, has usually been condemned.

CHAPTER NINE

Three Case Studies
of *Borassus* Utilization

TO GAIN SOME idea of the potential of *Borassus* utilization and its variations, we must consider specific instances of its use—three case studies from areas of intensive exploitation. The first case will be a detailed examination of the Rotinese use of the lontar and will elaborate on what was only briefly sketched earlier in this study. It will reflect on previous considerations and establish the starting point for a new set of comparisons. The second case for comparison will be that of the Madurese, an Islamic lontar-tapping people who live on an island off the northeast coast of Java. This case is of particular interest because it deals with another Indonesian population noted for its reliance on the lontar palm. The Madurese are a people who are religiously and culturally distinct from the Rotinese. More significantly, they have pursued their exploitation of the lontar within a region of Indonesia that is historically famous for the commercial production of sugar. The third case cannot be narrowly focused, but relates generally to the tapping populations of south India, and specifically to the Nadar or Shanar caste groups of the Tinnevelly District of Madras. All of these Tamil-speaking groups were Hindu until about the beginning of the nineteenth century. Their exploitation of palms forms part of the traditional Indian hierarchical pattern of social specialization and is difficult to consider except in relation to this hierarchy. Since the nineteenth century these caste groups have attempted by various means to alter their social position within the hierarchy. Not unlike the Rotinese, many have converted to Christianity and have resorted to western education for their advancement.

THE ROTINESE CASE: THE ETHNOBOTANY OF THE LONTAR

The lontar is a massive dioecious palm with solitary trunk and thick, broadly based, spiny-edged leafstalks that mount wide, fan-like fronds. At its crown are lateral inflorescences with slight fibrous sheaths. The inflorescences on the male palm develop branched rachillae on which appear numerous tiny flowers that open in basipetal succession, about one flower each day; the inflorescences on the female palm develop clusters of large, dark, smooth-skinned fruit consisting of a fibrous pulp surrounding one to three seeds. This, in a few lines, is a reasonable, semitechnical description of the lontar palm. Not surprisingly, the distinctions in this somewhat cumbersome description translate effortlessly into Rotinese. The Rotinese terminology is as follows:

(a) The palm itself is *tua;* the male palm is *tua mane,* the female palm is *tua feto.*

(b) The trunk of the tree is *tua-huk; huk* being the "counter" term for trees (*tua-huk hitu:* "seven trunks of lontar").

(c) The leafstalk itself (the petiole proper) is *beba tua* or *tua-beba;* the spines on the leafstalk are the *nggou.*

(d) The young leafshoots are *tua-polok* and these develop into the full fan leaf, the *sosonga* (also *songa-dok* or *sosonga-dok*).

(e) The spine or back of each leaf section of the full fan is the *lidak;* as such, *lidak* is used as the counter term for leafsections (*sosonga lidak hitu:* "seven sections of leaf," the number needed to make a certain type of basket).

(f) The entire inflorescence, whether on a male or a female palm, including its sheath and branches (*ai*), is the *sumak.*

(g) The open sheathing spathes around the peduncle are the *tua-tapis* or *tapi-tua.*

(h) The inflorescence of the male tree with its branches or rachillae is the *tua-nggi;* the rachillae are the *tua-pule.*

(i) The tiny flowers of the male tree are the *tua-buna;* these flowers appear "singly in repeated succession," *kikisa.*

(j) The fruit of the female tree is the *saiboa;* its fibrous flesh is the *saiboa sesek* and its seeds the *saiboa deëk.*

We can consider the lontar palm in terms of the products of its major parts, which are its trunk, fruit, leafstalk, fan leaf or frond, and the juice or sap that issues from its inflorescences.

Tab. X.

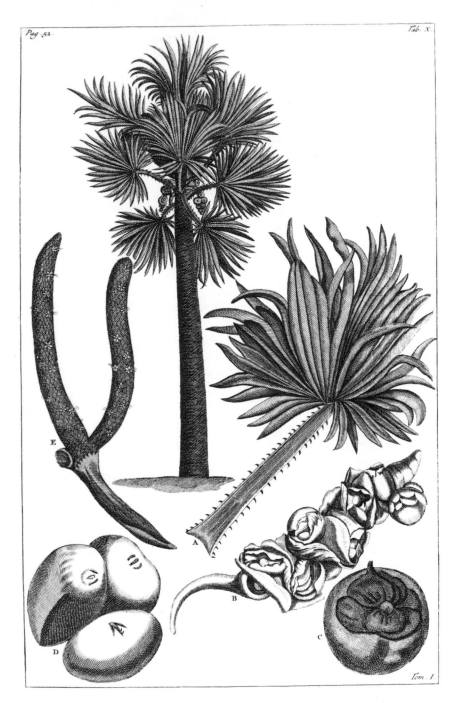

A drawing of the lontar palm from G. E. Rumphius' *Het Amboinsche Kruydboek* (1741), showing (*A*) a leafstalk; (*B*) a female inflorescence with young fruit; (*C*) the fruit; (*D*) three seeds; and (*E*) a male inflorescence with tiny flowers.

(*a*) *The Trunk*. From the trunk comes lumber for a wide variety of purposes. Felling a tree for lumber prevents the further use of its other parts. The older a tree grows, the harder its wood becomes; hence the better its yield of hard timber. As a general rule among the Rotinese, older trees are felled for their lumber. These happen to be the tallest and therefore the most dangerous and difficult to climb. It would be considered foolish to fell a young, productive tree and even trees that are not productive of juice can still be pruned of their leaves. If a choice had to be made, however, an unproductive tree would certainly be felled before a juice-producing palm. The male palm is said to have a harder, darker wood than the female and is therefore preferred for lumber. Female trees, on the other hand, are said to produce more juice; but tapping them requires more effort, for their inflorescences are less easily crushed to initiate the flow of juice. Furthermore, there is the question of distance. A tapper prefers to work a number of trees that are near one another, so that a lone tree a fair distance from other trees would be an ideal candidate for felling. Thus, as a set of decisions: older trees are preferred to younger ones, nonproductive trees to productive ones, males to females, and lone trees to those that are part of a cluster. Certain cultural rules also affect, in a minor way, the cutting of trees. If a tapper dies in a fall from a tree, the offending lontar must be felled for his coffin. For symbolic reasons, women ought to be buried in a coffin made from the trunk of a female lontar, men in a coffin made from a male lontar. But the discussion of calculated choice in regard to the felling of trees is somewhat academic since, for Rotinese in most areas, there is a surplus of untapped trees. Trees for lumber are utilized chiefly for building and for household needs. On Roti, the production of lumber has not been organized into an industry.

(*b*) *The Fruit*. Rotinese make little use of the fruit of the lontar. There are a few trivial uses to which an occasional lontar fruit is put; for example, in the distillation of Rotinese gin, capping a cooking pot with the fibrous flesh of the fruit imparts a pleasantly sweet taste to the liquor. Most lontar fruit, however, is left to rot on the ground where it falls. On occasion, pigs eat some of it but there is no conscious attempt to use lontar fruit as a source of pig feed. With no great pressure yet on the supply of trees, the thought of planting lontar seeds is considered slightly ridiculous; as a result, there is no market for the seed. From a comparative point of view, given the many possible uses of *Borassus* fruit, the Rotinese neglect of it indicates a disregard for one of the major potentials of this palm.

(*c*) *The Leafstalk*. A lontar palm is crowned with anywhere from 30 to 60 leafstalks, each of which opens into a wide fan leaf. A leafstalk can grow to

1.5 meters in length, and a fully formed leaf may have a radius of almost a meter with approximately 60 folds to its fan. The average number of leaves is about 40 per tree. Since a palm grows at its apex, the rhythm of leaf succession is an index of its growth. Leaves open, grow out, yellow, and eventually fall, leaving the cicatrices that ring the trunk of the palm. This succession of leaves has a regular and calculable interval.[1] Empirical studies indicate that the lontar forms 12 to 14 leaves a year and that the life of a leaf is between 3 and 4 years.[2] However, the pruning of a palm for leaf and leafstalk has an effect on the growth of leaves and, in fact, on the growth of the entire tree and its production of juice.

This raises a question which, though seemingly trivial, is fundamental to palm-tapping. Careless pruning can destroy a tree or render it unproductive. For reasons that are not yet fully understood, the productive life of a tree and the level of its yield of juice are dependent on selective pruning. I have never heard Rotinese make any direct statements that would connect pruning with the yield of juice. But given what is known of *Borassus* palms, the traditional methods of pruning seem intended to maximize juice production. Trees are always pruned of their leaves before they are tapped, but they are not denuded. More importantly, they are cleared of their oldest leaf structures—which are, in fact, for the Rotinese more useful than the young leaves.

A leaf structure is both a hard fibrous stalk and a wide fan leaf. The products of these parts must be considered separately. Leafstalks (*tua-beba*) may be interlaced to make excellent material for fences, or may be used to make partitions in a house, or may be worked to make ropes, bridles, halters, and a host of other products. Normally, however, they are not. This is because Rotinese palm utilization is based on two palms. The gewang and the lontar occur in equally large numbers and in close proximity on the island. The leafstalk of the gewang (*tula-beba*) is a harder, longer-lasting stalk than that of the lontar. For any use for which Rotinese need a leafstalk (with the exception of cheap firing material for the cooking ovens) the gewang leafstalk is superior and therefore reduces significantly the need to prune lontars for their leaf structures. The effect of this is to safeguard the lontar palms for tapping.

(*d*) *The Leaf.* Structurally, the leafstalks of gewang and lontar are similar; their leaves, however, are markedly different. The lontar has a broad undivided fan leaf; the gewang's fan leaf extends outward in long narrow spikes. There are certain products for which only the gewang is suitable; its layered leaf is strong and durable and it can be woven into a variety of forms. The thin, tough, inner layers of the leaf are especially needed for tying threads in patterns for the dyeing process in tie-and-dye weaving; they are also wound and woven to make coarse clothes (*lapik*) for work in the fields. Since it can be separated into layers, the gewang leaf does not dry as a flexible, indivisible strip, nor can it be split into fine slivers or rasped thin as the lontar leaf can. Since it is an undivided fan leaf, it is less suitable for making leaf-buckets. For buckets as well as for most basketry, for hats, and for cigarette paper, the lontar leaf is more commonly used. The ribs or spines of the lontar leaf have a number of special uses as well: for stringing objects, or for braiding to make small, porous containers for meat. Finally, the broad lontar leaf is used for thatch. Discarded lontar leaves—the remains of a season's pruning, old basketry, and former thatch—are burned to fertilize the gardens. Therefore, while the gewang alleviates some of the need for pruning, it does not relieve it entirely. The two palms function together. The dual exploitation of both palms, and especially of their leaf products, is a distinctive feature of the Rotinese palm economy.[3]

(*e*) *The Juice from the Inflorescences.* The physiology of sap circulation in the lontar is still only poorly understood.[4] In palms, starch reserves are converted to sugar and are transported upward toward the stem apex. In the lontar, men breach this apex via the inflorescence. By injuring the fibrovascular tissues of the inflorescence, they induce a flow of sweet juice. On the evidence of *Borassus*-tappers throughout Asia, a partial crown of leaves is necessary for the tapping of trees. A limited pruning of young trees induces an earlier flow of juice, but total pruning has exactly the opposite effect.

The amount of juice that a lontar can produce is prodigious. A palm with five productive inflorescences will, by my calculations, yield an average of over 6.7 liters of juice a day or 47 liters in a week, while a palm with only one inflorescence will still produce about 2.25 liters of juice or over 15 liters a week. Were a tree to produce at its maximum for only one month, it would yield over 200 liters of juice or—at a conversion rate of approximately 15 percent—over 30 liters of cooked syrup.[5] Minimally, a tree with but one productive inflorescence would yield 67.5 liters of juice in a month or about 10 liters of syrup. Given the fact that a Rotinese is capable of tapping 20 to 25 palms and, with skill, would certainly be able to keep them producing near the maximum for two months and perhaps longer, simple arithmetic should indicate the potential productive capacity of these palms.[6]

The fact is, however, that the Rotinese tap their palms to meet their needs. Since most households produce for themselves and since there is only a very limited market for the sale of the syrup or hardened sugar, there is no attempt on Roti to maximize the full productive capacity of the island's palms. Tapping a few trees at the time of their first blossoming and intensive tapping for about six weeks to two months after their second blossoming will provide a sufficiency for the rest of the year. At most a man will tap 10 to 15 trees during this peak period, and even if they are not his own trees and he has to give a portion of his yield to the owner of the trees, he will still have more than enough for both his family and his animals.

Given a situation of some surplus, there is an advantage—especially for owners of a few scattered trees—to tapping someone else's trees, provided they form a large enough cluster. The consolidation of potentially productive trees is probably the first criterion for efficient and intensive lontar-tapping. Efficiency from the tapper's point of view has less to do with obtaining a maximum yield than it does with obtaining a satisfactory yield with a minimum of labor. A grouping ideally should have from 10 to 20 palms and should contain more palms than are actually tapped at any one time. (This is because not all trees blossom at exactly the same time. Thus if the yield from certain palms drops off as others begin to blossom, a tapper has some leeway to switch trees.)

Height is also an important factor. The taller the tree, the more difficult and the more dangerous it is to climb. Preference is therefore given to tapping younger, shorter palms, and this also ensures that the same cluster may be used several years in succession.

Another factor is the location of the cluster in relation to the cooking area. At the height of the tapping season, quantities of juice are gathered and must be cooked as soon as possible after collection. Transporting this juice a considerable distance can be a disadvantage, for sugar inversion begins and the juice sours rapidly. Cooking during this period is an unrelieved occupation that must be done throughout the early part of the day and late in the evening. While the cooking is preferably done near the tapper's house, it is also possible to erect ovens near the main cluster of trees. In brief, ideal conditions involve a consolidated cluster of relatively young palms near the household where their yield is to be cooked.

ROTINESE TECHNIQUES OF LONTAR-TAPPING

Seven simple instruments are employed in tapping (*ledi*):

(*a*) The *kakabik* is a pair of wooden tongs, roughly a yard in length and tied at one end to form an effective vice or pressing instrument.

(*b*) The *boboik* is a simple water container made from the hollowed shell of a coconut into which is inserted a long neck or spout of bamboo.

(*c*) The *kikik* is a short broom-like instrument, made by beating and fraying one end of a fibrous lontar leafstalk.

(*d*) Three kinds of *haik*, or carrying buckets made of lontar leaf, are used in tapping. The smallest is the *hai seseluk*, which is hung in the tree to catch the lontar juice. There is always a pair of hai seseluk for each inflorescence bundle. The second haik is the *hai kuneuk*, which is carried by the climber to the crown of the tree to gather the juice from the various hai seseluk; the third haik is the *hai sasalik*, into which is poured the combined juice from numerous ascents.

(e) The *kepisak* is a small rude basket of lontar leaf, which supports each juice-catching hai seseluk that hangs in the crown of the tree.

(f) The *kakaik* is a double-hooked piece of buffalo horn. One end is tucked over the belt of the tapper, while on the other end hang the kakabik, boboik, and haik.

(g) The *dope* is a convenient hand-size knife with a small sharp blade. A *dope-tuak* can be used for no other purpose. This knife must be razor sharp and is usually resharpened each morning before the tapper begins to climb.

In selecting his tree, the tapper chooses male trees with well-developed inflorescences (*tua nggi nanda*), all of whose branched rachillae have emerged (*basa-basa nggi pule-na kalua nala deak*) and begun to produce tiny individual flowers (*nggi pule-na nabuna kikisa*). Female palms must be chosen just before their inflorescences begin to develop fruit; if the fruit has already begun to develop, the Rotinese insist that it is no longer possible to tap the tree. As it is, the labor involved in crushing or squeezing the inflorescence is greater than for a male palm. This is enough to produce a definite bias in favor of tapping male palms, even though females are said to produce more juice. In my limited experience, it would seem that if a man decides to tap only a few trees, he will tend to choose female palms. By expending more labor initially, he will reduce his climbing labor later. Men who tap many trees, on the other hand, tend to tap male palms.[7]

The preparation of a tree is done in several stages. First, the tree must be prepared for climbing. Methods vary in different parts of the island. In west Roti and parts of central Roti, trees are permanently notched for climbing. According to a local myth, which is a simple ad hoc explanation of clearly observable practices, this notching was done by a man from the sea who began notching trees in Ndao and stopped in Termanu when his machete grew dull. In east Roti, the leafstalks from either the gewang or the lontar are tightly bound to the trunk of the tree to form a kind of ladder. An alternative method of climbing in east Roti is by means of a circlet of fiber or buffalo hide (*lalabak*) into which one slips both feet to mount the tree.

On his first ascent a tapper cleans the crown of the tree, cuts away awkward or broken leafstalks, and removes the thorny spines from the sides of

A Rotinese squeezing the inflorescences at the crown of a male lontar palm prior to tapping.

those that remain. To each of the inflorescences he is likely to use, the tapper ties a leafstalk for additional support. He then waits for the flowering of the rachillae on the inflorescence; when this occurs, he climbs again to cut the interfering spathes and to break off the rachillae he does not intend to tap. He takes the remaining rachillae between the tongs of his *kakabik* and softens them by squeezing. This is said to open wide the inner tissues of the spikes and promote the flow of juice (*mbule mata-na namaloa de oe-na nakando*). The inflorescence is left for two or three days and is then squeezed again. The second squeezing is called the *na-male tua:* "the softening (or weakening) of the lontar." After this final weakening, all the rachillae on each inflorescence are bound together and left for another day or two.[8]

The next stage is called the *dulun:* "the tying in order." The bonds holding the bundles of rachillae are undone and the rachillae are retied, usually in groups of two; the peduncle or base of the inflorescence is broken or bent so that all of its rachillae hang downward. This stage is described as *basa-basa tua nggi mbule-na lakabubua nakabali nana atu dua-duak-ka:* "All the rachillae of the lontar's inflorescences are gathered together as if arranged in twos." These drooping inflorescences with their rachillae tied in pairs are now ready for tapping; the tip of each rachilla is sliced off evenly and slivered again once or twice to begin the flow of juice. At each subsequent ascent, an additional sliver is sliced from each rachilla to continue this flow. One of the great skills in tapping is to be able to sliver just enough from the rachilla, or the inflorescence in the case of the female, to continue the flow of juice. The finer the slivering, the longer the palm will produce. The flow of juice comes to an end only when the rachillae or inflorescences are reduced to their base.

The Rotinese tap their palms twice a day, in the early morning and the late afternoon. The tapper ascends the tree, carrying a small knife (dope), his water container (boboik), his brush (kikik), and a medium-sized leaf-bucket (haik). When he reaches the crown, he pours the lontar juice from all the small haik suspended in the tree into his carrying haik. He cleans each of the smaller haik with water from his boboik, brushing the inside of the haik with his kikik. At each producing pair of rachillae are hung two haik, which are used alternately to allow the other haik to dry. The Rotinese say this prevents the juice from souring. On comparative evidence, it turns out to be a critical feature of Rotinese tapping. By using two haik, one of which is cleaned and left in the sun to dry, the Rotinese have developed their own means of slowing the fermentation of the fresh juice. Instead of using clean receptacles, other populations add various kinds of inhibitors that lessen fermentation but also render the fresh juice unpleasant to drink.

In the crown of each tree there may be as many as five or more producing inflorescences, each with two haik and one lontar basket (kepisak) to protect the receiving haik. When a tapper has emptied all the haik, cleaned and exchanged them, and cut a sliver from the spiked tips of all the rachillae or inflorescences, he descends, adds what he has gathered to his large collecting haik (hai sasalik), and ascends another tree. He continues until he has finished his round of trees and carries the accumulated juice home to be cooked.

By Rotinese calculations, all lontar produce twice as much juice during the night as they do during the day. A morning's ascent should yield twice as much juice as an evening's ascent. But reducing climbing to once a day does not effectively gain two-thirds the yield for half the labor. The heat of the day turns the collected juice sour. The critical Rotinese tapping procedures—and indeed those of other lontar-tappers—are intended to prevent this souring. Tapping once a day gains only a sour inferior yield. To Rotinese, the tapping of trees twice a day is a mark of intensive tapping. In their legends it is seen as a major step in the development of their lontar economy.

Lontar-tapping is confined to the dry season. Since on Roti this dry season comprises as much as nine months of the year, there are two distinct tapping periods within the dry season. In the Rotinese division of their year, there exist two seasons. The dry season (*fai hanas*) is associated with the east monsoon (*ani timu*), while the wet season (*oe fak*) is associated with the west monsoon (*ani mulis*). In actuality, the winds are variable and these seasons are not tidy bisections. The west wind begins sometime in December, bringing with it occasional rain; it begins to slacken by March. April is unpredictable; it is the month when dangerous tropical cyclones may swing in from the northeast. By May the east wind begins and rises in intensity until in July it has become a strong, gusty, desiccating force. In August it slackens, and October and much of November are the calm windless months that precede the west monsoon. What is considered the dry season may begin as early as mid-March and extend to December.

Lontar-tapping is explicitly attuned to the winds. Implicitly it is attuned to the blossoming inflorescences of the palms. The two periods for tapping are the *tua timu* and the *tua fanuk* (or simply *fanuk*). Tua timu refers to the tapping period at the beginning of the east monsoon, tua fanuk to the tapping period after the east wind has subsided. These correspond to the two periods in the year when the palm's inflorescences blossom. Studies on the Indonesian lontar identify these two blossoming periods, at the same time revealing that growth of the tree's inflorescence is greatest during the east monsoon.[9] This explains why the yield during fanuk greatly exceeds that during tua timu.

Between mid-March and mid-April tappers prepare their trees. Late April is usually the beginning of tua timu, and tapping continues through the months of May and June. The labor of this tapping period is borne almost exclusively by men. Most of the juice that is gathered is drunk directly; very little of it is cooked to syrup. Most of what is cooked is made into hard sugar (*tua batu*) and sold. One practical reason is that women have little time for cooking; May and June are the months of harvest and women are mainly occupied in the fields.

In July and early August tapping decreases and the east wind mounts. The lontar buckets, it is said, are agitated by the wind in the trees and their juice sours quickly. Because of the wind, climbing is risky. Furthermore, with most of the harvest in, there is usually sufficient food. Fishing is also good and herds are at about their fattest, having fed on the grass of the early dry season and having been left to pasture on the stubble of the harvested fields. These are the months of feasting. They are also the time for major construction, such as house-building and stone-fencing around the lala fields. From Thie and Dengka especially, there is often an exodus of laborers to work on

A young Rotinese woman plaiting lontar leaf.

this kind of construction in east Roti, particularly Termanu. Tappers, therefore, either limit the number of trees they tap or cease entirely.

Tapping resumes in earnest in late August or early September. Fanuk includes the months of September and October and may extend into November. The Rotinese view this period as a progression that rises to a pitch and then tapers off slowly. Its initial segment is *fanu mbedak;* its intensive segment is *fanu nambesak;* its decline is *fanu loe-na.* Emphasis is on the cooking process, women's work from which there can be no relief. A steady fire is required, and the boiling pots need constant tending, since the cooling juice tends to spill over suddenly. Froth must be continually ladled off and saved for the pigs. The cook must be ready with what is called a *dodombok* (a leaf-stalk, branch, or piece of dried coconut on the end of a stick) to thrust it into the bubbling pot just as it is about to spill over. The intensive segment of fanuk is referred to by the phrase *lao-la balanggeo:* "the blackening of the cooking ovens." The early rains that signal the end of fanuk are called the *uda poli-afuk:* "rains that soak the ash." This rain ends the tapping season, and the cooked syrup is stored in pots and vats within the house.

CRITICAL FEATURES OF THE ROTINESE *BORASSUS* ECONOMY

Estimates of the number of lontar on Roti always run into the hundreds of thousands. Ormeling had access to the report of a Dutch forestry expert, Th. Rahm, who surveyed the island in 1923. One local estimate for this period set the number of lontar palms at 150,000 and gewang palms at 100,000. According to Ormeling, Rahm considered these local estimates remarkably low. He himself considered the number of palms on Roti to be "far greater," but he did not hazard a more likely estimate.[10] Although lontar grow throughout the island, they are so irregularly scattered and clustered that any exact calculation of their number is extremely difficult. I can only venture to guess that there are at least 500,000 lontar on Roti.

Rahm also noted in his report that there was a considerable differential in the number of trees owned by individuals, varying "from some tens to many hundreds of trees per owner," but with many Rotinese possessing no trees at all.[11] The ownership of trees is one of the most difficult topics on which to obtain information. Unlike coconuts, lontar are not marked by their owners and trees abound everywhere, individually and in large numbers. Where they occur individually, they are counted by trunk (*huk*); where they occur in large numbers, they are reckoned in clumps or clusters (*nanga*). At best, a stone or two may mark the boundaries between clusters. The ownership of trees provides a potential source of litigation, and trees are indeed the cause of numerous court cases. Given the vagaries of ownership and the Rotinese predilection for litigation, it is surprising that there are not more disputes than do occur.

Most trees belong to the nobles and the rich, who themselves have only a general idea of the number of trees they possess. Some higher nobles, clan lords, and a few rich persons do not tap their trees. Some claim, as a sign of status, that they would be incapable of climbing a tree. By contrast, there are many commoners who own no trees at all and many more who own only a few. Most commoners and a large percentage of the noble class, unless physically disabled, tap trees. With a surplus of trees, those who do not own their own are not at too great a disadvantage, since there is competition among tree-owners to find, attract, and hold men who will tap for them. The tapper makes a payment in cooked lontar syrup (called *kefek*) to the owner of the trees he taps. The traditional payment varies from state to state. In central and east Roti kefek is lower than in west Roti, particularly Thie and Dengka where the demand on the trees is greater. In Termanu, for example, the traditional kefek is said to vary between one *blek* of syrup (19.5 liters) per ten trees to one blek regardless of the number of trees tapped during the season. In all the specific cases on which I have reliable data, however, kefek was decided upon after some bargaining between the tree-owner and the tapper. Most of these negotiations are worked out among kinsmen and are often settled in quantities of less than a blek—in "small pots" or *nggusi ana* that contain only 10 liters. Kefek is always determined for a clump of trees and for one season, but before that season begins; so the risk or advantage falls to the tapper depending on the number of inflorescences the palms put forth during the season.

Obviously, heavier demand for trees results in higher kefek payments. A kefek demand that is too high, however, is disadvantageous to any owner of a large number of trees, since it will force tappers to look elsewhere. It is possible that high kefek may have been a stimulus to the nineteenth-century emigration to Timor. More often, it can lead to temporary shifts of labor not only from one tree-owner to another within a particular state, but also from owners in one state to owners in another. At present, the somewhat lower kefek payments that can be negotiated in Termanu attract temporary labor from both Dengka and Korbaffo, though not on a very large scale. As long as there remains a surplus of trees in the Timor area, kefek cannot be too onerous. And the clear indication is that the limits on lontar-tapping for Roti in particular, and for the area as a whole in general, have not yet been reached.

One of the most important features of the Rotinese economy, then, is this surplus of palms. Equally important is the lack of any developed market for palm products. Lontar utilization, particularly on Roti, is still largely for subsistence needs. In the Kupang area, there is a limited market for leaf-stalks for building. Fresh juice is actually sold by peddlers in the streets of the town, and thin cakes of crystallized sugar are regularly sold in the local market. There is also some demand for lontar syrup to be distilled to make gin. Most of these products are supplied by the Rotinese on Timor.[12] It would seem that the Rotinese emigration to Timor has made the economy of the island of Roti even more subsistence-oriented than it was a century ago. The Rotinese settled in and around Kupang now supply a great deal of the demand that previously was met directly from Roti.

Wealth on Roti can be reckoned in a variety of goods. Gold is a form that can be displayed or sold. Livestock can be killed for feasts or sold from time to time, mainly to the few Chinese merchants who live in Baä. (Pigs and chicken can easily be transported by perahu for sale in Kupang.) Rice, maize, millet, and sorghum can also be sold, and there is always some demand for agricultural products in Kupang. Rice, especially, can be used for feasting. But lontar syrup—the primary subsistence food—ranks least among all these forms of wealth. A tapper will offer fresh juice to anyone who encounters him at work and every visitor must, at the very least, be given syrup mixed with water (*tua hopo*). This has been a Rotinese tradition since Rumphius described it in the seventeenth century.

One factor that puts a price on syrup is the demand for gin. All official stills are licensed by the government and the price of a license is, relatively speaking, very high. The cost of a bottle of gin, therefore, reflects the price of the license more than the cost of the syrup. The whole system results in a great deal of illicit distilling. Fermented lontar beer (*lalu*) can also be a substitute for gin. The government recognizes this fact and, at certain times of the year, allows everyone to distill their own liquor without license. Thus even the demand for gin can be met at the individual household level.

In 1972, when I tried to determine the price of a lontar palm, I was told that the cost would be 500 rupiah or approximately $1.25. This would be an extraordinarily low price to pay for a productive tree that might yield 200 to 400 liters of juice a year for 20 or more years, but the point was, of course, that the price was an arbitrary quotation to answer a naive question. Although they may be transferred among individuals, lontar trees are not bought or sold. The market has not yet begun to affect this basic mode of production.

It is possible to summarize the critical features that distinguish this particular *Borassus* economy. An important factor relative to other such economies is that Rotinese are able to convert extra sugar production to animal protein via their pigs. The fact that they do this on an ever-increasing scale, as lontar production increases, has already been established. Also significant is the fact that lontar utilization is not an exclusive occupation. It forms the pivot to the economy, since syrup is the key to intensive animal husbandry, and leaves, as fertilizer, are the key to intensive gardening. But a Rotinese tapper is not bound to his trees alone. At the same time that he is a tapper, he may also be a cultivator, a fisherman, and a herder. Neither economic pressures nor social institutions confine him to a single occupation. By the nature of this labor, he has time to engage in other pursuits and even indulge in education.

In terms of technique, the double-haik method for collecting fresh juice must be seen as a superb solution to one of the most difficult problems of tapping—how to retard fermentation. It is a solution that allows the Rotinese to drink fresh juice for half the year without having to depend entirely on syrup, which is a reduced product. Also, the reliance on gewang for leaves alleviates the need for overpruning of the lontar which, in turn, would affect the production of juice.

Finally, it should be noted that, despite the importance of the lontar, there is very little ritual and a minimum of legend or mythology associated with the tree and the processes of production. The Rotinese view the development of their lontar economy in historical terms. The two features that they consider to mark the full exploitation of the lontar are double-tapping —morning and evening—and the creation of the underground cooking oven, exactly the same sort of oven that fascinated Cook on his visit to Savu. (In Appendix D, I provide a commentary and translation of some verses and the major legend from Termanu about the lontar.) What is interesting is that the Rotinese in Termanu attribute these innovations either to someone who came from Thie or to a Ndaonese resident of Thie. In west Roti and especially in Thie, lontar-tapping is attributed to Ndaonese or Savunese influence. Savunese, in turn, attribute their knowledge of tapping to legendary figures who came from the western region of Indonesia. In view of these traditions, it is useful to consider another area of intensive lontar-tapping, the northeastern portion of the island of Madura, which lies some 600 miles to the west of Roti.

THE MADURESE CASE:
MARKET DEMANDS ON LONTAR PRODUCTS

Madura lies off the northern coast of the eastern hook of Java, at the center of what is regarded as Inner Island Indonesia. This is the area of Indonesia's highest population concentration. Unlike Java with its tropical climate, lush volcanic soils, and proverbial fertility, Madura is a dry island and suffers a long, hot east monsoon. The eastern sections of Madura, along a line from Sepulu to Pamekasan, are the driest parts of the island. Throughout this area the center of which is Sumenep, the lontar flourishes. The palms abound on low limestone hills, the least fertile of Madura's soils.

Madura has more than climatic similarities to Roti and Savu. The island is a source of considerable emigration—to a number of islands, but mainly to Java. Surabaya, like Kupang for the Rotinese, has been the urban magnet that has attracted Madurese; but this migration has extended, not inward toward central Java, but along its north coast and particularly the east hook of the island. Dutch reports in the nineteenth and early twentieth centuries read much like the reports on the Rotinese penetration into Timor. Each successsive report marks a point of farthest migration and usually declares the migration will continue no farther—only to be contradicted, at a slightly later date, by one of the next reports. In contrast to the elaborate inner refinement of the traditional Javanese, the Madurese are characterized as dynamic, aggressive, and at times outwardly offensive. The unpredictable, uncontrolled Madurese have not infrequently been viewed with misgiving.

The social history of the Madurese has yet to be studied. The parallels with the Rotinese and Savunese situations can only pose a variety of questions. Madurese emigration to Java has been going on for a considerable period. In the nineteenth century, the areas into which they migrated were not as populous as they are now. Nevertheless, the Madurese have, for over a century, sustained an emigration to one of the most densely populated islands in the world. This emigration continued even after officials began to sense an impending crisis in Java's population and to consider plans for the transmigration of Javanese to other islands. And it occurred, in spite of Dutch disapproval, during a period when the ordinary village-based Javanese peasant was subjected to generally effective colonial control. The economic means by which the Madurese supported their migration have not been examined, and the role of the lontar in this regard is entirely unknown. Our consideration of the case of Madurese lontar utilization is limited to a specific period in the recent past.

In the mid-1920's, the Dutch Resident on Madura became alarmed at the wholesale pruning of lontar trees for the production of mats, mainly for export to Java. He therefore requested and commissioned the first, and seemingly the only, detailed investigation of lontar utilization in the Netherlands Indies. The investigation was undertaken jointly by an agricultural consultant, L. Gebuis, and a local agricultural superintendent, R. Abdul Kadir. Their report was published in the journal *Landbouw* in 1928-1929, and this discussion is based largely on their valuable findings.

Madurese implements and methods of tapping differ hardly at all from those of the Rotinese. But on Madura it is clear that the utilization of the lontar, while less diverse, is far more intensive in certain respects. Lontar, for example, are not left to grow where their seeds fall. During the west monsoon, the period of rain on Madura, baskets are hung in the best-producing female palms to catch their ripe fruit as they drop. There is a market for this seed fruit. The soft, ripened, sweet-smelling fruit are preserved in baskets until the onset of the next west monsoon. The seeds are then removed and are planted in orderly close proximity. Six meters is considered the proper distance between trees, so that when they have grown to full size, their leaves touch. This ensures maximum efficiency in tapping and pruning. It is possible then to connect the trees near the crowns by a kind of bamboo ramp, so that the tapper is able to move from one tree to the next without descending. He has only to lower the juice of each tree that he taps by means of a rope.

While the tapping implements and methods of the Madurese may be similar to those of the Rotinese, the fact that their palms are systematically planted and their climbing procedures are rationalized indicates a greater pressure on their trees. Even more radical are the differences in use of the palm products. On Madura, especially in the 1920's, there was already a developed and almost insatiable market for such products. Their export to Java was a well-organized fact of Madurese life. Instead of using palm products to meet subsistence needs, the Madurese tailored their utilization to meet the specific demands of a largely external market. To maintain the comparison with Roti, we can consider, in turn, the use made on Madura of the trunk, the fruit, the leaves, and the juice of the palm.

(a) *The Trunk.* The Madurese describe a special category of unproductive trees as "false" (*letjek*) trees. These produce neither juice nor fruit. They could be kept for their leaves, but are generally the first category to be felled for their wood. Firewood has long been scarce on Madura. Some young trees are reported to have been used for this purpose, while older trees were felled for timber to be used for house posts and for rafters. The price of a tree for timber, in the 1920's, was one Dutch guilder or florin, to which was added another guilder (f. 1) for the cost of felling the tree. Gebuis and Kadir give no indication that there was any kind of major timber industry on the island.

(b) *The Fruit.* A good female lontar palm may produce as many as 220 fruit, with the average being 150. During the west monsoon the palm will produce about twice as many fruit as during the east monsoon. From first appearance it takes about three months for these fruit to ripen. Some Madurese climb their trees to thin out the fruit clusters, which results in a smaller number of larger, more attractive fruit.

Unlike the Rotinese, who make little use of the fruit, the Madurese eat the ripe fruit of the lontar and reserve the best fruit for seed. The largest fruit that grow during the west monsoon season are left to ripen on the tree for about six months and then are picked for their seeds. Gebuis and Kadir calculated that the sale of the fruit of a female palm would average about one and a half guilder (f. 1.50) per year. The price of seed fruit was slightly higher than that of fruit to be eaten. The price depended upon the number of seeds: one cent for two seeds; one and a half cents for three seeds. From the hard seed nuts that were not planted, the Madurese fashioned spoons and other small utensils.

One point of comparison needs to be emphasized. That the Rotinese allow the fruit of many of their trees to ripen to the fullest and to fall where they may, in effect, leaves the propagation of new trees to chance. This relative noninterference allows certain trees the maximum natural possibilities of reproduction. On the other hand, the very fact that there is a market for fruit on Madura necessitates that, if the trees are to continue, they must be planted. The Rotinese do exert some selection on their trees, if only in a negative and indirect way, by tapping a considerable number of female palms that therefore do not bear fruit for the tapping season. Madurese selection is more direct and would seem to be more positive.

(c) *The Leaves.* The use made of the lontar's leaves marks another difference between Madura and Roti. In the 1920's, leaf-pruning for mats and baskets was a major industry on Madura. In fact, the fear of permanent damage to the palm population by unabated pruning was the reason for the Gebuis-Kadir study. To underline the seriousness of the situation, these authors quote a Madurese saying that as soon as a lontar has a stem, its pruning begins. Nowhere was the trade-off between pruning and tapping more apparent than on Madura at this time.

If a lontar palm is left intact, it can have a juice-producing life of 30 to 40 years. If it is moderately pruned on an annual basis beginning at an early stage of its growth, it can still produce juice for 20 to 30 years. There are indications that initial pruning before a tree begins to produce and modest pruning thereafter increases juice production, although it may shorten the productive life of the tree. On Madura, however, according to Gebuis and Kadir, most lontar had a juice-producing life of only 8 to 10 years. This was because the trees were heavily pruned twice a year, once during the east monsoon and again during the west monsoon. The greatest market demand was for newly opened leaves, because they made the finest mats and baskets.

With a potential crown of up to 60 leaves, the lontar produces new leaves at a rate of 12 to 14 per year. On Madura, those trees that were used only for their leaf production would be pruned of all but their 8 most recent, un-opened leaves. According to Gebuis and Kadir, a good juice-producing tree ideally should be allowed to retain about 40 leaves including the newest. Most young trees were pruned down to 10 to 20 leaves and completely cleared of all but their unopened leaves just before it was reckoned that they were about to produce juice.

Gebuis and Kadir concluded that this improvident use of the lontar was not entirely irrational in the circumstances of the market that the Madurese had to face. They give a number of reasons for their conclusion. In some parts of Madura, sugar production was uneconomical because of competition with the highly efficient colonial cultivation of sugarcane on Java. This was especially true in areas located at a distance from the main market centers, where the lack of a sufficient source of cheap firewood for sugar cooking added significantly to production costs. (Although the Madurese used leaf-stalks as firewood, these stalks by themselves were apparently not a sufficient source of wood. A partial reason for this insufficiency was the Madurese folk assertion that trees should not be "startled" by having both leaves and leaf-stalks cut at once. The Madurese practice was therefore to prune the leaves first and leave the leafstalks to be trimmed later.) Just as important, how-ever, from Gebuis and Kadir's point of view, was the fact that there was a good market for leaves and need among the Madurese for a quick and early income from their palms. Like old trees that were difficult to climb and false trees that never produced juice or fruit, immature trees could be made to produce an immediate income through the sale of their leaves. Pruning a tree was also easier labor than tapping.

The price of a half-leaf varied from one-half to one cent. More profit could be made if the leaves were fashioned into various finished products. A fine mat that could be made by a woman in 12 hours using 10 leaves would sell at 45 to 50 cents. A small container that could be made in 4 hours using only half a leaf might sell at 4 to 5 cents. Similarly, a leaf-bucket like a Rotinese haik which required only half a leaf but skill to make, might sell for as much as 10 cents. The making of these leaf products was a spare-time activity in most villages. Traders who came through the villages bought them for sale in larger markets or for shipment to Java.

As on Roti, the gewang palm (Madurese: *potjok*) is found in roughly the same areas as the lontar. Although the Gebuis-Kadir study does not men-tion these palms, their occurrence had a direct bearing on lontar utilization. The leaves of the gewang can be split into layers and used to weave high-quality mats and baskets. On Madura and elsewhere in Indonesia, this kind of matting is referred to as *agel*. American coffee merchants, for example, used to stipulate that all coffee shipped from Java to the United States be packed in agel matting, which was said to improve the flavor of the coffee. Thus rather than reducing the need to prune the lontar, the gewang was itself the source of another minor industry. The existence of the gewang also resulted in a price structure that relegated lontar leaves to a secondary position.

(*d*) *The Juice from the Inflorescences.* Madurese tapping procedures are so similar to Rotinese that they need hardly be recounted. Within one month of the time the lontar begins to blossom, as its inflorescences develop, the tree is ready to be tapped. The first task is to clean the crown, then to remove spines from the leafstalks, and to break off four to six superfluous rachillae from the inflorescences that are to be tapped, leaving less than half to be first scraped and then twice pincered with tongs. The only difference in the preparation of a male and a female lontar is that the female inflorescences require more squeezing with heavier tongs. The rachillae are bound, in pairs, and bent downward. They must usually be sliced twice at their tips to initiate the flow of juice. Leaf-buckets are hung under these inflorescences and, as on Roti, each receiving bucket is protected with a large lontar basket. But Madurese do not change receiving buckets after emptying them; instead, they add to each bucket a small quantity of finely stamped *kesambi* (*Schleichera oleosa* Merr) bark to retard fermentation.

Lontar blossom twice, at the beginning of the east monsoon and again in the west monsoon. The onset of the west monsoon brings an earlier rain to Madura than to Roti, and these rains inhibit tapping by making the trees more difficult to climb. But yields are much higher during the west monsoon, although the sugar content of the juice is lower. (To what extent this is the result of dilution by rainwater is not discussed.) A good tree is reported to supply 400 liters of juice with a 10-percent sucrose content in the west monsoon, and 200 liters of juice with a 15-percent sucrose content during the east monsoon. The tapping season for male lontars lasts for three to four months during the west monsoon and about two and a half months during the east monsoon. Female lontar produce for an appreciably shorter time (one to one and a half months) and are preferably not tapped in the rainy season to permit development of their fruit. Thus, even on Madura, there is a bias toward tapping male lontar. In season and despite the rains, tapping cannot be interrupted. Trees are tapped twice a day with the morning's climb returning the bigger yield. Except in the way fermentation is retarded Madurese lontar-tapping is strikingly like Rotinese tapping.

The processing of the juice, however, is less similar. Cooking is done in earthen pots as soon as possible after the day's first climb. It is continued until the juice forms lumps, hardens, and then, as it cools, becomes a hardened sugar (*gula trebong*). The evening's juice is boiled only slightly to a thin liquid (*kelang*), which is added to the next morning's regular cooking. This hard sugar is sold either by the pot or in different-sized baskets. In the 1920's merchants bought sugar in the villages and transported it to markets in Prenduan, Aéngpanas, and most importantly, Pamekasan, where other merchants purchased it to be shipped on to Java.

By adding shredded coconut or cassava meal, the Madurese produce other sugar foods (*gula kelapa* and *djubadha*). After the juice is strained of kesambi, it can be drunk directly, sold, or cooked slightly and then sold in local markets. By not adding kesambi to their buckets, the Madurese gather juice that will, within three days, turn to a serviceable vinegar. By introducing even more kesambi bark, the Madurese induce a slow fermentation. Vats of the liquid are buried for at least three to four months and then dug up. This powerful alcoholic drink is Madurese *towa*. Despite Islamic injunctions, the Madurese too have their own special liquor.

By Gebuis and Kadir's estimates, a productive lontar can yield a total of 600 liters of juice during the two tapping seasons of the year. Cooked, this comes to 70 kilograms of sugar and could be sold for as much as 9 guilder (f. 9.00). The cost of firewood might, however, reduce these profits by one-third. Since a man could tap many trees—Gebuis and Kadir set the limit at about 12—the possibilities for gaining a reasonable livelihood from the sale of lontar sugar did exist on Madura. What Gebuis and Kadir do not explain is how many trees would have to be pruned of their leaves and how many baskets and mats would have to be made to surpass the profits from the sale of lontar sugar. (To gain a rough idea of what this might be, one could calculate that 18 fine mats requiring 180 leaves and probably a month's labor might equal the maximum profits from tapping a tree for a year.) It is apparent from their report, however, that the profits from the sale of leaves tended to be greater than those from the sale of lontar sugar. The labor involved may also have been less. Nevertheless, the amount of lontar sugar exported from Madura in the early 1920's remained remarkably high. Figures for the years 1919 to 1923 from the Customs Office at Sumenep indicate that this region of Madura, in fact mainly the Panjurangan area, exported from a million to a million and a half pots of lontar sugar each year. This export averaged 184,000 Dutch florin annually. Although the figures fluctuated over this five-year period, there is no evidence of a decline in production.[13]

Madura thus provides another example of an economic system based on the productive possibilities of the *Borassus* palm: one dominated by market demands that had developed within the confines of a well-regulated colonial regime. Religious and cultural factors also had an effect on the use of the palm. As Moslems, the Madurese do not keep pigs as the Rotinese do. Without pigs, they do not have the means of converting their juice, syrup, and cooking wastes to protein. In fact, since there was a steady market for sugar, it cannot even be said that the Madurese had a surplus of syrup—unlike the Rotinese for whom a surplus means that which is not needed for human consumption. The Madurese village economy in the 1920's was clearly oriented toward a large outside market, and their utilization of their *Borassus* palms reflected this fact.

PALMYRA UTILIZATION IN CEYLON AND SOUTH INDIA

A single species of *Borassus* palm, referred to in the English literature as the palmyra palm, grows in incalculable numbers along both the Malabar and Coromandel coasts of India. Its distribution extends well into the interior of India and into the northern regions of Ceylon. In certain areas the concentration of these palms is so dense that they constitute vast forests. Pate, in the *Madras District Gazetteer* for the Tinnevelly region, estimated that some of these palmyra forests reached a density of 8,000 trees to the square mile,[14] while Ferguson, in the previous century, made what he considered a modest estimate that on the Jaffna peninsula of Ceylon and the surrounding islands there were some 6,400,000 palmyra palms.[15]

The palmyra palm is the special resource of the Dravidian-speaking populations of south India and Ceylon, and this tree is of such great importance that it has become the subject of legends, proverbs, and poetry. The great Pandava kings are said to have lived on palmyra fruit during their exile in the wilderness, and for this reason they and other rulers of south India supposedly adorned themselves with garlands of palmyra blossoms.

The Tamil poet, Arunachalam of Kumbakonam, wrote a long and famous poem, the *Tala Vilasam*, extolling the wonders of the tree. According to the *Tala Vilasam*, Brahma created the world without adequate provision to meet the wants of the people. They turned to Siva, who directed Brahma to create a *kalpa*-tree, a tree that would by itself provide the people of the earth with everything they needed. Brahma created the palmyra. As a tree of life, the palmyra is one of five trees permitted to grow in the Indian paradise. The *Tala Vilasam* enumerates the 801 uses of its products. Without naming all 801, we can concentrate on some of the major uses of the palmyra's trunk, fruit, leaf and leafstalk, and juice. These seem to exceed, by several orders of magnitude, anything found in Indonesia.

(a) *The Trunk.* In India and Ceylon, the palmyra is the center of a large timber industry. In Ceylon this industry was already well developed by the seventeenth century when the Dutch ruled the island. As rafters for building, the palmyra has been described as "the first wood in India"[16] and since its durable qualities increase with age, even after it has been felled, there is a Tamil proverb that asserts: "The palmyra lives a thousand years and lasts another thousand when it dies." The palmyra rafters of old Dutch houses on Ceylon are said to have improved as the rest of the house aged and showed need of repair. The hardest dark wood of very old trees was once also used as a fancy wood to manufacture umbrella handles, canes, rulers, and boxes.

Palmyra timber is further used for making troughs, spouts, drains, and water-raising equipment for the irrigation of fields. In a practice somewhat similar to that found on Roti, the hollowed trunk of a large palmyra can be lowered into a well to prevent its collapse and to keep it clear of debris. Ferguson further reports what appears to be one of the more peculiar uses of this wood: "The trunks of young trees or the top parts of old trees are often cut up into pieces, split and placed where game is plentiful in the Patchelepalla district of Jaffna. The wild hogs and hares are very fond of the soft, white, spongy hearts of the logs, and, in resorting to them to eat them, are frequently shot by the natives."[17] This use of the palm as wild hog bait is the closest Indian or Ceylonese approximation of the Rotinese practice of pig-feeding.

(b) *The Fruit.* The fruit of the palmyra is another major locus of elaboration in India and Ceylon. It is so developed, in fact, that a complex native classification of palms seems to exist based on four critical dimensions of their fruit: color, smell, taste, and shape. A small amount of fruit is eaten fresh; most of it is roasted or preserved in a form popularly referred to as *punatoo.*

In India and Ceylon, most palmyra fruit ripens during a brief period in August and September. Punatoo is the means of preserving the sweet, mellow, carroty pulp of this fruit. Platforms are constructed four or five feet above the ground and on these are spread mats of palmyra leaf. The ripe fruits are collected, their smooth epicarps opened, and their fibrous pulp removed. This pulp is soaked in water in palmyra baskets and squeezed to form a jelly. The mats are covered with successive layers of the jelly to half an inch in thickness, and this gelatinous mass is allowed to dry in the sun. Approximately a thousand fruits are used to make each single mat and the resulting punatoo is sold either by the whole mat or in smaller squares. For the poor classes of India and Ceylon, punatoo—mixed with grain, soups, cakes, smoked, or eaten raw—is a dietary staple for several months of the year.

A further use is made of the seed nuts of the fruit. These nuts are collected and planted in beds six to eight layers deep under loose, sandy soil. The bulbs that sprout from these nuts in two or three months are dug up, stripped of their enveloping sheaths, and dried in the sun. Fresh bulbs are called *kelingoo* and, after they have been boiled, *odial*. Odial can be reduced to an all-purpose flour that is another of the essential ingredients in lower-caste Tamil cooking.

(c) *The Leaf and Leafstalk*. The leaves of the palmyra, in India and Ceylon as in Indonesia, are made into the usual array of multisized mats, baskets, bags, fans, temporary umbrellas, and hats; they provide a cheap and plentiful thatch and are also used to make water buckets. Somewhat inferior to *tallipot* or *Corypha* leaves, palmyra leaves have been employed for centuries as writing material. Ferguson reports that palmyra leaves are also commonly used to fertilize fields, but not in a burned form as on Roti: "In Jaffna and doubtless in India the leaves are used extensively for manuring the rice fields: the fan parts are put into the ground til they rot off, and this is found to be an excellent manure, giving a quantity of silicious and other matter to the soil."[18] There is no indication in the literature, present or past, that the market demand for leaf products in India ever led to a situation like that on Madura.

(d) *The Juice from the Inflorescences*. William Ferguson, during his stay in Ceylon, seems to have developed an interest in the palmyra that approached obsession. In his monograph not only did he attempt to cite and translate every major reference on the palmyra, he went so far as to try, for example, to identify the birds that most often congregated at the crown of the palm. Compared with literally dozens of accounts that either are misleading in their explanation of the tapping process or summarize it in such a way as not to explain it, Ferguson's description of tapping is outstanding. Since nearly every accurate portrayal of palmyra-tapping in English directly or indirectly relies on Ferguson, it is worth quoting his description at length:

> When the proper season arrives, which is in November and December, the too frequently degraded and drunken toddy drawers are seen and heard busy at work in the Palmyra groves throughout the Peninsula of Jaffna. Their practised eyes soon fix on those trees that are fit for the "scalping knife," and if they have not dropped the footstalks of the leaves, the first operation, if the trees are valuable, is to wrench these off. This done, the toddy drawer, armed with his leathern protector for his breast, his raceme-batten of wood, his small thongs, straight and crooked knives, with the side leather pouch to contain them, procures a piece of tough jungle vine, or a strip of the footstalk of a fresh leaf of a young Palmyra or Coconut tree, which he thoroughly twists,

and then converts it into a sort of loop of such dimensions as to admit of his feet getting through to a span large enough to allow them to clasp the tree. This done, he puts his feet in this thong, stands close to the tree, stretches himself at full length, clasps it with his hands, and pulls his feet up as close to his arms as possible; again he slides up his hands, and the same process is repeated, until, by a species of screw process, he ascends to the summit of the tree. When the trees are high, some use hoops of the same material, large enough to encircle both the tree and the toddy drawer, who slides it up the tree, so that it is always a support to the body while the climber is in the act of taking a fresh grasp.

Arrived at the summit, amongst the leaves, the climbing apparatus is laid across a leafstalk, and the pruning and phlebotomy commence. One or two of the lower leaves are left as a support to the toddy drawer until the operation is completed. He then draws his crooked knife, which, on a small scale, a good deal resembles a reaping-hook, and rids the tree of all the accumulated dirt, such as old leaves, the network which supports them; and, if an old tree that bore fruit before, the stumps of the fruitstalks. Then all the leaves are cut off, excepting 3 or 4, and the young top bud of the tree. Besides the removal of all these, the crooked knife is now used in shearing off the outer covering of that part of the tree from which spring the leaves and the racemes. These latter are supported during this operation by being tied up by several thongs to the footstalks of the uncut leaves. The pruning having been completed, all or most of the spathas are effectually encompassed from end to end by thongs, to prevent the membrane which covers the inflorescence from bursting. The racemes thus tied are then beaten and crushed between the wooden battens to wound them, and to hurry on the flow of toddy. This done and the spathas being secured to stalks of the remaining leaves, the toddy drawer descends. The operation of beating and crushing takes place for 3 successive mornings, and on each of the 4 following a thin slice is cut from the points of the racemes, to encourage the flow of sap and keep them from bursting. On the eighth morning a clear sweet liquor begins to flow from the wounded racemes, which is indicated by the "Toddy Birds" and crows fighting and chattering amongst the trees. The toddy drawer then ascends with a chatty or toddy receiver stuck to his belt behind. He places the ends of the racemes in these, and when secured leaves them till evening, when they are found to contain quantities of this liquor. The operation of attracting the juice is repeated every morning and evening, or in the mornings only, until the whole of the raceme is sliced away.

The trees are drained in this way for several months of the year, but if the operation is repeated on the same tree for three successive years, without allowing any of the racemes to burst naturally, the trees are said to die.[19]

Caldwell gives an abbreviated but reliable account of the palmyra in south India, which indicates only minor variations in tapping from the techniques of Ceylon.[20] A loop for climbing is not used in the Tinnevelly and Travancore districts; a palmyra leaf-bucket is utilized by climbers in ascending to gather juice, but not for collecting juice from the inflorescences; and during the peak tapping season, the palms are commonly climbed three times a day. The only significant difference in any of these methods and those on Madura and Roti is in the means of inhibiting fermentation. The Rotinese avoid rapid fermentation by cleaning and exchanging leaf-buckets and, for the production of syrup, by immediate cooking. The Madurese add kesambi bark and therefore need not fully cook the juice of the evening's ascent. But in order to drink fresh juice, they must (usually by slight heating) precipitate out the kesambi bark. In south India and Ceylon, tappers use earthen pots to collect the juice in the trees and sprinkle the insides of the pots with lime to prevent fermentation. This use of lime is regarded as indispensable and there exists a native distinction between the two kinds of fresh toddy. Toddy from limed pots may be drunk, but that from unlimed pots—whatever its state of fermentation—is regarded as alcohol. Drinking this liquor, and apparently by implication the sugar made from it, is polluting and for some castes is a direct violation of their ritual rules.

In the nineteenth century the major tapping caste of south India, the Shanar or Nadar caste, regarded itself as a caste that abstained from liquor. Trees for the production of alcohol had to be individually licensed and liquor distillation was ideally left to other lower castes. The Nallavas and Pallas toddy-drawers in Ceylon at this time seem to have been less rigid in the maintenance of similar distinctions. Most of the juice of the palms in south India was therefore cooked to a hard sugar or jaggery. The same was largely the case in Ceylon, although large quantities of the juice were fermented to make either liquor or vinegar.

For the lower castes in south India and Ceylon, a meal could consist almost entirely of palmyra foods: punatoo fruit pulp cooked with odial flour and eaten with jaggery sugar. Possessed of their own integral food source and of a potentially profitable system of production, the tapping castes of India and Ceylon might appear to have been in a position of economic importance. Yet all accounts in the eighteenth and nineteenth centuries indicate exactly the opposite. Ferguson describes the tappers of Ceylon as poor and degraded: "From time immemorial up to 1843 these unfortunate people were in a condition of slavery."[21]

The price of juice from the palmyra was astonishingly low. Ferguson notes that the average value to the tapper of an entire year's yield of toddy from a male palm amounted to only 6 pence—and half of this went to the tree's owner. The tapper was in servitude to a single economic function, that of climbing and drawing juice. He did not own the trees he tapped and did not even have full control over the cooking of jaggery. In south India, the situation of the tapping castes was only slightly better. Hardgrave describes the climber's position in the early nineteenth century as follows:

> The climber owned neither the land nor the trees which he tapped— only the sharp tapper's knife, a few earthen pots, and meager clothing. His home was a palmyra-thatched hut, and if the palmyra tope, or grove, was situated far from his own village, he would leave to take seasonal residence with his family among the trees. The tapper received no money for his labor, but a share system gave the produce of alternative days to the climber and to the owner. Whether in the districts to the north of the Tambraparni, where the owners of the lands were Maravars, Naickers, Vellalas, or others of high caste, or in the barren palmyra forests of Tiruchendur, where the Nadans held the land, the climber was bound to the trees by tradition and an accumulation of debts. The profits of climbing were small and usually exhausted by the *panaiyeri* [climber] two or three months after the end of the season, and, even with the cottage industries from the by-products of the palmyra, such as mat- or basket-making by the women, the climber had little recourse other than to seek the enfettering advances from the owners.[22]

In the southernmost regions of Madras a subcaste of Nadar, known as Nadan, was granted by Nayak conquerors extensive tracts of land over which they exercised an exclusive proprietorship in return for the taxes they gathered. Although still ritually inferior by reason of their association with the entire caste, these Nadan are reported to have amassed enormous wealth and, when not in dispute among themselves, maintained an exacting control over their palmyra forests.

HERE ANY COMPARISON with either Roti or Madura should end. The scale on which power is exerted on either of these islands does not seem to be comparable with south India or Ceylon. Tappers on both islands have a relatively wider control over their resources and the products of their labor. Rotinese, in particular, pay only a fraction of what most Indian tappers paid for the right to use others' trees. The presence of a variety of petty states and of new tapping land on other islands seems to have created a dynamic that keeps tapping payments low. Furthermore, Rotinese, in groups or as individuals, have a sufficient control over production and resources to be able to allocate them in a variety of economically advantageous ways. They are not exclusively tappers, or cookers, or wood-fellers as would be the case in south India. They may be cultivators, herders, fishermen, traders, and even teachers—all or any of these, at the same time.

Comparison of these three cases thus suggests some of the variety of economic and social institutions that can be developed from the productive capacities of the *Borassus* palm. As on Roti, the palm can act as the pivot for a wide range of subsistence activities. Its use can be channeled to meet specific demands, as on Madura in the 1920's. But equally, its great productive capacities can be exploited to their fullest without necessarily benefiting its users, as in south India where tapping castes ranked at the lowest levels of the ritual hierarchy and could secure only a meager living from their labor. It is, therefore, not the *Borassus* itself nor the techniques of production, but the use made of its products, that is significant.

PARALLELS IN NADAR SOCIAL HISTORY

It would be appropriate here to conclude this study, were it not that certain aspects of Nadar social history call for a comparison with the social history of the Rotinese. The history of this south Indian tapping caste, with its parallels in development through conversion, education, migration, and political assertion, telescopes in a shorter period and on a larger scale the history of the Rotinese, yet in a cultural context radically different from that of eastern Indonesia. The history of this caste is marvelously well documented in an excellent monograph, *The Nadars of Tamilnad* by Robert L. Hardgrave, whose concern was to provide a case study of the development of caste as a political force in India. His book and that of the Scottish missionary Robert Caldwell, who after 36 years' work among the Nadar became their first bishop, provide a wealth of information for the purpose of comparison with the Rotinese. The historical parallels in the developments of the two palm-tapping peoples, occurring as they do within such different cultural contexts, provoke still further reflections on the nature of *Borassus*-based economies.

To begin with, there can be little doubt that the tapping castes of south India had, by their intensive palmyra utilization, harnessed an extraordinary source of productive wealth. In a desert-like region at the southern tip of India, "sandy, burnt up, barren, and uninviting,"[23] these populations were ruled by a succession of conquerors from the north. The fabled kings of the area, the Pandyans, were defeated by Moslem invaders in the fourteenth century and, having reestablished their dynasty, were defeated again by Telugu Nayaks. The Nayaks, who reigned in Madurai, parceled out their territory among their own military leaders and the local Maravar chieftains of the region. These *poligars* or chieftains, in time, fortified their lands and disputed one another's positions, while nominal overlordship of the southern districts passed into the hands of the Nawab of the Carnatic.

The arrival of the British East India Company profoundly altered political and economic relations in the area. Initially the Nawab called upon the British to restore control over his rebellious districts. Beginning in 1751, the East India Company sent a series of expeditions against the poligars and in return was given administrative jurisdiction over the areas it was able to control. The last of these ''poligar wars'' was in 1801, but already in 1785 and again in 1790 when its contracts with the Nawab expired, the Company unilaterally ''assumed the management'' of these territories, in some instances doling them out to cooperative poligars. For the first time in centuries the incessant warfare of the poligars was ended, banditry was curtailed, and with astonishing acceleration, in the nineteenth century, a network of roads and rails was established in the Madras Presidency.

In the wake of the Company came missionaries. Some were sent to India under the auspices of the London Missionary Society, which had served as the inspiration and model for the Netherlands Missionary Society. At a purely formal level, therefore, the institutional channels of western influence in south India were superficially similar to those in eastern Indonesia. And the group that responded most readily to the altered relations produced by the British was the tapping caste, then known as Shanar, whose members were divided into dozens of subcastes and scattered in large numbers throughout the entire southern part of India. In the nineteenth century, the Shanar population was estimated at a half million, a figure that has increased rapidly to one and a half million in the present century.

The first missionaries to arrive in the southern area were astonished at what they found and overwhelmed by the success of their mission:

> The staple produce, however, of the sandy districts is the palmyra. If one were to judge from abstract probabilities, he might expect to find those districts uninhabited; but Divine Providence is there as well as here, and it has pleased Providence to ordain that the palmyra palm should flourish more luxuriantly in those sands than in any other part of the East, and should feed an abundant population with its saccarine sap. The sandy districts in the South-East teem with human life, and it is remarkable that it is amongst the inhabitants of those districts that Christianity has made its greatest progress. Hitherto, from a variety of causes, Christianity and the palmyra have appeared to flourish together. Where the palmyra abounds, there Christian congregations and schools abound also; and where the palmyra disappears, there the signs of Christian progress are rarely seen.[24]

There was nothing mysterious about this association of palmyra palm and Christianity. While continually disclaiming any desire to meddle in worldly affairs, the missionaries organized their Christian communities on a sound foundation. The first converts in the Tinnevelly district, persecuted in their own villages, were purchased land to found a new settlement called Mudalur in 1799. Other Christian settlements soon followed: Bethlehem, Nazareth, and later Sawyerpuram (named after a British merchant, Sawyer, who had willed his land to the mission). By 1803 there were 5,000 Shanar converts, at which point whole villages of Shanar began to convert en masse. The simple but effective organizational principles of these villages were set forth by Bishop G. E. L. Cotton: "When a village becomes Christian, it forms itself at once into a Christian municipality, in which Church and State are united together . . . The catechist is received as the counsellor and director of the headman; and the missionary, resident at the central station of the district, is recognized as the superintendent of all the communities scattered through it."[25] Missionaries actively supported their communities against the intense opposition of other caste groups as well as the Nadan subcaste overlords of the Shanar. As one missionary wrote: "If [the Shanar] continue to grow in mind, intelligence, and character, they must gain influence, and that influence must be felt, and felt for good . . . Already other castes are beginning to be jealous of the advantages the Shanars are gaining from their connexion with us."[26] Another missionary, in a letter to the London Missionary Society, listed some of these advantages: "We have raised them in a civil point of view—delivered them from unjust taxes and oppressive customs and a grievous poll tribute, the cause of much cruelty in its collection . . ."[27] By 1849 there were nearly 40,000 Shanar converts in Tinnevelly on the southwestern coast and another 20,000 in Travancore on the southeastern coast. Caldwell could write, without exaggeration, that "the number of this one caste that have placed themselves under Christian instruction is greater than that of all the other converts in India, in connexion with all Protestant Missions,"[28] while at this same time another missionary, writing from Travancore, proclaimed: "The whole Shanar community, amounting together [in Travancore] to about 150,000, is open to us."[29]

Christianity became known as the "Shanar Church." With Christianity came education and, shortly thereafter, a number of possibilities for migration. Because of the mass conversion of Shanar, there was little possibility for the "out-casting" of converts. Hindu and Christian Shanar remained within the same caste, marrying among themselves and attending mission schools together. Nearly one-third of the pupils at the mission schools were non-Christians. By 1820 twelve Shanar youths entered teacher training because "the inhabitants of the palmyra forest preferred Shanar Christians to teach them."[30] Soon afterward Shanar formed a considerable majority of the teaching profession of the Tinnevelly district. Both Christians and Hindus, from a position of growing economic prosperity and a supremacy in western-style education, began agitating for a more appropriate status for their caste. In particular, the Shanar wished to be identified with their subcaste overlords, the Nadan. Alternatively, they wished to be known as Nadar. The changing marks of status adopted by Christian Nadar were almost immediately copied by Hindu Nadar. The privilege of Nadar women to cover their breasts, as befitting "Christian modesty," a privilege denied the Nadar by their caste position, was adopted in Tinnevelly where Nadar formed a majority. But when this custom was also copied by the minority of Nadar in Travancore, it took 40 years of agitation and finally a decree of the Governor of Madras in 1859 to be accepted. To other castes the Nadar were an undifferentiated group, shared a common social position in the caste hierarchy, and posed an obvious threat to the social order.

Nadar had, even before the British arrival, some seasonal mobility. By moving back and forth between the west and east coasts, from southern Tinnevelly to southern Travancore, they were able to take advantage of alternate tapping seasons. With the opening of plantations on Ceylon and later in Malaya and with the systematic recruitment of labor from Madras, between 1843 and 1867 one and a half million laborers emigrated. According to Hardgrave, a substantial number of the emigrants to Ceylon and Malaya were Tinnevelly Nadars, and "of the Nadar migrants, the greatest number were drawn from the Christian community."[31] Those abroad regularly sent remittances to their families in Tinnevelly. Of the million and a half emigrants from Madras, half are estimated to have returned; included in this figure is a considerable number of Nadar who returned to buy land and shops in Madras. Returning migrants stimulated an internal migration within the Presidency.

Before the arrival of the British, some Nadar had the task of driving bullock carts among the palmyra groves to collect cakes of jaggery sugar. This sugar was actually a medium of exchange in the southern area, and a few Nadar plied a trade based on the exchange of jaggery for dried fish, salt, and other products. With the establishment of the British peace and the expansion of the road system, Nadar—traders and dealers in the sugar currency of the region—by a simple transformation became the middlemen and money-lenders along a trade route opened by the British East India Company linking Tinnevelly with the north.

On this route, moving in the direction of the town of Madurai, Nadar settled at six main centers, called the "Six Towns of Ramnad"; each of the six became a fortified and prosperous island in the midst of higher castes (the Maravars, Kallars, Pallans, and Vellalas). Established in small shops but tightly organized by common well-funded caste councils, these merchants (mostly Hindu) pressed for ritual privileges in accordance with their new economic standing. The first Nadar town was built near Sivakasi, the site of an East India Company cotton warehouse. Nadar merchants began by carrying on "extensive commerce especially in tobacco and cotton."[32] By 1891 they numbered 80 percent of the town's population, but because of their low caste associations they were still denied access to the local Siva temple. In their attempt to claim a Kshatriya status as descendants of the Pandyans, the "palmyra-climbing kings," Nadar repeatedly tried to gain admission to the temple and eventually provoked what became known as the Tinnevelly riots. In 1899 the dominant Maravars of the area attacked the town of Sivakasi to rid their area of Nadar, only to be repulsed by outnumbered but armed Nadar in the town. The attempted sack of Sivakasi marked a significant, though largely symbolic, turning point in Nadar history; it gained them a degree of direct British protection but, more importantly, enormous attention and support, especially in the "enlightened" national press.

Hardgrave documents in detail the continuing Nadar advancement in trade, education, and political life in the twentieth century. One pattern emerges. While still availing themselves of some of the benefits offered to "depressed castes," the Nadar elite and particularly the Nadar Christians consistently abandoned the economic system that originally launched their prosperity. This process was already evident in the last century. In 1871 a British settlement officer reported that "many Shanar have nothing to do with climbing" and that "through the increased wealth and comfort of the Shanars as a class, owing to the spread of education among them, and remunerative means of subsistence, it has become every year more difficult for owners of palmyrahs to get people to climb trees."[33] In 1901 it was noted that Christian Nadar had "given up tapping the palmyra palm for jaggery and toddy as a profession beneath them; and the example is spreading so that a real economic *impasse* is manifesting itself."[34] In 1940 a survey revealed that "about 40 percent of the Nadars of the Tinnevelly District are estimated to be engaged in tapping, but among Christian Nadars, tappers would form about 20 percent since, as a result of education and development of trade with Ceylon, several families have given up this vocation."[35]

Thus, in less than two centuries, the Nadar were able to avail themselves of a variety of opportunities afforded under British colonialism. By their readiness to convert to Christianity, they gained both political protection and economic emancipation from their previous overlords. They could harness for themselves the productive capacities of their palm economy and were allowed to trade in the commodities they produced. By obtaining an early access to western education, they were also able to assume positions of prominence in the newly emerging political hierarchy created by the colonial regime. Their palm-tapping skills were easily adapted to the skills required in British plantations abroad, particularly on the rubber and oil palm estates of Malaya. And the cash obtained from their labor gave them, on their return to India, a purchasing power that other caste groups, still enmeshed in the traditional agricultural system, lacked.

This pattern of recent Nadar history certainly recalls that of the Rotinese. But a detailed consideration indicates that a pattern of parallel development cannot be found at the level of particular events. If parallels are to be found, they consist in a series of general structural resemblances entailed by the constraints and capacities of similar social and economic factors.

The British in south India, like the Dutch in eastern Indonesia, encountered certain populations who had a number of nonagricultural skills and a particularly productive, though externally vulnerable, mode of livelihood. In south India, the British resorted to a direct protection of these populations; in eastern Indonesia, Dutch protection of the Rotinese was less direct but no less effective. An economic motive alone would be insufficient to account for the conversion of the Nadar to Christianity. Careful inquiry would probably reveal a tangle of motives and events leading to this conversion, as was true with the Rotinese in the eighteenth century. Yet in both cases there were undeniable economic and political advantages accorded those who did convert. In both cases, as well, their position vis-à-vis the colonial government was radically altered.

The education offered to both of these populations could reasonably be considered similar. The formal learning of an established lingua franca removed both from exclusive dependence on their local communities. And the generation-by-generation development of their educational attainments—from a system of elementary schools, to teachers training colleges, and finally to universities—followed a well-established western pattern. It could be argued that, by the nature of their palm economies, both populations had the means to support educational specialization, the social discipline to accept it, and youth with enough free time to take advantage of it. It could also be argued, less convincingly perhaps, that the traditions of palm-tapping (involving the daily application of fixed skills in a monotonous routine) prepared these populations for the regimentation encountered in their early schools. Apart from this, it is difficult to determine a specific contribution made by their distinctive economies. The developments among the Nadar and Rotinese only reconfirm the capacity of their economies to support densely settled and highly organized populations. The pattern of their development conforms, in rough outline at least, to models established by western influence. The distinctiveness of this pattern derives, in large part, from the fact that both populations began their educational development well in advance of other groups or peoples in their local area.

At a certain point, even general resemblances between these two cases cease. The Rotinese have retained their subsistence economy to a remarkable degree. Since their products never became major marketable commodities, they had fewer opportunities than the Nadar to move into trade. At best, on Timor they could become peddlers and intermediaries between the mountain peoples and the Chinese merchants of Kupang. They were never able to challenge the centuries-old Chinese domination of trade on the island. Furthermore, their migration to Timor was quite unlike that of the Nadar. Rotinese migration led to permanent settlement and the creation of a way of life like that on their home island. The Nadar migration, on the other hand, was a temporary movement of labor to other colonial areas. Even when it led to permanent settlement, it involved an adaptation to plantation life in a foreign land.

Emigration from Roti left the economic structure of the island relatively unchanged. Rotinese on Timor, however, moved to the forefront of development on their new island home. Via the school system, Rotinese on Roti could join their contemporaries on Timor and both could acquire an education that often led to future prominence in national life. While a sense of identity with a particular state on Roti has always been of profound importance to most Rotinese, their individual successes have not, until recently, prompted any attempts to alter conditions on the island itself. What is most striking about the Nadar case is their concerted attempt, based on altered economic circumstances, to change their position as a caste in the ritual hierarchy. The success of individual Nadar has remained inextricably bound up with the status of their caste. Among the Nadar, this quest for an altered status has led to the wholesale abandonment of palm-tapping as an occupation, especially among Christian Nadar; as a caste they are rapidly abandoning the economy that initially supported them. Among the Rotinese, individuals for generations have given up tapping for more prestigious occupations; but by contrast with the Nadar, the Rotinese on Roti as well as on Timor have retained their palm-centered economies. They have been involved in no radical transformation of the systems that sustain them, nor have they effected any sharp break with their traditions. They have neither inherited some shattered world nor rejected their previous culture. They are a people conscious of the continuity of their way of life and confident of their cultural traditions.

CONCLUSIONS

The focus of this book has been first on the ecological and economic situation, as it exists today, on Sumba, Savu, Roti, and Timor; then on the historical circumstances and external pressures that have fostered present-day adaptations; and finally on certain of those adaptations in the light of comparable cases. At this stage the study should be able to stand on its own without further justification or summary. Yet I feel it important to note that this book is also a prelude to the next stage of my consideration of the Rotinese, which will be a study of Rotinese political traditions—the history of the formation of one state on the island and of the internal development of its political categories.

One of the issues I have tended to emphasize throughout has been the need for a historical perspective in anthropology. History, in this sense, need not be seen as a unique and privileged means of explaining social action, but rather as the necessary dimension without which anthropology, as a discipline with its own distinctive concerns, cannot deal with the problems of change and continuity in social life.

While societies may differ in their consciousness of the past and may even develop conceptions that serve to negate the past, they still undergo historical change. The ahistoricism of early anthropology may once have been partially justified by the claim that reliable evidence on such historical change was simply unavailable for the majority of societies that anthropologists tended to study. But the spread of western influence in its various guises has now stimulated some degree of historical consciousness in most of the cultures of the world. Moreover, the structures by which this influence has spread have prompted change on an unprecedented scale, at the same time providing records of at least the recent past. An anthropology, therefore, that would deny history or ignore the effects of the West can only be judged to be a suspect discipline of little ethnographic relevance for the study of the societies of the present.

The integration of a historical perspective within anthropology requires a critical recognition that the methods of social inquiry are intimately and inextricably associated with the climate of political and social opinion. The complementary study of history and anthropology must therefore also involve the sociological study of historiography and, indeed, of social anthropology itself. In the words of the late Professor Sir. E. E. Evans-Pritchard, what is needed is the "study of historical knowledge as part of the content of social thought of a changing present."[36]

Insofar as this study is itself a product of the concerns of our present period, we may reflectively speculate on what that coffee broker from Amsterdam, Batavus Drystubble, would have thought of it. Since this book has nothing to do with coffee, he would find little that would be useful for his profession. Still, as a self-proclaimed "man of the world"—whose world has now passed—he may be credited with further opinions. He would conceivably have approved of the social betterment that has occurred among the Rotinese, Savunese, even the Nadar. But he would hardly have condoned the litigiousness of the Rotinese, the aggressiveness of the Savunese, or the seemingly unnecessary caste-consciousness of the Nadar. The economic system of which he was an exponent permitted the advancement of these populations as it constrained others in the same areas. All three populations deftly exploited the colonial system, but have now, in the process, become the minority inheritors of precarious positions in new nations. One doubts whether the practical Heer Drystubble would have had the empathy to appreciate their achievements or to recognize their new dilemmas. And even as he could not foresee the transformation of his world, we today cannot foretell the future conditions to which these populations will have to adapt.

APPENDIXES

NOTES

BIBLIOGRAPHY

INDEX

Appendix A Official population figures for west Timor, Sumba, Roti/Ndao, and Savu/Raijua: 1961 and 1971.

Location	Area (sq km)		Population		Density	
	1961	1971	1961	1971	1961	1971
Kupang	5,301	5,199	149,868	187,525	28.3	36.1
North central Timor	3,038	2,636	101,708	116,785	33.5	44.3
South central Timor		4,259	202,964	241,913	47.7	56.8
Belu		2,139	130,350	153,156	60.9	71.6
Total for west Timor	14,737	14,233	584,890	699,379	39.7	49.1
East Sumba		7,713	94,902	104,073	12.3	13.5
West Sumba	3,439	4,200	156,224	187,209	45.4	44.6
Total for Sumba	11,152	11,913	251,126	291,282	22.5	24.5
Roti/Ndao		1,223	72,783	76,227	59.5	62.3
Savu/Raijua		502	44,956	51,002	89.6	101.6

Note: Figures for 1961 are based on data in *Symposium I Pembangunan Ekonomi dan Keuangan, N.T.T.,* 1966: 36. Figures for 1971 are from *Sensus Penduduk Propinsi Nusa Tenggara Timur, Tahun 1971* (Kupang, 1972: 17). The regency of Kupang includes Roti, Savu, Ndao, and Semau; in these calculations, I have excluded Roti, Savu, and Ndao but included Semau as part of Kupang. There is no explanation in the sources for the different area calculations for Timor or Sumba.

Appendix B Computer analysis of the populations of men and livestock on Roti, Ndao, and Savu.

The purpose of this appendix is to provide some explanation of the analysis that serves as the basis for discussion of the interrelations among men and livestock on Roti, Ndao, and Savu in Chapter 1. The analysis was done utilizing SNAP/IEDA, a computing package based on the statistical techniques developed and presented in J. W. Tukey's *Introduction to Exploratory Data Analysis* (1970). The program was run on the Stanford S360 by Dr. Perry Gluckman, at the Center for Advanced Study in the Behavioral Sciences, Stanford, California.

A series of step-wise regressions was utilized, the first stage of which involved removing land area as a covariant factor. Since the number of items was small, with at least an order of magnitude increase over the range, a log metric was used. Each population, human and animal, was related to land area on Roti, Ndao, and Savu by regressing the log of that population over the appropriate log of its land area. The regression resulted in a measure that was the ratio of the actual to the expected population based on land area. This measure was proportionally greater than one if the particular population was larger than expected, and proportionally less than one if the population was smaller than expected on the basis of land area. The ratio measures for the human population could then be related to the appropriate ratio measures for each animal population. This offered a means of determining whether there was any significant correlation between men and their animals or among the different populations with the effect of land area removed. Appendix Table B-1 gives the residuals or ratios of actual to expected population in log metric, as used in this analysis.

In the correlations based on the regression of these residuals on one another, the most significant relation to emerge was that between the human population and the pig population. As regards other correlations of animal and human populations with land area removed, there was a 0.57 partial correlation between the human population and the combined total of goats and sheep. Separately, there was a 0.52 partial correlation of humans with goats and a 0.47 partial correlation of humans with sheep. With buffalo, there was a low partial correlation of 0.15. There were, as well, partial correlations among the various animal populations: 0.73 between pigs and combined goats and sheep, with separate partial correlations of 0.69 of pigs with sheep and 0.54 of pigs with goats. Appendix Table B-2 gives the partial correlation matrix of these various populations.

Appendix Table B-1 The residuals or ratios of actual to expected population in log metric for the analysis of human population and livestock on Roti, Ndao, and Savu.

State or island	Human population	Water buffalo population	Pig population	Goat-sheep population	Goat population	Sheep population
Landu	0.3067	0.3559	0.3426	0.9410	1.0832	0.9800
Ringgou/Oepao	1.4160	1.6623	0.4382	0.4407	1.1188	0.1103
Bilba	1.2821	2.0441	0.4260	1.4987	0.9444	2.0502
Diu	0.5772	1.1083	0.4145	1.2493	0.6356	1.7944
Korbaffo	1.0620	2.3721	1.6151	1.6506	1.6528	1.8996
Lelenuk/Bokai	0.2849	0.6178	0.3396	0.2538	0.2922	0.2706
Termanu	0.9192	1.2586	0.3379	0.4974	0.7140	0.4479
Baä	1.3428	4.8344	1.9395	1.9915	2.4577	2.0262
Talae	0.6401	1.3182	0.7612	0.5681	0.9535	0.4181
Keka	0.6362	0.7083	0.4046	0.8337	0.9112	0.9215
Loleh	1.4181	0.7115	0.5458	0.4738	0.8304	0.3422
Dengka/Lelain	1.4932	0.9307	3.0972	2.3993	3.7444	2.0128
Thie	2.4992	1.5620	3.0982	1.9707	1.8254	2.3202
Oenale	0.9850	0.4333	1.7685	0.9218	0.3527	1.3876
Delha	0.7148	0.3305	2.8873	1.2656	0.4394	1.9743
Ndao	2.7760	0.6180	3.8275	1.9508	2.1876	2.1544
Savu	1.9781	0.9789	3.3280	1.2850	0.9701	1.4837

Appendix Table B-2   Partial correlation matrix of human population and livestock.

	Buffalo	Pigs	Goats/sheep	Goats	Sheep	Human population
Buffalo	1.00	-0.00	0.37	0.39	0.29	0.15
Pigs	-0.00	1.00	0.73	0.54	0.69	0.73
Goats/sheep	0.37	0.73	1.00	0.80	0.92	0.57
Goats	0.39	0.54	0.80	1.00	0.50	0.52
Sheep	0.27	0.69	0.92	0.50	1.00	0.47
Human population	0.15	0.73	0.57	0.52	0.47	1.00

The object of this analysis was not only to evaluate the various subsystems of animal husbandry associated with a lontar economy, but also to devise a scale or index to relate these subsystems to one another as coherent, comparable economic strategies. To do this, the ratios of all animal populations for each of the states were divided by the sums of the ratios of buffalo, pigs, and goats plus sheep. This gave an estimate of the ratio of each of the animal populations to the total livestock in each state, again with the effect of land area removed. By means of this standardization, it was possible to examine whether there is a pattern or strategy to the way in which different states proportion their livestock. Appendix Table B-3 provides, for each state, the proportion of total livestock that is divided into buffalo, pigs, and goats and sheep, and a cumulative figure that is the total of the ratios of all livestock. This table forms the basis for the barycentric diagram of Figure 2.

Appendix Table B-3   Ratios of the various animal populations on Roti.

State or island	Buffalo	Pigs	Goats and sheep	Cumulative livestock index
Landu	0.22	0.21	0.57	1.64
Ringgou/Oepao	0.66	0.17	0.17	2.54
Bilba	0.51	0.11	0.38	3.97
Diu	0.40	0.15	0.45	2.77
Korbaffo	0.42	0.29	0.29	5.64
Lelenuk/Bokai	0.51	0.28	0.21	1.21
Termanu	0.60	0.16	0.24	2.09
Baä	0.55	0.22	0.23	8.77
Talae	0.50	0.29	0.21	2.65
Keka	0.36	0.21	0.43	1.95
Loleh	0.41	0.32	0.27	1.73
Dengka/Lelain	0.15	0.48	0.37	6.43
Thie	0.23	0.47	0.30	6.63
Oenale	0.14	0.57	0.29	3.12
Delha	0.07	0.65	0.28	4.48
Ndao	0.10	0.60	0.30	6.40
Savu	0.18	0.59	0.23	5.59
Mean	0.35	0.34	0.31	

Appendix C Computer analysis of the censuses of the Rotinese states: 1863 to 1961.

This appendix provides a partial explanation of the analysis that serves as the basis for the discussion of Rotinese migration and population density in Chapter 5.

The problem for analysis in this instance is not unlike the problem dealt with in the analysis described in Appendix B. The data—in this case, a series of exclusively human populations for the various states—are also equivalent. Therefore the initial stages of this analysis resemble those of the earlier ones. To compare the populations of the Rotinese states over time, land area must be removed as a covariant factor. The territory of the states varied somewhat prior to 1888, but for present purposes one can only use the figures for land area after that date. (The results must be evaluated with this stipulation in mind.) The population figures used are those of the six censuses from 1863 to 1961. The states of Ringgou/Oepao, Lelenuk/Bokai, and Dengka/Lelain were combined for the simple reason that, for at least one census, their joint populations were recorded as a single figure. The data thus consist in land area and six censuses for fifteen states. As in the previous analysis, these data were converted to a log metric and the log of the population for each state in each census was regressed over the log of that state's appropriate land area. The results were, again, a log measure—the ratio of the actual to the expected population based on land area, with values larger than one indicating a population greater than expected and values less than one, a population smaller than expected. At this point, the similarities to the previous analysis end.

To obtain a grouping of states in accordance with their population patterns, the log measures for each state were compared in pairwise fashion; one way, by computing their covariance (without the means), the other way, by computing their interproduct (with the means). Each method gave a 15 x 15 matrix of relationship. The computation of the covariance, it was assumed, would emphasize the microeffect in each population pattern, while the computation of the interproduct would emphasize the global effects in each of these same populations. A multidimensional scaling was then done on the set of computations by means of a program called the M-D scale. A simple rotation produced two scales, each based on one of the ways for comparing the data. The result is the set of figures in Appendix Table C-1.

The diagram used in Chapter 5 (Figure 3) is thus a scale; each state's location represents its position relative to the other states of the island. Com-

Appendix Table C-1   Scaling dimensions for the populations of the Rotinese states.

State or island	Covariance (without means)	Interproduct (with means)
Landu	-0.889	-1.674
Ringgou/Oepao	1.554	1.266
Bilba	1.471	1.244
Diu	-1.163	-1.679
Korbaffo	0.926	0.954
Lelenuk/Bokai	-1.450	-1.697
Termanu	1.090	-0.688
Baä	-1.316	1.387
Talae	1.310	-1.424
Keka	-1.165	-1.467
Loleh	0.209	1.211
Dengka/Lelain	-1.298	1.423
Thie	-0.551	1.466
Oenale	1.551	0.945
Delha	-0.279	-1.265

putation of the covariance apparently reveals the aspects of these data that have to do with their pattern of relative loss or gain over time, whereas computation of the interproduct tends to reveal their pattern relative to land area.

This particular analysis may be judged to enhance the general line of argument, provided one accepts the techniques that have been applied. Certain elementary cautions are warranted. To begin with, the procedure for removing the effect of land area is clear from the previous discussion. But the scaling techniques applied to these data need justification. The object of the analysis was to develop two indices by which to plot each state, and in a sense the procedures that were eventually adopted came about through manipulating various possible techniques and observing their results. Conceivably factor analysis (if there were more data) or something far simpler would have been preferable. In this analysis a program utilizing the M-D scale was used to compute, for both the covariance and the interproduct, the best fit of the six dimensions of the data in two dimensions. Since this program does not allow for reduction to a single dimension, summing the two dimensions of the covariance and the interproduct produced the final two dimensions employed to plot the diagram. The reason for summing these separate dimensions, which amounted to a simple rotation of the data, was to obtain the single dimension not provided by the program. Essentially what one obtains with the interproduct is the mean after a rescaling selected by the M-D program. The covariance, on the other hand, selects the composite census with most information and deemphasizes the censuses with least information. Given the large amount of manipulation in this program and the small amount of data to which the manipulation was applied, there is a distinct possibility that these techniques may produce an artifact that happens to coincide with the substantive data.

The overall approach in this analysis was proposed by Dr. Perry Gluckman of the Center for Advanced Study in the Behavioral Sciences at Stanford, who was unaware of the line of argument the analysis was intended to serve; some of my other colleagues at the Center, in particular David Wiley and Roger Shepard, favored some simpler form of analysis. Two other procedures were tried. One used, instead of the interproduct (with means), the means of the residuals of each state's population, together with the M-D scale based on the covariance, to plot these states. Another procedure compared the slope of the data in the various censuses simply by taking the relative increase or decrease in population between the 1863 and 1961 censuses and plotting this against the mean for each state. A better means of estimating the slope could be devised, since this estimate effectively ignored half the census data. Finding a way to use all the data was one motivation for the scaling procedures. In both cases the alternative procedures produced plots similar enough to the present diagram to suggest a basis for the interpretation advanced in Chapter 5.

Included in Appendix Table C-2 are both the means of the residuals of the population and the figures for the relative increase or decrease of these populations over the hundred-year period. Those who would prefer the less complicated analysis may replot the states using these data. As an anthropologist, I admit a fancy for *bricolage*, however involved such model-building may at times seem. An extremely valuable source book on multidimensional scaling and its applications is the two-volume collection of essays entitled *Multidimensional Scaling* (1972) edited by R. N. Shepard, A. K. Romney, and S. B. Nerlove.

Appendix Table C-2   The residuals or ratios of actual to expected population in log metric for the population analysis of Roti.

| State or island | Census of— | | | | | | Mean | Increase/decrease, 1863/1961 |
	1863	1885	1921	1954	1957	1961		
Landu	-0.5760	-0.5888	-0.5088	-0.4612	-0.4661	-0.4381	-0.5065	0.1379
Ringgou/Oepao	0.5099	0.3668	0.2111	0.1250	0.1241	0.1350	0.2453	-0.3749
Bilba	0.4360	0.4075	0.1662	0.0409	0.0467	0.0452	0.1904	-0.3908
Diu	-0.4768	-0.4486	-0.1821	-0.1945	-0.2147	-0.1701	0.2811	0.3067
Korbaffo	0.1215	0.1831	0.0835	0.0393	0.0257	0.0076	0.0768	-0.1139
Lelenuk/Bokai	-0.6505	-0.4392	-0.4805	-0.1926	-0.1466	-0.1818	-0.3485	0.4687
Termanu	0.0609	0.0941	-0.0345	-0.1223	-0.1349	-0.1323	-0.0448	-0.1932
Baä	-0.0067	0.0596	0.1968	0.3066	0.3182	0.3465	0.2035	0.3532
Talae	0.0803	-0.1871	-0.1058	-0.1239	-0.1506	-0.1467	-0.1056	-0.2270
Keka	-0.3108	-0.0420	-0.1208	-0.1038	-0.1254	-0.1002	-0.1338	0.2106
Loleh	0.1611	0.0335	0.1964	0.1235	0.1244	0.1442	0.1305	-0.0169
Dengka/Lelain	0.1414	0.2898	0.1707	0.2731	0.2553	0.2616	0.2320	0.1202
Thie	0.3286	0.0456	0.4328	0.4178	0.4706	0.4133	0.3514	0.0847
Oenale	0.3543	0.2434	0.0475	-0.0013	0.0009	-0.0634	0.0969	-0.4177
Delha	-0.1732	-0.0176	-0.0725	-0.1266	-0.1276	-0.1209	-0.1064	0.0523

Appendix D   Rotinese myths and legends of the lontar.

Lontar-tapping is the main source of subsistence on Roti. The lontar palm forms what I have termed a "primary symbol" of Rotinese culture (Fox 1975:99-132). As an icon of sexuality, as a model of growth and maturation, and as a source of products both sweet and sour, male and female, the lontar gives rise to a wealth of cultural imagery. Yet compared with rice and millet, the tree is not the object of a great deal of ritual. Moreover, the tree is mentioned only briefly in the major mythological poems of the Rotinese. Instead of myths about the "origin" of the tree, Rotinese tell various legends about the "discovery" of the techniques of tapping.

A functionalist interpretation for this lack of myth and ritual about the tree would assume that the dependability of the lontar and the consistency of its production evoke less concern than food crops such as rice and millet, whose growth can indeed be precarious. This type of explanation is plausible, but almost impossible to prove. From a comparative point of view, however, it is apparent that the Rotinese concern with rice, and by association millet, is part of their pan-Indonesian inheritance. The myths and rituals of rice have been elaborated by the Indonesian peoples for perhaps thousands of years. Almost all Rotinese myths and rituals are recognizable variants of these ancient forms.

For the lontar, to my knowledge, there is no equivalent Indonesian mythology. The lack of this mythology on Roti would also accord with what the Rotinese themselves assert about their past, namely, that they were cultivators of rice and millet long before they began to develop their techniques of palm-tapping. The object of this appendix is to summarize the principal mythological references to the lontar and to recount one of the chief legends about the processes of tapping and cooking. I have relegated this information to an appendix not because it is unimportant, but because I have already indicated its main features in Part Three of this study.

As are many important plants and most Rotinese cultural objects, the lontar is identified with the sea. Native folk etymology derives the word for "lontar fruit," *saiboa,* from *sai(k)* ("sea depths") and *boa* ("fruit"). Thus it is the "fruit of the sea." Ritual language associations make similar identifications. The word *tua* ("lontar") forms a proper pair or dyadic set with either *meti* ("tide") or *tasi* ("sea"). Ritual chants call upon the sun and moon "to bring the abundance of the tide, the juice of the lontar palm." In one of the major chants that relates the origin of fire are interpolated sections that further confirm these mythological links. In addition, the beings credited with the first notching of lontars in west Roti are known by the dyadic name, *Nggeo-Nggeo Sain ma Fula-Fula Liun:* "Black-Black of the Sea and White-White of the Ocean."

There is a simple ritual that may be performed when the tapping implements are taken down from the house at the beginning of the season; special offerings may also be made, in east Roti, to ensure that the climbing strap or rope (*lalabak*) does not break; cooking ovens are usually hung with *maik* (three-pronged lontar-leaf representations of the ancestors) to guard against evil spirits and there is the belief that the chief storage vat kept in the loft of the house, the *bou nitu inak* ("the great spirit vat"), should never be empty. But these beliefs and practices are not at all as prominent or as necessary as the elaborations associated with the cultivation of rice and millet.

While the lontar tree's origin is not given prominence in Rotinese mythology, there are various important legends about the development of the techniques of tapping and cooking. These developments did not take place at the beginning of time; they took place gradually over time. This distinction, between myth and legend is relevant. Rotinese mythology consists in those oral traditions that are related in a special ritual language. They form something of an esoteric tradition; their recitation, in chant, is confined to ceremonial occasions. Legends, on the other hand (which include those that explain the development of lontar-tapping), are "historical tales." They are attributed to certain clans, in specific states, and even to particular ancestors. They may vary from state to state, but within each state they form part of a stable tradition.

In west Roti, especially in Thie, lontar-tapping is attributed to Savunese influence. In Termanu, lontar-tapping, cooking, and certain other technical innovations are associated with one clan, Dou-Danga. All traditions agree that the founder of this clan came from Thie; in some tales he is, by implication, a Ndaonese resident of Thie who, for services to the Lord of Termanu, was granted land, rights to water, and a court position in the state. There are four technical innovations attributed to Dou-Danga and they are remembered in a short poem with a single refrain:

Ledi tua lai dua	Tapping lontar twice a day
Neme Dou-Danga mai	Comes from Dou-Danga
Kali dae tapa laö	Digging earth to plaster an oven
Neme Dou-Danga mai	Comes from Dou-Danga
Feä fi puni uma	Pulling alang to roof a house
Neme bei Dou-Danga mai	Comes still from Dou-Danga
Pele pado lelelu	Torch-fishing carefully for octopus
Neme Dou-Danga mai.	Comes from Dou-Danga.

All of these innovations involve the lontar. Octopus-fishing requires a special kind of lontar torch. The use of *alang-alang*, a kind of *imperata* grass, to roof a house serves as a replacement for lontar-leaf roofing. Gathering and bundling this grass demands more labor than do lontar leaves, but the roofing lasts nearly twice as long. The large houses of nobles and wealthy individuals are usually, for practical as well as prestige reasons, roofed in alang-alang. This reduces, to a limited extent, one of the major demands for lontar leaves on the island.

The two other innovations, double tapping and the cooking oven, are, for the Rotinese, the critical features that led to their full exploitation of the lontar. Double tapping prevents the souring of the juice. All intensive *Borassus*-tapping peoples tap the palm twice each day. The "oven," however, is a somewhat unusual and ingeniously simple adaptation to the local conditions, both on Roti and on Savu.

A shallow hole is dug in the earth and a hollow clay mound is raised over it with openings into which may be fitted cooking pots. After drying in the sun, this hollowed mound is filled with wood (often the dried hard seeds of the lontar) and covered with leafstalks and sheaths. The whole thing is then fired to produce a crude, temporarily serviceable cooking oven.

Throughout Roti there are areas of clay soil. But the predominance of heavy clay soils in west Roti reinforces the association of this area with lontar-tapping. The better the clay soil, the better the possibilities of making a good oven. Dengka, in particular, has excellent clay; in fact, one of the names of this state is *Dae Mea:* "Red Earth."

Supposedly the ancestor of Dou-Danga built the first oven on the plan of a Rotinese house. He erected two poles to support a ridgepole, laid spars across this ridgepole, and covered the structure with clay. Ovens now have a variety of shapes: some raised, enclosed, and well made; others of the simplest form: a tunneled shaft of slightly raised clay open at both ends, on which four or five pots may be placed to cook juice. The following narrative, from Termanu, relates the development of these innovations:

According to the tale, in former times, here in the domain of Termanu, there was no one who tapped the lontar twice a day, in the morning and in the afternoon; everyone tapped just once in the morning. Because of this, no one drank sweet lontar juice; they only drank a sour lontar juice which was like vinegar.

One day early in the morning, an old man of clan Dou-Danga—his name is not told—went fishing for octopus in the sea. On returning from the sea, half-way home, he noticed a lontar palm that was being tapped. He put down his scoop-net and climbed up into the lontar to drink some lontar juice. He drank some but it was sour. So he poured it out; then with his knife, he sliced the tip of the rachilla at the point where it drips. After that, he reattached the leaf-bucket in the basket in the usual place, climbed down, picked up his things and went home.

That afternoon, the old man went scoop-fishing again in the sea. He returned by the same path on which earlier that morning he had tapped the lontar. There he put down his scoop-net and climbed up into the tree. He took some lontar juice and drank it. When he drank it, it was not extremely sour but tasted sweet and only slightly sour. At this, the old man realized that if one tapped both in the morning and in the afternoon, one would get sweet tasty lontar juice. So he climbed down, picked up his scoop-net, and returned home.

That old man was a tapper; he tapped a number of lontar palms near his house. When he began tapping his lontars in the morning and in the afternoon, his wife and children were able to drink delicious, sweet lontar juice. His neighbors saw him tap in the morning and in the afternoon and they thought to themselves saying: "Why does that old man tap twice a day, while we tap only once in the morning?" One villager spoke to another, saying: "We tap our lontars once a day in the morning, but that old man taps his lontars twice a day." Finally everyone knew about the old man's tapping.

One day, a man whose house was near that of the old man went to the old man's house. He wanted to ask him what his lontar juice tasted like when he tapped twice a day. When he came to ask, it happened that the old man and his wife and children were drinking and still had some fresh lontar juice; they poured some for him to drink. He drank and discovered that this fresh juice was sweeter and more delicious than anyone else's juice. After he had finished drinking, the man left and he told this news to members of his household. They told it to all the tappers in the village; everyone heard and knew about it. Then all the tappers in that village copied the old man's tapping so that they all drank delicious, fresh lontar juice. Men in other villages saw this and they began to tap like the old man and his village so that, in the end, everyone in the domain tapped twice a day, morning and afternoon, and everyone had delicious fresh lontar juice to drink.

Now everyone drank delicious lontar juice, but no one knew how to cook the juice to make a sweet syrup as we do now. They thought that they had only to gather several large buckets of sweet juice and pour them into a vat and they would not turn sour. Actually, after the tapping season, when they drank the juice in the vats, it was more sour than vinegar.

One reason why no one was able to cook juice to syrup was because in former times no one knew how to make a lontar cooking oven on which to set pots as we do now. So the old man from clan Dou-Danga sought some way to make an oven so that he could cook his juice to syrup.

He went to look for clay and he carried this back to his house. After that he went to look for *memengok* [a kind of epiphytic creeper, red and without leaves, that entwines itself around other trees]; he removed and brought back a large coil of this. He then cut the memengok into small pieces and he mixed these with the clay. After that, he soaked this mixture with water for about an hour; then he treaded this so the earth and memengok pieces were thoroughly mixed. After that, he began to make the oven. First, he gathered a number of stones larger than a gewang core to make a surrounding wall that was long and wide. Then he cut two pieces of wood the length of a folded arm [that is, a forearm, about one cubit] and made these into poles the width of a thumb and into thin straight sticks the width of a finger to form the spars. After finishing the surrounding wall of stones, he dug a hole to insert two upright poles and laid on top of them one piece of wood lengthwise to form his ridgepole. After that, he laid eight sticks crosswise on either side with one end resting on the ridgepole and the other end resting on the surrounding stones; these were the spars. Then he took clay and plastered it over the spars and plastered it to cover all the gaps between the poles from top to bottom, leaving only four holes in the middle on which to set the pots. When the framework of the oven was thickly plastered with clay, he took his pots one by one and measured them against the holes in the middle. He smoothed more and more clay over them until they were just right. When the plastering was finished, he let the wind blow on it for three or four hours so that the oven would begin to dry. Then he took dry leaves and the brittle leaf sheaths of the lontar and wrapped them around the outside of the oven and he gathered the seeds of old lontar fruit and heaped them inside the oven. He fired these until the oven had completely dried. Early the next morning when the oven had completely dried and the old man had finished his tapping, he immediately instructed his wife to set four clay pots on the four holes of the oven, to fill them with lontar juice, and to make a fire inside the oven so she could cook lontar syrup.

But still no one understood how to cook lontar syrup; thus when the lontar juice boiled up and its froth was removed, they scooped it out and poured it into vats. At the end of the lontar season when there was no more juice and they had to drink syrup for the wet season, the syrup was sour because the juice had not yet become a proper syrup.

The following year, the old man tapped again and his wife cooked, but her cooking was not like that of the year before. When the syrup boiled up and the froth was removed, she kept the fire going until the syrup went down and finally began to turn reddish-brown. When the syrup was a fine red-brown, it had become a proper syrup; she scooped the contents of the four pots into one leaf-bucket to be poured into vats. But before they poured it into vats, they mixed some with water to drink; they drank and found that it was truly delicious, not sour at all.

From that day forward, the old man's wife cooked syrup in this way and poured it in vats to keep for themselves to drink during the wet season with the extra to sell to the people of the village. People drank and found that cooked syrup was delicious, so they bought some from the old man and asked how the old man was able to cook such delicious syrup. Even before the old man told them anything, people saw the lontar cooking oven inside a little hut and they all went to see how it was made. Everyone was amazed that the old man had made such an oven, with holes in the middle on which to set pots. When they repeatedly asked him, the old man told them how to make a lontar cooking oven and how to cook lontar syrup. The people who came asked the old man to demonstrate to each of them how to plaster and make a cooking oven and how to cook juice to a delicious syrup so that later they would know how to plaster an oven and cook syrup. The old man agreed; he told each of them to gather clay at their homes and some small sticks.

When the clay and pieces of wood were ready, the old man went from house to house showing each person how to plaster an oven. And the old man cooked juice for each person to show how lontar juice could be made into delicious syrup.

Thus everyone in the domain learned from someone else until each understood how to plaster an oven and to cook syrup. Everyone has drunk delicious lontar syrup to this day and until this time.

There is much that can be gleaned from this tale. The Rotinese do not consider themselves to have been a palm-tapping people at the beginning of their history, nor at the time when they first reached the island of Roti. This is another reason why what I have called their mythology is concerned mainly with the origin of cultivated plants. Even in the legends about their early ancestors, the Rotinese describe themselves as cultivators. The picture these legends present of this earlier period is not unlike that of the present-day Timorese cultivators. In these legends changes occur gradually. At the point in time when this particular legend is supposed to have occurred, the Rotinese were already tapping palms in a casual way. This again is not unlike some Timorese today whom the Rotinese regard with derision because they know how to tap trees but do so only irregularly. The change that the Rotinese see crucial to the transformation of their economy came with the start of regular tapping twice a day.

One can see how this seemingly minor change could be of major significance. It imposed a regularity and discipline that attached men to trees rather than to swidden fields. It is virtually impossible to tap trees twice each day and watch over distant fields as well. The shift to regular tapping was a change from which all further developments in the economy can be seen to follow. With the ability to convert fresh juice to syrup and store it, the transformation was assured. Whether one considers the legend as ancestral truth or as an allegory about cultural change, it points toward that step which, though one of many in a series of gradual changes over time, may suddenly have vaulted the Rotinese people from swidden agriculture to a lontar-based economy.

Notes

Introduction

1. Jesuit and Dominican missions to the Timor area began in the sixteenth century. Their effects are difficult to assess. Early missions seem to have been of limited duration, sustained on the strength of determined individuals, and frequently these efforts were counteracted by the feuding political factions. After 1750, the political alignment of local areas and religious allegiance stabilized to form approximately the pattern that has persisted to the present.

2. The Bunaq people, a majority of whom live in east Timor, have been extensively studied by Louis Berthe and Claudine Berthe-Friedberg. Two of their papers (Friedberg 1971 and 1974) are of particular relevance for this study.

3. These figures for the Indonesian populations are taken from the *Sensus Penduduk Propinsi Nusa Tenggara Timur, Tahun 1971,* a stenciled document produced in Kupang in August 1972. My experience leads me to suspect that these figures may be a slight underenumeration of the present population. Appendix A gives further details on these populations. East Timor's population figures are from official Portuguese sources; I have no idea how accurate they may be.

4. Research on the economy and ecology of various regions of east Timor is now under way and in several years we may have a clearer picture of the situation on this part of the island.

5. For short ethnographic sketches of the Helong and Ndaonese, the least known of these populations, see Fox 1972c and d. For a longer discussion of the linguistic and cultural situation affecting both populations, see Fox 1974. A major study of the Helong was done by Nikolas Kadafuk, an anthropology student from the University of Udayana who carried out fieldwork under my general supervision in 1972-1973. His preliminary findings are embodied in *Laporan Tentang Helong* (1973), a 190-page typescript report.

6. Most Ndaonese men are gold- and silversmiths, who travel throughout the Timor area in search of work.

Chapter 1   The Contrast of Economies

1. See Geertz 1963:12-37.

2. The figures for the carrying capacities of swidden systems in southeast Asia quoted from Geertz (1963:26) come from van Beukering 1947, Freeman 1955, and Conklin 1957. It is noteworthy that these swidden systems are based chiefly on the cultivation of cereal crops; higher carrying capacities have been observed for swidden systems based on root crops in, for example, New Guinea or southeastern Nigeria. See Harris 1972.

3. Ormeling 1956. This study remains a major source book on Timor, since many of the government documents on which it was based were subsequently lost.

4. This figure can only be taken as a general indicator of the situation on the island. Timor is characterized by an extreme variability and irregularity in rainfall. For rainfall figures for Timor, see Ormeling 1956:17-21.

5. Detailed descriptions of Timor, of Atoni swidden agriculture, and of the Atoni in general can be found in Ormeling 1956, Cunningham 1963 and 1967, and Schulte Nordholt 1971. Comparative material on the swidden agriculture of the Bunaq, a small population on the border between east and west Timor, can be found in Friedberg 1971 and 1974. For a recent bibliography of sources on Timor, see Schulte Nordholt 1971:482-494. Henceforth in this study, I shall use the term "Timorese" explicitly in reference to the Atoni.

6. These and subsequent census figures for 1930 are taken from *Volkstelling,* 1936.

7. Conklin 1959.

8. Ormeling 1956:198-202.

9. Ormeling 1956:26. Ormeling's breakdown of this average (see his fig. 8, p. 27) shows that much of the area inhabited by Atoni still had a population density below 25 persons per square kilometer. The highest population densities were to be found around Kupang, in the areas inhabited by Belu, and in the Atoni highlands.

10. Comparative figures for 1961 and 1971 on the populations and population densities of the different regions considered in this study are given in Appendix A.

11. These rainfall figures for Sumba come from unpublished tables compiled by the Governor's office in Kupang for the entire province of Nusa Tenggara Timur.

12. Major sources on Sumba are Roos 1872, Roo van Alderwerelt 1906, Nooteboom 1940, and Onvlee 1973. For a bibliography of Sumba, see Fox and Fox 1972.

13. On Timor, rice is planted on newly cleared land and is followed, after the first year or two, by maize. In east Sumba, Nooteboom reports that rice and maize are intercropped in the same field. Such intercropping, if it occurs, is somewhat unusual. Other sources indicate separate fields for dry rice and maize, with rulers alone possessing rights to the few wet-rice fields on the island. See Nooteboom 1940:74-76 and Schulte Nordholt 1971:52-55.

14. Koopmans 1921.

15. Wainwright 1972.

16. Wijngaarden 1890b.

17. Radja Haba n.d.

18. These recent rainfall figures for Savu come from unpublished tables compiled by A. J. Tilla, head of the Kecamatan Sabu Barat.

19. Wainwright 1972.

20. In previous literature, this palm is also referred to as *Borassus flabellifer* L. See Part Three for a discussion of the botanical classification of *Borassus* palms.

21. The third part of this volume provides a comparative examination of the uses of *Borassus* palms in south and southeast Asia, and is intended as a qualification of this statement. A detailed examination of lontar-tapping, its techniques and its strategies, would distract from the main argument at this point.

22. For comparative calculations of lontar yields, see Ormeling 1956:154. Ormeling estimates the yield of a single lontar at about 56 liters of syrup per tapping season, and he claims that this is a conservative estimate.

23. On other Indonesian islands, products derived from bamboo, coconut palms, and banana trees provide typical articles of daily need. On Roti and Savu, the same semiarid conditions that severely limit the occurrence and development of these tropical plants allow a proliferation of the lontar and gewang palms, which in turn creates the possibility of an almost exclusive reliance on their products.

24. In 1973 local government officials, without calculating the importance of seaweed in the Rotinese diet, began a drive to force the Rotinese to plant vegetable gardens. This campaign caused some disruptions in Rotinese agriculture, because success was being judged in terms of land planted rather than yield. In certain areas, to achieve quotas, Rotinese were forced to adopt swidden techniques, which they described as a "waste of seed." The long-term effects of this kind of campaign remain to be seen.

25. The probable identification of this seaworm is *Leodice viridis*. Only its free-swimming sexual segments rise to the surface and are gathered by the Savunese and Ndaonese. Taken in small quantities as an appetizer, perhaps with gin, these *nyale* are a special treat that I can attest to having enjoyed.

26. Rotinese whom I questioned about this practice regarded the burning of lontar leaves less as a pragmatic attempt to restore the fertility of the soil and more as a truncated and transformed continuation of older dry-field agricultural practices. Over a hundred years ago Ferguson (1850) noted that *Borassus* leaves were used as fertilizer in Ceylon and south India. For further discussion see Part Three.

27. Control of water appears to have been a critical factor in the historical expansion of certain states on the island. I hope to be able to deal with this question at greater length in a subsequent study.

28. See Ormeling 1956:198-200.

29. See Schulte Nordholt 1971:52-91 (in particular 53-61).

30. Heyne (1927:976-977) reports that the use of *Lannea grandis* for fencing is common on Java. Savunese claim that this is a relatively new method of fencing on their island.

31. When I once suggested to a group of Rotinese in Termanu that they might consider planting lontar, my suggestion was greeted with outright laughter.

32. See Fox, "The Ceremonial System of Savu" (forthcoming).

33. See Ormeling 1956:155-161 and Kana 1966:24-29.

34. This use of the water buffalo in wet-rice cultivation also accounts for their retention in large numbers in certain areas of Timor (such as Amabi and most of the Belu region) as well as in west Sumba.

35. These data for Roti and Ndao come from Koopmans 1921, and for Savu from Heiligers 1920. See also Table 2.

36. One of the peculiar features of local government records about Savu is that they report a progressively diminished surface area for the island. Heiligers' unpublished "Memorie" (1920) reports Savu's surface area as 747 square kilometers; the *Sensus Penduduk* (Kupang, 1961) lists it as 502 square kilometers, whereas the *Sensus Penduduk* (Kupang, 1971) gives this surface area as 458 square kilometers. In this study I have based all my calculations on Heiligers' figure. If, in fact, Savu's area is less than Heiligers indicates, my arguments about the carrying capacity of Savu's lontar economy would be that much further strengthened.

37. The only data for an analysis of livestock-raising are those found in unpublished reports of the Dutch colonial administration. These data relate to the islands in 1920. Since Rotinese and Savunese are masters at evading official inquiries, it would be hazardous to maintain that these figures portray the exact number of animals on the islands. At best, one must assume that the figures are representative samples of each area's animal population—in effect, that no one group of Rotinese or Savunese was more successful than another in avoiding this enumeration. The concern is not, however, with absolute figures but with their relative proportions, and the one thing that can be said in support of these data is that they appear to represent the most thorough census ever undertaken of these islands.

38. Grazing animals fatten after the rains have produced new grass on the islands; pigs, because of their special diet, fatten during the dry season while other livestock lose weight.

39. Professor Shepard Forman informs me that horses are used extensively as plow animals in east Timor. True plowing is not to be found in west Timor, nor on the other islands of the outer arc. Several Dutch attempts to introduce the plow were made, but failed (Ormeling 1956:125-126). Field-treading occurs in place of plowing and although cattle can be used for this task, buffalo are everywhere the preferred animal. Bali cattle are, for example, often too small to be particularly effective.

40. The partial correlation matrix for all these populations is included as Appendix Table B-2.

41. Appendix Table B-3.

42. For a discussion of the use of barycentric representations, see Mosteller and Tukey 1968:114-119.

Chapter 2   The Clash of Economies

1. There is a definite trade-off between tapping a palm and pruning for its leaves. Too much pruning inhibits tapping and may shorten the juice-producing life of the tree. For further discussion see Part Three.

2. Ormeling 1956:61.

3. Some of the comparative evidence for the spread of this palm-tapping technology is analyzed in Part Three. A Rotinese legend concerning the origin of certain of these techniques is discussed in Appendix D.

4. A critical question here for future investigation is how the east Sumbanese

have maintained one of the lowest rates of population increase of any people in Indonesia.

5. Ormeling (1956:154), for example, refers to the Rotinese lontar-tappers' professional disdain of the inefficient and amateurish way in which the Timorese use the palms available to them.

6. Historical evidence suggests that to the Timorese neither the Rotinese occupation of certain stretches of land nor their use of unexploited palm savannah was seen as an immediate threat. The source of most disputes during the early settlement period was livestock. Somewhat the same situation may have been true of the Savunese settlements on Sumba.

Chapter 3   The Intricate Background of Island Relations

1. Wolters 1967:65-66.
2. Groeneveldt 1880:116.
3. For a more extended discussion of the history of this period, see Boxer 1947 and Schulte Nordholt 1971:159-185.
4. Leitão 1948:161-172.
5. From a letter by Scotte quoted in Schulte Nordholt 1971:167.
6. This stretch of beach is still called Pantai Solor.
7. Boxer 1947:12.
8. For information on Sonba'i, I have relied primarily on Schulte Nordholt's attempt (1971:159-185) to sort out local political relations on Timor during the Company period. Ormeling (1956:94-103) also provides a history of the early sandalwood trade.
9. For a discussion of the internal structure of these separate states, see Schulte Nordholt 1971:262-306.
10. Perhaps because Kupang was considered an outpost, men of diverse origin were able to find employment in the Company's service there. The Company's logbook reveals names of Dutch, German, Danish, Scottish, Italian, and Portuguese origin. Even in the eighteenth and nineteenth centuries, shipwrecked sailors of other nations were pressed into service in Kupang.
11. This kind of compact seems to have been a Dutch adaptation of a traditional native oath that required the drinking of cat's blood.
12. For centuries one of the leading slavers in eastern Indonesia was the Sultan of Bima, who regularly raided the Manggarai region of western Flores.
13. Quoted from the Corpus Diplomaticum Neerlando-Indicum, Commentary on the Company Treaty with Solor and Timor, Treaty No. CCXV, 2 July 1655, in *Bijdragen tot de Taal-, Land- en Volkenkunde*, vol. 87:75.
14. Various non-Austronesian or "Papuan" languages are spoken on Timor, Pantar, Alor, and Wetar in eastern Indonesia. Dr. C. L. Voorhoeve of the Research School of Pacific Studies has indicated that present evidence suggests the classification of all these languages in what is called the Trans-New Guinea phylum of languages. On Timor the principal speakers of these languages are the Bunaq who inhabit the central border region between west and east Timor, and the Makassae and Fatuluku of east Timor.
15. Domesticated animals provide supporting evidence for the antiquity of

agriculture on Timor. Recent archaeological excavations in east Timor have uncovered, in a sequence calculated to have begun 4,500 to 5,000 years ago, the remains of pigs and goats, followed later by dogs and water buffalo (Glover 1971). Although these cave sites have not provided evidence of the foods grown at the time, this early date can be taken as the likely inception of agriculture on Timor. By about 1000 B.C. Timor was in regular contact with southeast Asia.

16. Thus, for example, both Old and New World taro (*Colocasia esculenta* and *Xanthosoma*) are cultivated by the same groups on Timor. Dr. William Clarke of the Research School of Pacific Studies at the Australian National University identified these two types of taro for me during a brief visit to Timor.

17. Despite an undoubted convergence of influences, root crops have never been as important as cereals in the subsistence diet of the peoples of the Timor area. Indonesian influence, and with it "Indonesian" food crops, have always predominated.

18. This discussion makes no attempt to cover the history of all the food crops now grown in the Timor area. Many newer vegetables, such as peanuts, onions, garlic, squash, and eggplant, outrank the older staples. A Mennonite agricultural mission that began work near Kupang in the early 1950's has been responsible for the introduction and dissemination of many new varieties of food.

19. Glover 1971:17. For early references to Job's tears on Roti, see van Lynden 1851:391 and Jonker 1908:82.

20. The green gram is sometimes referred to in English as the mung bean. The Dutch botanical literature uniformly classifies this particular bean as *Phaseolus radiatus* L. and calls it green gram, as distinguished from *Phaseolus mungo* L., which is the distinct designation for the mung bean (Heyne 1927:836-838). In the revision of this nomenclature, the term *Phaseolus aereus* Roxb. seems to have been adopted to cover earlier usages (Purseglove 1971:290-294).

21. Ormeling 1956:108.

22. Coolhaas 1968:III, 782.

23. Dampier's evidence on this point is conclusive: "Indian corn thrives here, and is the common food of the Islanders" (1939:168). It is essential to realize, however, that his description of Timor relates specifically to the north coast between Kupang and Lifao. Although he anchored for two months in the Bay of Kupang, he could not have seen maize growing at the time he was there; but he gathered information from both the Dutch and Portuguese, probably bought some maize to supply his ship, and certainly witnessed the clearing and planting of fields by the Timorese (see 1939:170).

24. In the Belu region, which is the center of sorghum and green gram production on Timor, these crops are apparently grown in separate fields.

25. Kol. Arch. 1123, *Timor Book 1661,* 22 November 1660.

The *Timor Book* to which I refer so extensively is the major source of information on the Company's activities in the Timor area. It consists of letters and documents sent annually from Kupang to Batavia that were copied in Batavia, translated if necessary from Malay to Dutch, and sent on to the various Company councils or *Kamer* in the Netherlands. Each year the *Timor Book* was bound, according to no coherent system, with other books originating from other Dutch factories in Indonesia and Asia. Hundreds of these large bound volumes, divided into individual books, are to be found in the *Algemeen Rijksarchief* in the Hague. They are referred to as the *Overgekomen Brieven en Papieren,* and a typed catalog provides references to the separate books. Athough duplicate copies of most of these materials are available from both the Amsterdam and the Zeeland *Kamer,* the catalog is based on the collection from the Amsterdam *Kamer.*

When quoting from the *Timor Book,* I cite the Colonial Archive Number (Kol. Arch.) for the particular volume; unless otherwise specified, this refers to the Amsterdam *Kamer.* I also cite the volume date, with the understanding that each contains letters and papers written during the previous year. Where possible, I have indicated either the date of the particular letter referred to or a page number if one exists. Since the *Timor Book* was merely the bound collection of papers received from Kupang in any one year, rarely are these books systematically arranged. For the above references, for example, Kol. Arch. refers to the Archive Number of the *Timor Book* for 1661; the report from which I quote was actually written on 22 November 1660.

26. Rumphius 1741:vol. 1, bk. 8, chap. 9, p. 51.

27. This comparison of Rotinese and Savunese, it must be admitted, is based in part on a knowledge of their present institutions. However, many features of these societies are indicated in the early description of the islands. I plan to deal more extensively with the development of indigenous Rotinese institutions in a future monograph to be entitled *Termanu: The Political History of an Indonesian State.*

28. Ndaonese can be considered as a dialect of Savunese. Both the Savunese and Ndaonese people assure me that despite certain differences, they can understand one another (see Jonker 1903:85-89).

29. The first account of dialect variation on Roti was written by a Rotinese, D. P. Manafe, in 1889. He concluded that there were nine dialects on Roti, and these divisions were used by Jonker in his dictionary (1908). It must be realized, however, that nine is for the Rotinese the number of a totality and that virtually all enumerative schema comprise nine items. There are nine ''seeds'' in the agricultural cult, nine clan lords, nine ancestral sons of the moon, and so forth.

30. Ten Kate 1894:221. See Fox 1974 for a more detailed discussion of dialect differences and their cultural significance.

31. See Fox 1971a and *Termanu* (in preparation).

32. Savu's name is supposedly based on that of an early ancestor of the Savunese, Hawu Miha. The lack of a single native name for Roti as a whole may explain some of the vicissitudes in the naming of the island. See Fox 1969.

33. See Fox 1971b, 1974, and 1975.

34. Teffer 1875:225.

35. Fox 1965:203-209.

36. See Fox, ''The Ceremonial System of Savu'' (forthcoming).

37. See Cunningham 1965 for comparable material on Dutch appointments of secular figures on Timor.

Chapter 4   Roti, Savu, and the Dutch East India Company

1. *Daghregister 1656,* 1904:11.
2. Leitão 1948:161-172.
3. See Jonker 1905:451-453.

4. *Daghregister 1653,* 1888:154; Coolhaas 1964, II:750.

5. Kol. Arch. 1107, *Timor Book 1657:218-219.*

6. Kol. Arch. 1116, *Timor Book 1659,* 3 October 1658:510.

7. Kol. Arch. 1123, *Timor Book 1661,* 22 November 1660:725.

8. *Daghregister 1661,* 1889:217.

9. Kol. Arch. 1123, *Timor Book 1661,* 22 November 1660:725.

10. Corpus Diplomaticum, Treaty No. CCLVIII, 27 July 1662, in *Bijdragen,* vol. 87:212-214.

11. *Daghregister 1664,* 1893:272.

12. *Daghregister 1676,* 1887:161.

13. *Daghregister 1681,* 1919:616; *Daghregister 1682,* I, 1928:262-264; and *Daghregister 1682,* II, 1931:1183-1185. The kati was equivalent in weight to 0.617 kilogram.

14. *Daghregister 1682,* I, 1928:263.

15. Corpus Diplomaticum, Treaty No. DXXXIII, 24 November 1690 to 3 February, and 4 May 1691 in *Bijdragen,* vol. 91:538-544.

16. Corpus Diplomaticum, Treaty No. DCXI, 9 October 1700, in *Bijdragen,* vol. 93:185-189.

17. Fox 1971a:60.

18. In translating certain names, terms, or phrases from letters in the archives, I occasionally include, for the sake of accuracy, the Dutch word or phrase in parentheses spelled just as it appears in the archives. In numerous instances this spelling is unlike modern Dutch usage. Thus, for example, *"een goede spijscamer"* is ter Horst's exact phrase in Kol. Arch. 1119, *Timor Book 1660,* 4 October 1659:865.

19. Coolhaas 1971, IV:490.

20. Coolhaas 1971, IV:407.

21. The Dutch pound during this period was the Amsterdam pound, which was equivalent in weight to 0.494 kilogram or 1.09 pound (avoirdupois).

22. Kol. Arch. 1992, *Timor Book 1729:65-66.*

23. Coolsma 1901:42.

24. Ibid.

25. Kol. Arch. 2488, *Timor Book 1744:96-103.*

26. Ibid.

27. Strictly speaking, all of these dates in the *Timor Book* refer to the tribute of the previous year. Thus the determination of the price of a schoolmaster is reported in a letter to the Governor General dated 17 September 1750, Kol. Arch. 2653, *Timor Book 1751:61-65.*

28. Kol. Arch. 2775, *Timor Book 1757,* 28 September 1756.

29. Kol. Arch. 2951, *Timor Book 1763.*

30. Leitão 1948:162.

31. Heeres 1895:422-429, 474-478.

32. Ibid., 424.

33. Coolhaas 1971, IV:108-109. The teyl (also spelled *tael* or *thail*) varied in weight from 0.38 to 0.54 kilogram.

34. Haga 1882:394-399.

35. Corpus Diplomaticum (Part VI), Treaty No. CMXCVII, 9 June 1756, in Stapel 1955:81-107.

36. Van der Chijs 1879:27-28.

37. The *Endeavour*'s visit lasted five days, from 17 to 21 September 1770. The fullest accounts of this visit are to be found in Hawkesworth's 1773 edition of Cook's *Voyages,* III:265-299, and in Beaglehole's 1962 edition of Banks's *Endeavour Journal,* II:149-177. It should be noted that Banks's papers were originally used by Hawkesworth in editing Cook's official account. Banks's account therefore serves as both a check on and an amplification of what was written in Cook's name.

38. Cook 1773:277-278.

39. Banks 1962:150.

40. Cook 1773:295.

41. Ibid., 294-295.

42. Banks 1962:160.

43. Cook 1773:295.

44. Ibid., 288.

45. Ibid., 288-289.

46. Ibid., 268.

47. Ibid., 276.

48. Ibid.

49. Ibid., 289.

50. Banks 1962:151.

51. Cook 1773:269.

52. Ibid., 298.

53. Ibid., 295.

54. Ibid., 291.

55. Ibid., 290.

56. Ibid., 288.

57. A descendant of six generations from Lomi Djara, D. D. Bireludji, was until recently *camat* (or subdistrict head) of Seba and continues to reside in one of the old royal residences; his friend and associate, G. R. Manu, a descendant of five generations from Manu Djami, is the Fetor of Seba. Both gave me invaluable assistance during my stay on Savu.

58. Banks 1962:153.

59. Cook 1773:276.

60. Ibid., 273.

61. Ibid., 284-286.

62. A description of the similar Rotinese oven is to be found in Part Three.

63. Cook 1773:286.

64. Ibid., 293.

65. Ibid., 276.

66. See the description of the uses of the lontar on Roti for the year 1780 in van Hogendorp 1825-26, II:423-424.

67. Dentrecasteaux 1808:172-173.

68. Wijngaarden 1890b:367.

Chapter 5   The Rotinese in the Nineteenth Century

1. Van Hogendorp 1825-26, II:422.

2. Dicker 1965:19; Fox 1965:47-54.

3. In one article in 1864, Jackstein went so far as to defend the ritual rights of the "Head of the Earth" against interference by Dutch colonial officials.

4. Coolsma 1901:832.

5. Dicker 1965:79.

6. Buddingh 1861, III:326.

7. Jackstein 1864:283.

8. See van der Chijs 1879:10 for a list of Malay schoolbooks used in Rotinese schools.

9. See van der Chijs 1879 on rulers' attitudes toward school attendance.

10. Graafland 1889:242-244.

11. Coolhaas 1971, IV:338.

12. Jonker 1908:356.

13. Le Grand 1900:372.

14. Rotinese have often told me that they would rather hear Malay than listen to the dialect of some other Rotinese state. One former Rotinese official from east Roti even boasted that when he was in office he used a Malay interpreter in certain parts of west Roti. This behavior was prompted more by social factors than by problems of dialect intelligibility.

15. For a fuller discussion of this complex linguistic situation see Fox 1974.

16. This settlement of Chinese operated a kiln for manufacturing bricks and roof tiles. Whether these tiles, made in Termanu, were strictly for export to Kupang or were part of a larger export trade is not clear. According to the oral traditions of Termanu, there was considerable hostility toward these Chinese on the part of certain segments of the local population.

17. This is a simplification of a more complex situation. Termanu seems once to have controlled a part of eastern Loleh known as Kuli. At some point, possibly when control of Kuli was granted to the ruler of Loleh, a segment of Kuli's population moved to Diu.

18. *Register in Rade,* 16 December 1819.

19. Kruseman 1824:185-186.

20. The *paal* is an old linear measure of Javanese origin. It was equivalent to 1,506.9 meters. According to Ormeling (1956:117) who bases his comment on Francis (1832), this area comprised the coastal strip from Oesina to Sulamu.

21. Francis 1838:357.

22. This is such a significant feature of the Rotinese transmigration that it deserves special emphasis. The Rotinese migration recreated, in villages on Timor, the local division of the island itself. Even today one has only to enter any of the dozens of Rotinese villages on Timor and hear the particular dialect that is spoken to know precisely from which part of Roti its population came. More than a century of living on Timor has not significantly eroded these old identities, nor has it brought about any full-scale intermingling of the separate, settled Rotinese populations. Roti is close enough for there to be considerable visiting between specific villages on Timor and certain states on Roti. New migrants almost always move to one of their state's village settlements on Timor, where they are assured of support by family and friends. This fundamental notion of identity in terms of one's particular state was made strikingly clear to me by a man from Dengka who had lived on Timor for years. He determined to explain to me where other "Rotinese" were settled, but by this it turned out that he meant only other men from Dengka!

23. Veth 1855:59.
24. Buddingh 1861, III:329-331.
25. Ormeling 1956:149.
26. Ibid., 152.
27. See Teysmann (1874:406-410) for a description of Rotinese settlements on Timor in the nineteenth century.
28. Donselaar 1864:34.
29. Van der Chijs 1879:12.
30. The first teacher training school for the area was not, in fact, in Kupang, but in Baä. Known as STOVIL (*School tot opleiding van inlands leraren*), this school was opened in 1902.
31. Manafe 1889; Fanggidaej 1892 and 1894.
32. These population figures are from the following sources: for 1824, Kruseman (1824); for 1831, Francis (1832); for 1863, Jackstein (1864); for 1879, Riedel (1889); for 1885, Wichmann (1892); for 1921, Koopmans (1921); for 1930, *Volkstelling* 1936; for 1954 and 1957, Gyanto (1958); for 1961, *Symposium I* (1967); and for 1971, *Sensus Penduduk* (1972).
33. Extract from Coorengel letter, in the *Algemeen Rijksarchief.*
34. Donselaar 1872:290.
35. The year 1879 is the only one for which Ndao has been included in the population figures of Roti; for all other years, Ndao has been purposely excluded.
36. Francis 1832:Bijlage 9.
37. Ormeling 1956:148.
38. For a study of the village of Sumlili, see Kadafuk 1971.

Chapter 6   The Savunese in the Nineteenth Century

1. Moor 1837:10.
2. Kruseman 1824.
3. Kruseman 1836:37.
4. Müller 1857, I:135.
5. Roo van Alderwerelt 1906:214-218.
6. Batiest 1823.
7. Roo van Alderwerelt 1906:242-245.
8. Francis 1838:366.
9. [Gronovius?] 1855:279-280. (In the introduction to this article, D. J. van den Dungen Gronovius is expressly thanked for supplying the material on which it is based.)
10. Ibid., 304.
11. Ibid., 309.
12. In the whole course of historical documentation, there is exactly one recorded visit to Raijua by a Dutchman, that of the missionary Wijngaarden for two days in 1889.
13. See Wijngaarden 1890b:376; Letterboer 1904; and Heiligers 1920.
14. Donselaar 1871:111.
15. Heiligers 1920:11.
16. Donselaar 1872:290-292.
17. Heiligers 1920:23.

18. These population figures are from the following sources: for 1824, Kruseman (1824); for 1831, Francis (1832); for 1869 and 1891, Donselaar (1872); for 1880, Riedel (1885); for 1890, ten Kate (1894); for 1920, Heiligers (1920); for 1924, Wetering (1926); for 1930, *Volkstelling* 1936; for 1961, *Symposium I* (1967); and for 1971, *Sensus Penduduk* (1972).

19. Humme 1876.

20. Quoted from Wielenga 1912:236.

21. *Koloniaal Verslag* 1877:37.

22. Wielenga 1912:236.

23. Wijngaarden 1893:368.

24. Letterboer 1904:350.

25. For a discussion of this lunar calendar and its attendant rituals see Wijngaarden 1892, Cuisinier 1956, and Fox ''The Ceremonial System of Savu'' (forthcoming).

26. Dicker 1965:79.

Chapter 7   Ethnic Relations in the Twentieth Century

1. For my discussion in this section, I rely heavily on unpublished documents by Schultz (1927) and Doko (1972).

2. These five parties were the *Partai Persatuan Timur Besar, Indo-Europees Verbond, Democratische Bond van Indonesia, Persatuan Kaum Maluku,* and *Persatuan Selatan Daya.* All originated in ethnic groups outside the Timor area.

3. Ormeling 1956:118.

4. Ibid., 145.

5. Ibid., 223.

6. Ibid., 222-223.

7. Ibid., 221.

8. Ibid., 67.

9. Ibid., 147-148.

10. Ibid., 152.

11. Ibid., 153.

12. Ibid., 144-145.

13. Ibid., 62-63.

14. Ibid.

15. Ibid., 115.

16. Ibid., 51.

17. Ibid., 161.

18. Ibid., 193.

19. Very little nutritional research has been done on Timor. One study (Tumonggor 1951), however, involved a comparison between Timorese and Rotinese in the Kupang area and pointed to a higher nutritional level among the Rotinese. The comparison was between Timorese cultivators and landless Rotinese lontar-tappers who worked as coolies in Kupang during the wet season. Even these, the lowest stratum of Rotinese on Timor, had a better and more varied diet than did the Timorese. Eighty percent of the Timorese diet was reported to derive from maize, whereas the Rotinese diet comprised lontar sugar, meat, and some fish, as well as maize.

20. Ormeling 1956:74-75.

21. Ibid., 124.
22. Ibid., 221.

Chapter 8   Introduction to the Borassus *Palm*   •

1. Corner 1966:1.
2. Beccari's initial study of the *Borassus,* "Studio sui Borassus" is found in *Webbia* 4:293-385. His monograph, *Palme della tribù Borasseae,* published posthumously in Florence in 1924 is essentially a reprint of his earlier work.
3. See Chevalier 1930, Dalziel 1937:496-497, Adandé 1954, Nicolas 1959, and Decary 1964 for a discussion of the uses of African *Borassus* palms.
4. Heyne 1927, I:324.
5. Burkill 1966:350-351.
6. Professor Harold E. Moore, Jr., has written several letters of comment on the materials sent to him from Timor. The following excerpt from a letter dated 1 March 1976 provides a succinct statement of his conclusions:

> As you will appreciate from your own work, there are not extensive study collections of *Borassus* available here or anywhere else. According to Beccari, both *Borassus flabellifer* and *B. sundaicus* are characterized by male flowers with the calyx divided to the base into three sepals while the remaining species, with the possible exception of *Borassus heineana* from New Guinea, have the calyx of the male flowers divided only to the middle into three lobes. *Borassus flabellifer* has orbicular petals in the perianth about the base of the fruit and these are not at all or scarcely overlapping. The leaves are said to be covered with scales (although I have not been able to verify this on material at my disposal). The seed is only superficially sulcate. *Borassus sundaicus,* on the other hand, has rounded-subreniform petals in the perianth at the base of the fruit and these are overlapping. Leaves are destitute of scales and the seed is deeply sulcate.
>
> My determination of your material as *Borassus sundaicus* is made on the basis of the shape of the petals and the fact that they overlap in fruit. No seed was available and to be honest I have not been able to verify the difference in the leaf as noted above. The photographs that you have so kindly provided further verify the nature of the petals at the base of the fruit.

7. Detailed and illustrated botanical descriptions of the Asian *Borassus* can be found in works such as van Rheede tot Drakenstein (1678-1703) and Rumphius (1741-1755), in Ferguson (1850), in Beccari (1914 and 1924), or in Corner (1966). These studies represent three hundred years of interest. From the ethnobotanical viewpoint, Ferguson's study is the most engaging. In nineteenth-century fashion, its full title is *The Palmyra Palm, Borassus Flabelliformis: A Popular Description of the Palm and Its Products, Having Special Reference to Ceylon, with a Valuable Appendix, Embracing Extracts from Nearly Every Author That Has Noted the Tree.*
8. Of more than minor importance for this study is the identification of the other major fan palm of the genus *Corypha,* commonly found in association with *Borassus* palms. In India and Ceylon, the *Corypha* is *Corypha umbraculifera,* the famed cultivated talipot of India whose leaves, like those of the palmyra, have served

for centuries as writing materials. In Indonesia, similar *Corypha* palms are called *gebang* or *gewang*. Both Roti and Madura have large numbers of these trees and in the Dutch literature they are variously named: *Corypha utan* Lamarck, *C. elata* Roxb., *C. gebanga* Bl., or *C. sylvestris* Mart. The major study of Indonesian *Corypha* is that of Douglas and Bimantoro (1957). On the basis of photographs and specimens sent from Timor, Professor Harold E. Moore, Jr. has identified the Timorese species as *Corypha elata* Roxb. Each of the three societies that we shall consider utilizes a species of *Corypha* along with a species of *Borassus*.

    9. Ferguson 1850:12.

    10. Cassier 1901:693.

    11. See Fernando (1970) for an interesting discussion of the unlikely alliance of British temperance organizations, Ceylonese nationalist leaders, and Buddhist monks in the campaign against the Excise Ordinance of 1912 regulating the sale of palmyra liquor.

Chapter 9   Three Case Studies of Borassus Utilization

    1. Corner 1966:44-45.

    2. Gebuis and Abdul Kadir 1928-1929:304-305.

    3. It is worth noting again that Savu has few gewang palms. I can give no botanical reasons for this fact. The Savunese, who have different methods of fencing from those of the Rotinese, have no need of gewang leafstalks. For tie-and-dyeing, they use the inner layers of coconut leaves or else they import *eke-nak,* the inner layers of gewang leaves, from Roti or Timor.

    4. The flow of sap in the lontar has been related by some to its system of transpiration, the means by which water is supplied to its leaves. Professor Moore informs me, however, that this is a controversial matter. According to Corner, the lontar has a high root pressure, more than enough to counter the negative pressure that develops in the root by the transpiring leaves. The flow of sap and the stream of transpiration thus may be mutually dependent, though inversely related. When transpiration is minimal, the flow of sap is at its maximum; when, during the heat of the day, transpiration is maximal, the flow of sap is reported to be minimal. (See Corner 1966:103, 135-136).

    5. The small hand refractometer that I used in the field to measure the sugar content of fresh juice consistently registered between 15 and 17 percent, which would seem to accord with the conversion rate that results from cooking.

    6. These calculations are based on conservative figures, but are in line with the estimates made by Ormeling (1956:154).

    7. I cannot substantiate that there is a definite difference between the juice production of the male and female lontar. Rotinese statements to this effect may reflect certain symbolic conceptions of the ideal nature of these trees.

    8. This description is of the preparation of a male palm. The preparation of a female palm is in no significant way different, except that the entire inflorescence must be squeezed instead of the separate rachillae. Afterward, then, there is no need to tie the separate rachillae together.

    9. Gebuis and Abdul Kadir 1928-1929:305.

    10. Quoted from Ormeling 1956:145.

11. In a future monograph dealing with the specific villages in which I have lived on Roti, I intend to publish detailed illustrations of the patterns of lontar ownership and payments by tappers to the owners. While I have considerable information on these patterns in Termanu, I am still collecting comparable material from west Roti.

12. It would be incorrect to overemphasize the lack of a market for lontar syrup. It is a relative matter, for the market in lontar syrup has fluctuated even in the recent past. The Rotinese have demonstrated that they are certainly able to respond to market demands when they arise. Ormeling reports that in the 1950's Chinese gin distillers in Kupang created a market for syrup by their purchases. The demand for syrup could not be met by the Rotinese on Timor, so syrup export from Roti rose considerably. In 1952, for example, Roti exported approximately 175,000 liters of syrup. When the Chinese ceased distilling, these exports dropped and picked up, on a much reduced scale, in the late 1960's, when a Rotinese in Kupang began his own distillery. In 1973, plans were being discussed for building a modern distillery in Kupang. This would have a major effect on the market for syrup.

13. Heyne 1927, I:326.

14. Quoted in Hardgrave 1969:25.

15. Ferguson 1850:39.

16. Ibid., 13.

17. Ibid., 16.

18. Ibid., 23.

19. Ibid., 27-28.

20. Caldwell 1857:31-37.

21. Ferguson 1850:30.

22. Hardgrave 1969:27-28.

23. Caldwell, quoted in Hardgrave 1969:19.

24. Caldwell 1857:31.

25. Quoted in Hardgrave 1969:55.

26. Quoted in Hardgrave 1969:57.

27. Quoted in Hardgrave 1969:58.

28. Quoted in Hardgrave 1969:47.

29. Quoted in Hardgrave 1969:57.

30. Quoted in Hardgrave 1969:51.

31. Hardgrave 1969:52.

32. Ibid., 97.

33. Quoted in Hardgrave 1969:53.

34. Hardgrave 1969:53.

35. Ibid.

36. Evans-Pritchard 1962:56.

Bibliography

Adandé, A. Le vin de palme chez les Diola de la Casamance. *Notes africaines* 61:4-7, 1954.

Banks, Joseph. *The Endeavour Journal 1768-1771*. J. C. Beaglehole, ed., vol. 2. London: Angus and Robertson, 1962.

Batiest, J. A. Zandelhout-eiland alias Tanna Tjumba. Nota van der gezagvoerder Batiest, van het schip Tjimanoh aldaar gestrand in 't jaar 1823 (?) In the G. J. Schneither collection, no. 130-131:24B b/s, Algemeen Rijksarchief, The Hague.

Beccari, Odoardo. Studio sui Borassus. *Webbia* 4:293-385, 1914.

———— *Palme della tribù Borasseae*. Florence: G. Pessari, 1924.

Beukering, J. A. van. Het ladangvraagstuk, een bedrijfs- en sociaal economisch probleem. *Landbouw* 19:241-285, 1947.

Blatter, Ethelbert. *The Palms of British India and Ceylon*. London: Oxford University Press, 1926.

Boxer, C. R. The Topasses of Timor. *Koninklijke Vereeniging Indisch Instituut*, Mededeling no. 73, Afdeling Volkenkunde no. 24, 1947.

———— *Fidalgos in the Far East 1550-1770*. The Hague: Martinus Nijhoff, 1948.

———— Portuguese and Dutch colonial rivalry, 1641-1661. *Studia* 2:1-42, 1958.

Buddingh, S. A. *Neerlands Oost-Indië*. 3 vols. Rotterdam: M. Wijt en Zonen, 1859-1861.

Burkill, I. H. *A Dictionary of the Economic Products of the Malay Peninsula*, vol. 1. Kuala Lumpur: Ministry of Agriculture and Co-operatives, 1966.

Caldwell, Robert. *Lectures on the Tinnevelly Missions, Descriptive of the Field, the Work, and the Results*. London: Bell and Daldy, 1857.

Cassier, A. Le palmier à sucre du Cambodge. *Bulletin économique de l'Indo-Chine* 38:689-693, 1901.

Chevalier, Auguste. Le Borassus aethiopum de l'Afrique Occidentale et son utilisation. *Revue de botanique appliquée et d'agriculture tropicale* 10:649-655, 1930.

Chijs, J. A. van der. Het inlandsch onderwijs in de Residentie Timor in 1871. *Tijdschrift voor Indische Taal-, Land- en Volkenkunde* 25:1-51, 1879.

Conklin, Harold. *Hanunoo Agriculture in the Philippines*. Rome: Food and Agricultural Organization of the United Nations, 1957.

———— Shifting cultivation and the succession to grassland. *Proceedings of the 9th Pacific Congress* (1957) 7:60-62, 1959.

Cook, James. *An Account of the Voyages for Making Discoveries in the Southern Hemisphere*. John Hawkesworth, ed., vol. 3. London: W. Strahan and T. Cadell, 1773.

Coolhaas, W. Ph. *Generale Missiven van Gouverneurs-Generaal en Raden aan Heren XVII der Verenigde Oostindische Compagnie*, vols. 1-4. The Hague: Martinus Nijhoff, 1960-1971.

Coolsma, S. *De Zendingseeuw voor Nederlandsch Oost-Indië*. Utrecht: C. H. E. Breijer, 1901.

Corner, E. J. H. *The Natural History of Palms*. London: Weidenfeld and Nicolson, 1966.

Corpus Diplomaticum Neerlando-Indicum, in *Bijdragen tot de Taal-, Land- en Volkenkunde*, vol. 73, pt. 1, 1907; vol. 87, pt. 2, 1931; vol. 91, pt. 3, 1934; vol. 93, pt. 4, 1935; vol. 96, pt. 5, 1938.

———— pt. 6 (1753-1799) F. W. Stapel, ed. The Hague: Martinus Nijhoff, 1955.

Cuisinier, Jeanne. Un calendrier de Savu. *Journal asiatique* 244:111-119, 1956.

Cunningham, C. E. "People of the Dry Land: A Study of the Social Organization of an Indonesian People." D.Phil. thesis, Oxford University, 1963.

———— Order and change in an Atoni diarchy. *Southwest Journal of Anthropology* 21:359-383, 1965.

———— Soba: an Atoni village of West Timor. In: *Villages in Indonesia*. Koentjaraningrat, ed., pp. 63-89. Ithaca, New York: Cornell University Press, 1967.

Daghregister gehouden in 't Casteel Batavia, anno 1624-1682. 31 vols. Batavia: Landsdrukkerij, and The Hague: Martinus Nijhoff, 1896-1931.

Dalziel, J. M. *Useful Plants of West Tropical Africa*. London: Crown Agents for the Colonies, 1937.

Dampier, William. *A Voyage to New Holland in the Year 1699*, vol. 3, pt. 2. London, 1703. Reprint London: Argonaut Press, 1939.

Decary, R. Les utilisations des palmiers à Madagascar. *Journal d'agriculture tropicale et de botanique appliquée* 11:259-266, 1964.

Dentrecasteaux (Jos. Ant. Bruny). *Voyage de Dentrecasteaux, envoyé à la recherche de la Perouse*, vol. 1. Paris: Imprimerie imperiale, 1808.

Dicker, Gordon. "The Proclamation of the Gospel in Timor. A Study of the Evangelical Church of Timor in Relation to Its Historical Antecedents." M.A. thesis, Melbourne College of Divinity. 1965.

Doko, I. H. "Sejarah Perjuangan Kemerdekaan di Nusa Tenggara Timur." Unpublished manuscript, 1972. Author's collection of documents on eastern Indonesia.

Donselaar, W. M. Het inlandsche christendom en schoolwezen op Timor in 1862. *Mededeelingen van wege het Nederlandsch Zendelinggenootschap* 8:24-60, 1864.

————— Een oude en een nieuwe akker, Timor en Savoe. *Mededeelingen van wege het Nederlandsch Zendelinggenootschap* 15:102-114, 1871.

————— Aanteekeningen over het eiland Savoe. *Mededeelingen van wege het Nederlandsch Zendelinggenootschap* 16:281-332; Naschrift: 332-340, 1872.

Douglas, J., and Bimantoro, R. R. Identification of the Corypha palms which flowered in the Hortus Bogoriensis 1953-1955. *Annales Bogorienses* 2:137-148, 1957.

Evans-Pritchard, E. E. *Essays in Social Anthropology.* London: Faber and Faber, 1962.

Fanggidaej, J. Rottineesche spraakkunst. *Bijdragen tot de Taal-, Land- en Volkenkunde* 41:554-571, 1892.

————— Beberapa tjeritera peroepamaan tersalin kepada bahasa Rotti jang dinamai tutui nakasasamak-ala. (Fabelen in 't Rottineesch, intr. H. Kern). *Bijdragen tot de Taal-, Land- en Volkenkunde* 44:450-460; 662-711, 1894.

————— *Het Evangelie van Lucas vertaald in het Rottineesch door* . . . Amsterdam, 1895.

Ferguson, William. *The Palmyra Palm.* Colombo: Observer Press, 1850.

Fernando, Tissa. Arrack, toddy and Ceylonese nationalism: some observations on the temperance movement, 1912-1921. *Ceylon Studies Seminar* 1969/70 series, no. 9, University of Ceylon, 1970.

Fox, James J. "Roti and Savu: A Literary Analysis of Two Island Societies in Eastern Indonesia." B.Litt. thesis, Oxford University, 1965.

————— "The Rotinese: A Study of the Social Organization of an Eastern Indonesian People." D. Phil. thesis, Oxford University, 1968.

————— Van Wouden's Types of Social Structure. *Man,* New Series, 4:650-651, 1969.

————— A Rotinese dynastic genealogy: structure and event. In: *The Translation of Culture: Essays to E. E. Evans-Pritchard.* T. O. Beidelman, ed., pp. 37-77. London: Tavistock Publications, 1971a.

————— Semantic parallelism in Rotinese ritual language. *Bijdragen tot de Taal-, Land- en Volkenkunde* 127:215-255, 1971b.

————— Sister's child as plant: metaphors in an idiom of consanguinity. In ASA Monograph 11: *Rethinking Kinship and Marriage.* R. Needham, ed., pp. 219-252. London: Tavistock Publications, 1971c.

————— The Rotinese. In: *Ethnic Groups of Insular Southeast Asia.* F. LeBar, ed., vol. 1, pp. 106-108. New Haven, Connecticut: Human Relations Area Files Press, 1972a.

————— The Savunese. In: *Ethnic Groups of Insular Southeast Asia.* F. LeBar, ed., vol. 1, pp. 77-80. New Haven, Connecticut: Human Relations Area Files Press, 1972b.

————— The Ndaonese. In: *Ethnic Groups of Insular Southeast Asia.* F. LeBar, ed., vol. 1, p. 109. New Haven, Connecticut: Human Relations Area Files Press, 1972c.

————— The Helong. In: *Ethnic Groups of Insular Southeast Asia.* F. LeBar, ed., vol. 1, p. 105. New Haven, Connecticut: Human Relations Area Files Press, 1972d.

————— On bad death and the left hand: a study of Rotinese symbolic inversions. In: *Right and Left: Essays on Dual Symbolic Classification.* R. Needham, ed., pp. 342-368. Chicago: University of Chicago Press, 1973.

——— Our ancestors spoke in pairs: Rotinese views of language, dialect, and code. In: *Explorations in the Ethnography of Speaking.* R. Bauman and J. Sherzer, eds., pp. 65-85. London: Cambridge University Press, 1974.

——— On binary categories and primary symbols: some Rotinese perspectives. In: *The Interpretation of Symbolism.* R. Willis, ed., pp. 99-132. ASA Studies 2. London: Malaby Press, 1975.

——— The ceremonial system of Savu. In: *The Imagination of Reality: Essays on Southeast Asian Symbolic Systems.* A. Becker and A. Yengoyan, eds. (forthcoming).

——— *Termanu: The Political History of an Indonesian State* (in preparation).

——— and Fox, Irmgard. "A Working Bibliography on the Islands of Roti, Savu, and Sumba." Unpublished manuscript, 1972.

Francis, E. A. "Verslag van den Kommissaris voor Timor, 1832." Koninklijk Instituut voor Taal-, Land- en Volkenkunde, manuscript collection.

——— Timor in 1831. *Tijdschrift voor Nederlandsch-Indië* I, i:353-369, 374-400; ii:25-53, 1838.

Freeman, J. D. *Iban Agriculture.* London: Her Majesty's Stationery Office, 1955.

Friedberg, Claudine. L'agriculture des Bunaq de Timor et les conditions d'un equilibre avec le milieu. *Journal d'agriculture tropicale et de botanique appliquée* 18:481-532, 1971.

——— Éleménts de botanique Bunaq. In: *Langues et techniques, nature et société.* J. M. C. Thomas and L. Bernot, eds., vol. 2. Paris: Editions Klincksieck, 1972.

——— Reperage et decoupage du temps chez les Bunaq du Centre de Timor. *Archipel* 6:119-146, 1973.

——— Agricultures timoraises. *Études rurales* 53-56:375-405, 1974.

Gebuis, Ir. L., and Kadir, R. Abdul. Enkele gegevens omtrent den Siwalan op Madoera. *Landbouw* 4 (Buitenzorg, Java):304-321, 1928-1929.

Geertz, Clifford. *Agricultural Involution.* Berkeley: University of California Press, 1963.

Ghose, Manmathanath. A neglected source of sugar in Bihar. *Agricultural Journal of India* 15, pt. 1:32-39, 1920.

Glover, I. C. Prehistoric research in Timor. In: *Aboriginal Man and Environment in Australia.* D. J. Mulvaney and J. Golson, eds. Canberra: Australian National University Press, 1971.

Graafland, N. Het eiland Rote. *Mededeelingen van wege het Nederlandsch Zendelinggenootschap* 33:239-277, 1889.

Grisard, Jules. Produits et utilisations du rondier. *Revue des cultures coloniales* 9:231-237, 1901.

Groeneveldt, W. P. Notes on the Malay Archipelago and Malacca compiled from Chinese sources. *Verhandelingen van het Bataviaasch Genootschap van Kunsten en Wetenschappen* 39, 1:1-144, 1880.

[Gronovius, D. J. van den Dungen?] Beschrijving van het eiland Soemba of Sandelhout. *Tijdschrift voor Neerlands Indië* 17(1):277-312, 1855.

Gyanto. *Pulau Roti: Pagar Selatan Indonesia.* Jakarta: Ganaco N.V., 1958.

Haga, A. De slag bij Penefoey en Vendrig Lip. *Tijdschrift voor Indische Taal-, Land- en Volkenkunde* 27:389-408, 1882.

Hardgrave, R. L. *The Nadars of Tamilnad*. Berkeley: University of California Press, 1969.

Harris, D. R. Swidden systems and settlement. In: *Man, Settlement and Urbanism*. P. J. Ucko, R. Tringham, and G. W. Dimbleby, eds. London: Duckworth and Co., 1972.

Heeres, J. E. *Bouwstoffen voor de geschiedenis der Nederlanders in den Maleischen Archipel*. The Hague: Martinus Nijhoff, 1895.

Heiligers. Memorie van overgave van de onderafdeeling Savoe. Afdeeling Zuid Timor en Eilanden. Seba, 1920. Copies of this document are to be found in the Wason Collection of the Cornell University Library, Ithaca, New York, and in the Bodleian Library, Oxford, as well as in the author's collection of documents on eastern Indonesia.

Heyne, K. *De nuttige planten van Nederlandsch-Indië*, 2nd ed. 3 vols. Buitenzorg: Departement van landbouw, nijverheid en handel in Nederlands-Indie; The Hague: Martinus Nijhoff, 1927.

Hogendorp, W. van. Beschrijving van het eiland Timor. *Verhandelingen van het Bataviaasch Genootschap van Kunsten en Wetenschappen*, vol. 1, pp. 192-214; vol. 2, pp. 405-434, 1779-1780. Reprint 1825-1826.

Humme, H. C. Aanteekeningen tot de bijdrage van den Heer Teffer over het eiland Savoe. *Tijdschrift voor Indische Taal-, Land- en Volkenkunde* 23:359-360, 1876.

Jackstein, A. Bijzonderheden omtrent den toestand der bevolking van het eiland Rotti. *Koloniale Jaarboeken* 4:265-283, 1864.

Jonker, J. C. G. Iets over de taal van Dao. *Album-Kern* (Opstellen geschreven ter eere van Dr. H. Kern):85-89. Leiden: E. J. Brill, 1903.

——— Rottineesche Verhalen. *Bijdragen tot de Taal-, Land- en Volkenkunde* 58: 369-464, 1905.

——— *Rottineesch-Hollandsch woordenboek*. Leiden: E. J. Brill, 1908.

——— *Rottineesche spraakkunst*. Leiden: E. J. Brill, 1915.

Kadafuk, Nikolas. "Usaha peternakan rakjat dalam hubungannja dengan aspek sosial dan tradisi masjarakat Rote Talae di desa Sumlili Kabupaten Kupang." Sarjana Muda thesis, Universitas Udayana, Den Pasar, Bali, 1971.

——— "Laporan Tentang Helong." Unpublished preliminary findings, 1973.

Kana, N. L. "A Preliminary Study of the East Sumbanese Social Organization and Religion." M.A. thesis, Cornell University, 1966.

Kate, H. F. C. ten. Verslag eener reis in de Timorgroep en Polynesië. *Tijdschrift van het Koninklijk Nederlandsch Aardrijkskundig Genootschap*, 2nd series, 11:195-246; 333-390; 541-638; 659-700; 765-823, 1894.

Koloniale Verslagen. The Hague, 1852-1930.

Koopmans, B. "Memorie van overgave van de onderafdeeling Roti: Afdeeling Zuid Timor en Eilanden." Baä, April 1921 (unpublished). Copies of this document are to be found in the Wason Collection of the Cornell University Library, Ithaca, New York, and in the Bodleian Library, Oxford, as well as in the author's collection of documents on eastern Indonesia.

Kruseman, J. D. Timor, 1824. March 15, 1824. In the G. J. Schneither collection: 24B[b]/3, Algemeen Rijksarchief, The Hague.

——— Beschrijving van Timor. *De Oosterling* 2:1-41, 1836.

Le Grand, G. J. H. De zending op Roti. *Mededeelingen van wege het Neder-landsch Zendelinggenootschap* 44:361-377, 1900.

Leitão, Humberto. *Os Portugueses em Solor e Timor de 1515 a 1702.* Tip. da Liga dos Combatantes da Grande Guerra. Instituto para a Alta Cultura. Lisbon, 1948.

Letterboer, J. H. Verslag over de zending op Savoe in 1903. *Mededeelingen van wege het Nederlandsch Zendelinggenootschap* 48:350-360, 1904.

Lynden, D. W. C. van. Bijdrage tot de kennis van Solor, Allor, Rotti, Savoe en omliggende eilanden. *Natuurkundig Tijdschrift voor Nederlandsch-Indië* 2:317-336; 388-414, 1851.

Manafe, D. P. Akan Bahasa Rotti. *Bijdragen tot de Taal-, Land- en Volkenkunde* 38:634-648, 1889.

Mateer, Samuel. *The Land of Charity: An Account of Travancore and Its Devil Worship.* New York: Dodd, Mead and Co., 1870.

Moor, J. H. Short account of Timor, Rotti, Savu, Salor, etc. In: *Notices of the Indian Archipelago and Adjacent Countries,* pt. 1, appendix:5-12. Singapore, 1837. Reprint London: Frank Cass, 1968.

Moore, H. E. Botany and classification of palms. *American Horticultural Magazine* 40:17-26, 1961.

Mosteller, F., and Tukey, J. W. Data analysis, including statistics. In: *The Handbook of Social Psychology,* 2nd ed. G. Lindzey and E. Aronson, eds., vol. 2, pp. 114-119. Reading, Massachusetts: Addison-Wesley, 1968.

Müller, Salomon. *Reizen en onderzoekingen in den Indischen Archipel.* 2 vols. Amsterdam: Frederick Muller, 1857.

Multatuli [Eduard Douwes Dekker]. *Max Havelaar.* Rotterdam: Elsevier, 1881.

Nicolas, François-J. La feuille de Borassus flabellifer utilisée comme support de l'écriture en Afrique occidentale. *Anthropos* 54:222-228, 1959.

Nooteboom, C. *Oost-Soemba, een Volkenkundige Studie.* The Hague: Martinus Nijhoff, 1940.

Onvlee, L. *Cultuur als Antwoord.* The Hague: Martinus Nijhoff, 1973.

Ormeling, F. J. *The Timor Problem: A Geographical Interpretation of an Underdeveloped Island.* Jakarta and Groningen: J. B. Wolters, 1956.

Purseglove, J. W. *Tropical Crops: Dicotyledons 1.* New York: John Wiley and Sons, 1971.

Radja Haba, M. C. "Future Development of Animal Husbandry in Raihawu (Savu)." Unpublished typescript, n.d. Author's collection of documents on eastern Indonesia.

Register in Rade. Algemeen Rijksarchief, The Hague.

Rheede tot Drakenstein, H. van. *Hortus Indicus Malabaricus.* 12 vols. Amsterdam: J. v. Someren and J. v. Dyck, 1678-1703.

Riedel, J. G. F. The Savu or Haawu group with a sketch map. *Revue coloniale internationale* 1:303-310, 1885.

———— Note sur l'île Rote. *Compte-rendu du IV Congrès Internationale des Sciences Geographiques à Paris,* 1889.

Roo van Alderwerelt, J. de. Historische aanteekeningen over Soemba. *Tijdschrift voor Indische Taal-, Land- en Volkenkunde* 48:185-316, 1906.

Roos, S. Bijdrage tot de kennis van taal, land en volk op het eiland Soemba. *Ver-*

handelingen van het Bataviaasch Genootschap van Kunsten en Wetenschappen 36:1-125, 1872.

Rumphius, G. E. *Het Amboinsche Kruydboek.* 6 vols. Amsterdam: Meinard Uytwerf, 1741-1755.

Schulte Nordholt, H. G. *The Political System of the Atoni of Timor.* The Hague: Martinus Nijhoff, 1971.

Schultz, C. Memories van overgave van den aftredenden resident van Timor en onderhoorigheden, July 1924-July 1927. Mailrapport 875/23, June 1927. Koloniaal Archief, Ministerie van Binnenlandse Zaken.

Sensus Penduduk 1961 [Population Census 1961] Republik Indonesia. Preliminary Figures. Jakarta: Biro Pusat Statistik, 1963.

Sensus Penduduk Propinsi Nusa Tenggara Timur, Tahun 1971. Kupang: Kantor Sensus dan Statistik Propinsi Nusa Tenggara Timur, 1972.

Shepard, R. N., Romney, A. K., and Nerlove, S. B., eds. *Multidimensional Scaling: Theory and Applications in the Behavioral Sciences.* 2 vols. New York and London: Seminar Press, 1972.

Symposium I Pembangunan Ekonomi dan Keuangan Daerah Propinsi Nusa Tenggara Timur, November 17-25, 1966 in Kupang. Kupang: Pemerintah Daerah Propinsi Nusa Tenggara Timur, 1967.

Teffer, M. De Savoe-Eilanden. *Mededeelingen van wege het Nederlandsch Zendelinggenootschap* 19:205-233, 1875.

———— Naamlijst en eenige aanteekeningen betreffende de geschiedenis der Savoenezen. *Tijdschrift voor Indische Taal-, Land- en Volkenkunde* 23:347-360, 1876.

Teysmann, J. E. Verslag eener Botanische Reis over Timor, en de daaronder ressorteerende eilanden Samauw, Alor, Solor, Floris, en Soemba. *Natuurkundig Tijdschrift voor Nederlandsch-Indië* 34:348-517, 1874.

Timor Boek. Overgekomen Brieven en Papieren, Amsterdam (or Zeeland) Kamer 1647-1798. Koloniaale Archieven in the Algemeen Rijksarchief, The Hague.

Tukey, J. W. *Introduction to Exploratory Data Analysis.* 3 vols. Reading, Massachusetts: Addison-Wesley, 1970.

Tumonggor, A. J. *Lapuran Pemeriksaan Makanan di Timor.* Jakarta, 1951 (unpublished).

Veth, P. J. Het eiland Timor. *De Gids* 8, 1:545-611, 695-737; 2:55-100, 1855.

Volkstelling, vol. 5: Inheemsche Bevolking van Borneo, Celebes, De Kleine Soenda Eilanden en de Molukken, 1930. The Hague: Landsdrukkerij (Departement van Economische Zaken), 1936.

Wainwright, M. *Potential for Water Resources Development—Savu, Rote and Timor, Nusa Tenggara Timur, Indonesia.* May/June 1972. Unpublished report prepared for the provincial government of Nusa Tenggara Timur.

Wallace, A. R. *The Malay Archipelago.* London: Richard Clay and Sons, 1869.

Wetering, F. H. van de. De Savoeneezen. *Bijdragen tot de Taal-, Land- en Volkenkunde* 82:485-575, 1926.

Wichman, A. Die Insel Rotti. *Petermanns Geographische Mitteilungen* 5:97-103, 1892.

Wielenga, D. K. De Savoeneezen op Soemba. *De Macedoniër* 16:235-240, 1912.

Wijngaarden, J. K. Het eiland Randjoewa. *Mededeelingen van wege het Neder-*

landsch Zendelinggenootschap 34:332-334, 1890a.

——— Eerste verslag. *Mededeelingen van wege het Nederlandsch Zendeling-genootschap* 34:366-383, 1890b.

——— Verslag wan mijne verrichtingen en bevindingen. *Mededeelingen van wege het Nederlandsch Zendelinggenootschap* 35:233-267, 1891.

——— Savoeneesche tijdrekening. *Mededeelingen van wege het Nederlandsch Zendelinggenootschap* 36:16-33, 1892.

——— Naar Soemba. *Mededeelingen van wege het Nederlandsch Zendeling-genootschap* 37:352-376, 1893.

Wolters, O. W. *Early Indonesian Commerce: A Study of the Origins of Srivijaya.* Ithaca, New York: Cornell University Press, 1967.

Index